The

Beethoven Sonatas and the Creative Experience

The Beethoven Sonatas and the Creative Experience

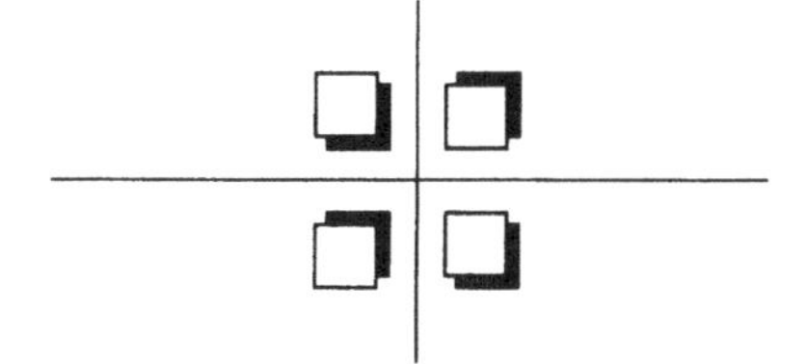

Kenneth Drake

INDIANA UNIVERSITY PRESS
BLOOMINGTON & INDIANAPOLIS

This book is a publication of

Indiana University Press
601 North Morton Street
Bloomington, IN 47404-3797 USA

http://www.indiana.edu/~iupress

Telephone orders 800-842-6796
Fax orders 812-855-7931
Orders by e-mail iuporder@indiana.edu

First reprinted in paperback in 2000

The paper used in this publication meets the minimum requirements of American National Standard for Information Sciences—Permanence of Paper for Printed Library Materials, ANSI Z39.48-1984.

Manufactured in the United States of America

Library of Congress Cataloging-in-Publication Data

Drake, Kenneth, pianist.
The Beethoven sonatas and the creative experience / Kenneth Drake.
p. cm.
Includes bibliographical references and index.
ISBN 0-253-31822-X (cloth)
1. Beethoven, Ludwig van, 1770–1827. Sonatas, piano. 2. Sonatas (Piano)—Analysis, appreciation. I. Title.
MT145.B42D7 1994
786.2'183'092—dc20 93-27719

ISBN 0-253-21382-7 (paper)

2 3 4 5 6 05 04 03 02 01 00

To Eskil Randolph,

the indispensable teacher of my youth,
who knew the language of music
and taught it in so unassuming a manner.

CONTENTS

PREFACE ix

I The First Raptus, and All Subsequent Ones 1

The Sounds of Involvement

II Technique as Touch 9
III Tempo and the Pacing of Musical Ideas 33
IV Dynamic Nuance and Musical Line 40
V The Role of Silence 48
VI Sound as Color 54

The Sonatas

VII Descriptive Music: Op. 81a, Op. 13 67
VIII Motivic Development: Op. 2 No. 1, Op. 57, Op. 110 84
IX *Quasi una Fantasia:* Op. 27 Nos. 1 and 2, Op. 26 113
X Line and Space: Op. 2 No. 2, Op. 101 128
XI Movement as Energized Color: Op. 53 144
XII The Moment of Creation: Op. 28, Op. 31 Nos. 2 and 3 159
XIII Facing Two Directions: Op. 49 Nos. 1 and 2, Op. 54, Op. 78, Op. 90 191

XIV	The Enjoyment of Fluency: Op. 10 Nos. 2 and 3, Op. 14 No. 2, Op. 22, Op. 31 No. 1, Op. 79	211
XV	The Cosmopolitan Impostor: Op. 2 No. 3, Op. 14 No. 1	239
XVI	Embracing the Dachstein: Op. 7, Op. 106	259
XVII	A Higher Revelation: Op. 10 No. 1, Op. 109, Op. 111	280
XVIII	The Witness Tree	305

NOTES 311
INDEX 317

Preface

It was an afternoon when Stanley Fletcher felt the need for a break before continuing teaching. We were joined by Alexander Ringer, and the conversation turned to the study of applied music. "The trouble with you people," he inveighed, "is that you teach skills but not what makes the music tick." No doubt Mr. Fletcher agreed in the privacy of his mind.

The desire to become a pianist is sustained by dreams, typically of study with a famous teacher, winning a competition, and playing concerts. Motivation feeds on examples of "legendary" performers who play throughout the world to "critical acclaim"—public relations phrases that never wear out however often they are run through the presses. For this, there is a science of performance to be learned in order that technique and musicianship can be reliably displayed. How else can one hope to reach the final round of the competition, or pass the DMA recital, or even one's recital approval audition? As a consequence, the loftiest model to which one is obliged to aspire becomes the flawless performance on the CD.

The years pass, and the anticipated rewards for years of study may not materialize, leaving a choice between believing in a mirage or believing that life, as José Echàniz reminded his students, is always more important than playing the piano. Stated another way, it is life—not the competition prize or the academic degree or rank—that lends significance to the act of making music. Whether a recital in Alice Tully Hall or an afternoon teaching privately in small-town America, the personal fulfillment of giving it away to however few or many—this love of the language of music—constitutes the real fabric of "culture," and culture, we often forget, is not restricted to a geographical location but is taken by the mind wherever it goes. As I think back on those years of study with Mr. Echàniz, his attitude toward the profession permeates the basic premise of this writing, that "each of us is gifted enough" and capable of being the medium for the composer's thought.

Understanding the language of music is the skill for which all the musician's other skills must be cultivated. Growing older, to quote Schumann, one should converse more frequently with scores than with virtuosi. The language of a Beethoven sonata is as precise as a legal document; it should not be played without discerning its uniqueness any more than a contract should be signed without understanding every clause. To that end, the player's tools are intuition, intelligence, and reflexes that respond to shapes in the score like fingertips reading braille—all coordinated by imagination. Imagination is like an unruly student with unbounded potential, brilliant but easily bored and irregular in class attendance. Once aroused, however, it becomes a tireless detective scrutinizing the score for the clue to what makes the piece "tick."

The standards of a degree program, however beneficial the intent, all too often compel conformity instead of fostering independent thought, whether or not the conclusion reached is one the teacher deems correct. Buckminster Fuller addressed the danger in becoming educated, saying that learning is not done with an injection or a pump but by working alongside a loving pioneer while he is still pioneering. Just such a pioneer, Charles Kettering, the inventor of the self-starter and the spray-lacquer finish process in the early days of the automobile, once remarked that he preferred *not* to work with university-trained assistants; intent upon pursuing an expected result, they frequently failed to notice the unusual along the way. The inventor, he said, may fail hundreds of times before making an important discovery, while, in our educational system, failure normally relegates one to the bottom of the heap. Like the inventor, an interpreter, instead of accepting dictated answers, deals with questions about the inner working of a piece of music, questions that probe far deeper than whether the tone is singing, the runs are clean, and the "style" is correct.

The present work is not an exercise in musicology or performance practice, nor does it offer measure-by-measure analysis. Instead, it is a work about meaning—a personal account of studying, teaching, and playing the Beethoven sonatas, the significance they assume in the innermost self, and, especially, the musical basis for their significance. The immediate purpose is to isolate ideas within the score and to perceive meaning *in* them and derive meaning *from* them. Meaning, the personal identification with musical symbols and relationships, is as difficult to measure as the moving air is to see. Nevertheless, like breathing, sensing meaning is divining the spirit within the music, in order to receive it into one's consciousness and be performed *by* it. Who has not been admonished at some point by a teacher, "Don't become so involved"? To be performed by the music *is* to become passionately involved with the relationship between musical symbols and human reasoning, impulses, and emotions—motivated by "inner necessity" (to borrow a phrase from Martin Cooper).

In dealing with meaning and the language of music in any period, one should not be deterred by the fact that interpretive choices are always, to a certain extent, subjective. Although determinations of this nature in the pages that follow have been shaped by weighing the evidence, one's understanding has no sooner been formulated in the written word than it is already incomplete. At best, the discussions that are presented may be regarded as a starting point for the reader's further reflection and formation of independent judgments.

Examples that occur within a quoted passage are not given measure numbers. Also, the numbering of measures, which follows the Henle edition, begins with the first pitches and ends with the last pitches, whether or not these form a complete measure (however, an upbeat to the opening of a work is not counted). I would like to express my thanks to Christopher Preissing of cp Music Engraving for his painstaking reproduction of the musical examples.

In addition to Eskil Randolph, José Echàniz, and Stanley Fletcher, my gratitude is extended to many others—to Alexander Ringer and the late Hubert Kessler, whose views about music are enduringly fresh and profound; to the late Jessie Kneisel, so patient and thorough, whose teaching of German at the Eastman School of Music introduced us to literature that shaped one's outlook upon music as a life work; to Margaret Saunders Ott, whose positive attitude toward teaching celebrates the uniqueness of each human being, and who is a model each day I enter the studio; to Paul Jackson, former Dean of the College of Fine Arts at Drake University, for his insightful ideas about interpretation during our many conversations; to the many students over the years who have taught me through their problems and their insights; and to my parents, who supported my training and my subsequent work with their labor and love.

The

Beethoven Sonatas

and the

Creative Experience

The First Raptus, and All Subsequent Ones

For approximately ten years, according to Anton Schindler, Beethoven considered preparing an edition of his works in which he would have described the extramusical idea or the psychological state that had led in each case to the composing of the work. The importance of extramusical stimulus in Beethoven's creative process was mentioned by others as well. Ferdinand Ries spoke of Beethoven's use of "psychological images" in his teaching. In a similar way, Czerny, the most important contemporary witness because of his long association with Beethoven and his stature as a professional musician, referred again and again to character, mood, extramusical events, and images.

In the Adagio of Op. 2 No. 3, Czerny writes, there is an evolving Romantic tendency, leading eventually to an integration "in which instrumental music was heightened to painting and poetry"; it was no longer a matter of merely hearing the expression of feelings, "one s e e s paintings, one h e a r s the narration of events."[1] Czerny describes the opening movement of Op. 27 No. 2 as being "extremely poetic" and easy to grasp—"a night scene, in which a plaintive ghostly voice sounds from far off in the distance."[2] The first movement of Op. 31 No. 2 will never fail to make a powerful effect "if the fantasy of the player stands on an equally high level with his artistic skill." The sixteenth notes divided between the hands in the finale must be played as evenly as possible "in order to sound, as it were, like the gallop of a horse." In a footnote Czerny continues: "Beethoven improvised the theme of this piece as once he saw a rider gallop past his window. Many of his most beautiful works originated through similar occurrences. With him every sound, every movement became music and rhythm."[3]

Czerny writes of the finale of Op. 57:

> If Beethoven (who was so fond of depicting scenes from nature) here perhaps thought of the waves of the ocean on a stormy night, while a call for help is heard from afar,—such a picture can always give the player a suitable idea for the appropriate performance of this huge tone painting. It is certain that Beethoven was excited to work on many of his most beautiful compositions through similar *visions* and images created from readings or from his own active fantasy, and that we would find the true key to his compositions and their performance only through an accurate knowledge of these circumstances, if such were generally possible.

Nevertheless, Beethoven himself

> was not prone to be communicative about such matters, only now and then, when in a confiding mood . . . for he knew that the listener would not feel the music in so unconstrained a manner, if one's power of imagination were to be fettered beforehand to a specifically expressed goal.[4]

Czerny's statement that *only through* a knowledge of Beethoven's extramusical stimuli, could they be known, would we find "the true key to his compositions and their performance" falls strangely on modern ears. Beside the professionalism of scholarly research or a concert career, night scenes, plaintive ghostly voices, galloping horses, and ocean waves are so much historical fluff. A well-trained pianist will play the sixteenths in the finale of Op. 31 No. 2 evenly anyway, and, in any event, the sound of a galloping horse would lead to an *allegro* instead of the indicated *Allegretto*.

Unlike any of us, Czerny actually *studied* with Beethoven and enjoyed his respect. However irregular their association may have been, Czerny was impressionable, observing in the working of Beethoven's vigorous fantasy how the extramusical image aroused the *raptus*—as Frau von Breuning described the young Beethoven's spells of moodiness—that in turn imbued a newly found musical idea with character. The musical idea became thereby more than a cerebral plaything. It became personally significant; it became *meaning*. Whenever Czerny played the finale of the D-minor Sonata, we may suppose, the imagery he remembered from Beethoven reached down to touch the motive of ongoing sixteenths, giving it a human dimension: the experience of repetitiveness, like time inescapable, a horse one cannot dismount. Were Czerny to return among us, it is likely that he would regard much that is applauded in our concert halls and schools of music as craft sanitized of human response and therefore lacking a sense of meaning.

Defining meaning is a highly subjective exercise, whether it refers to a more or less explicit musical depiction of an event or image or the *quality* of meaning. Do the stark contrasts in Mozart's B-minor Adagio, written in the year following

Leopold Mozart's death, reflect the younger Mozart's ambivalent feelings toward his father? Is the Baroque-like rhythmic continuity of the opening movement of the A-minor Sonata, written in Paris the summer of his mother's death, a musical depiction of fatalism? Since we can no longer ask Mozart, we cannot establish an indisputable link between composition and event. "Who cares what the fact was, when we have made a constellation of it to hang in heaven an immortal sign?" Emerson asked. The attribute of meaning that we ascribe to some external stimulus originates in the aloneness of the innermost self where the experiences of living are catalogued and stored. When threatened by some personal crisis, the self identifies with an immortal sign in the form of an equally troubled work, such as the B-minor Adagio or the A-minor Sonata. Through a mysterious mental alchemy, the piece becomes a symbol for the unspoken. A student, asked what the Arietta theme of Op. 111 made him think of, looked long at the piano in silence and then replied, "It is like crying on the inside about something you cannot cry about on the outside," an extraordinarily insightful remark from a young person hearing this music for the first time. He intuitively associated the inwardness of the falling motive, the flowing triple subdivision, the arch of the widely spaced lines, and the slow harmonic rhythm with a personal sadness deep within himself. The music had acquired meaning of the most sophisticated sort.

Were Czerny to return in the flesh, would he find virtue in our concern for performance practice? Would he be pleased to find his writings still consulted? Undoubtedly, but not if research results in a clinical demonstration instead of a humanly moving experience. It is reasonable to suggest that, for him, "correct performance" was an *attitude* toward the music. In describing Beethoven's visions and images as the true key to interpretation, Czerny was stating, as the one, all-encompassing rule of performance practice for the playing of Beethoven, total personal involvement.

"Total personal involvement" is becoming possessed by the music, cerebrally, muscularly, and subjectively. Every question that is raised, every touch that is learned, and every response that is recorded in the mind should establish more firmly the authority of the score within the player. Such a performance may not be flawless, but it will not deviate from a perceived spiritual standard. Fortunately, Beethoven and his contemporaries did not live in a world of electronic reproduction, or even reliable instruments, and consequently their imagination was not misled to believe in an external perfection that can be repeated over and over by pressing a button. At a time when a performance could not be heard beyond earshot of those present, the temptation to use the music to demonstrate skill on the instrument would have been, though just as alluring as it is today, beyond the imagination of what is now possible. We may daydream about contemporary accounts of Beethoven's playing being dependent upon his moods, yet we cannot escape the fact that such an attitude toward performance is alien to our age, in which inconsistency is regarded as amateurish.

Although involvement does begin with the basics of learning the notes and the phrasing in an indicated tempo, its eventual goal is a synthesis of technique, analysis, and imagination in an act that is both rational and irrational, both measured and unmeasured. Applied study that is limited to cosmetic refinement halts growth at an elementary level of involvement, where security is found in definite answers to simple questions: How slow? How fast? How soft? How loud? How short? How long? If unfailing technique and memory are of primary importance, why burden one's concentration with anything but the outer shell of the piece? Why speculate about the reason for a particular musical feature, such as the offbeat *sforzandos* in the development of the first movement of Op. 2 No. 1 or the alternation of *forte* and *piano* in the *Adagio espressivo* in the exposition of the first movement of Op. 109? Why question the composer's intent in indicating a *rallentando* preceding the E-minor theme in the exposition of the first movement of Op. 2 No. 2, or the segmented articulation of the opening theme of Op. 90, or the absence of conventional working-out in the development section of the first movement of Op. 110?

Musical playing alone is not necessarily interpretively convincing playing. Questions such as those above usher one directly into the mind of the composer, there with each performance to be involved with the original insecurity of choices made in the moment of creation. When playing, each musical "fact" must be assigned a human dimension. It is not enough to think of the opening four measures of Op. 7 as tonic E♭ major, however rational this observation may be. Because of the harmonic sameness, the listener's attention is drawn to the repeated eighth notes in 6/8 time, *Allegro molto e con brio,* which the imagination interprets as a "driving" rhythm, an adjective with a connotation of irrationality. Neither does it suffice to analyze the first six measures of the rondo of the same sonata as dominant harmony if one does not become aware of the many appoggiaturas, which the mind hears as "lingering" within the melodic line. The arpeggiated A-major sixth chord with which Op. 31 No. 2 opens is dominant harmony, but its harmonic function is uncommitted at this point, and, within *pianissimo,* the pianist's imagination hears only a quality of mystery.

What metronome marking can be assigned to "driving" or to "lingering"? What precise level of sound is appropriate for "mystery"? Any decision that involves the player's subjective (and, for the moment, infallible) judgment will be specific for only that moment; unlike the fixed perfection of a recording, performance that searches the depths of character can never be made totally predictable. There are two Urtexts, the one physical, black-on-white, that indicates the pitches, tempo, dynamics, phrasing, and articulation, and the other a human Urtext, a power within the printed page that performs *us,* enabling us to converse with the composer. The student who remarked, after playing the F-minor Fantaisie, "I felt like a giant for a moment," one might say had spoken with Chopin, personally.

For an interpreter committed to involvement, there is no station along the line to get off, for the music leads one always further into the composer's being and the humanness we share. The willfully philosophical in Beethoven is the spirit of one always dissatisfied and therefore driven to reach beyond his grasp, whether in formal construction, development of character, the treatment of the instrument, or in unceasing revision, even while works were being engraved. Finding meaning in struggle is the sentiment expressed in two letters to Countess Erdödy, one written in October 1815: "We finite beings, who are the embodiment of an infinite spirit, are born to suffer both pain and joy; and one might almost say that the best of us obtain *joy through suffering*";[5] and the other in May 1816: "Man cannot avoid suffering; and *in this respect his strength must stand the test,* that is to say, he must *endure without complaining and feel his worthlessness* and *then again* achieve *his perfection,* that perfection which the Almighty will then bestow upon him."[6]

The pianist who is an involved artist soon learns that the indefinite human dimension was and still remains too large for the definite canvas. How can the measure of the unmeasurable be expressed? What performer on what instrument can fill this ever-changing expandingness of the composer's imagination? How many performers, for that matter, are willing to risk failure trying to fill that beckoning void? We would rather believe that success and failure are mutually exclusive, and yet, joy through suffering and reaching beyond one's grasp both infer frustration and failure. As Lili Kraus was once quoted as saying, an audience that has been moved by a Beethoven sonata has experienced grace, and the performer who does not risk shame will never move anyone. Risking shame, being moved, experiencing grace—none of these sound like trustworthy advice for winning a competition. Consequently, she continued, each tries to escape into the perfection of the record player. Or, as the Ghost of an artist in C. S. Lewis's *The Great Divorce* reminisces,

> It was all a snare. Ink and catgut and paint were necessary down there but they are also dangerous stimulants. Every poet and musician and artist, but for Grace, is drawn away from love of the thing he tells, to love of the telling till, down in Deep Hell, they cannot be interested in God at all but only in what they say about Him. For it doesn't stop at being interested in paint, you know. They sink lower—become interested in their own personalities and then in nothing but their own reputations.[7]

To experience grace is to be forgiven for the one forgiven and to forgive for the forgiver. It is an act on the part of both performer and listener requiring a belief in meaning, and this is the ultimate involvement.

The Sounds of Involvement

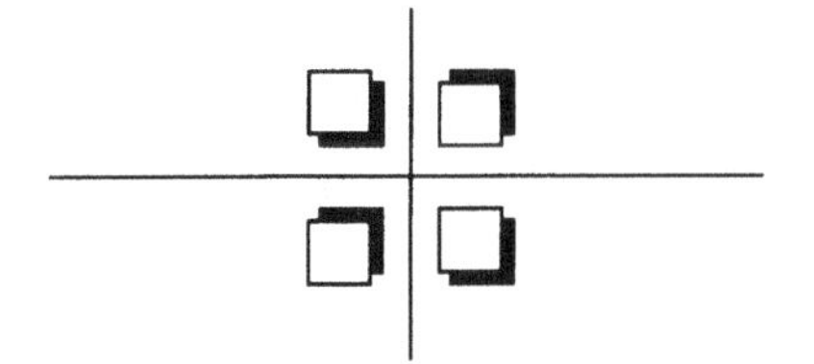

Technique as Touch

Among the misguided reasons for playing an early instrument is the intent to do a demonstration, as though dressing in its clothes will bring the past to life. Music making is not historical reenactment. An early piano should be used only as a medium to conjure up the spirit within the music. *The Spirit of St. Louis,* like the *Concorde,* enabled a person to fly nonstop across the Atlantic. Lindbergh, however, flew without the aid of sophisticated instrument systems, depending upon his skill and endurance. He came to know, as we cannot, the awesomeness of transatlantic distance and the elements, as well as the possibility for disaster.

Playing an early piano, though not life-threatening, also requires an exercise of judgment and skill. Lacking the resources of the modern piano, the player is responsible for believable dynamic levels and sensuous tone quality. When listeners remark that the period piano enabled them to *hear* the music for the first time, what they heard was the stimulus of the instrument to the player's imagination and ingenuity. In Beethoven, the player's involvement extends to the expressiveness of physical effort as well. As the historic piano is forced beyond the limits of its sonority, the music itself sounds more imposing. Because of the lesser sonority and the change in character from one register to another (as opposed to the homogenizing of sound on the modern piano), expressive details become as personal as words whispered directly in the ear of a single listener.

In program notes for a New York recital on which he used a clavichord, a harpsichord, an early piano, and a modern piano, Ralph Kirkpatrick compared playing

Mozart on the modern piano to walking "lace-beruffled" on eggs; it is, he wrote, as though one were to look through the wrong end of opera glasses and see the singers as pygmies on the stage. An early piano, he continued, its intimacy and nuance inherited from the clavichord and clarity and declamatory quality from the harpsichord, reveals "life-size" Mozart, there being no need to restrain the normal sound of the instrument, as one might playing a modern piano. Just as opera glasses reveal lines in the individual actor's face, the sound of the early piano makes it seem that we are walking shoulder to shoulder with Mozart, and that we can speak to him and he to us. Playing Beethoven (or Mozart of Haydn) on a piano of the period teaches that the technique required is primarily a control of touch, revealing infinite variety within the basic elements of piano sound, which is to say, intensity and duration.

The notation of Classic keyboard scores may be compared to the dots and lines and spaces in the engraving on paper currency, representing a precise calculation of pressure and duration in the fingertips that communicates musical ideas equally precisely. The fingertip must know the sensuousness of sound before the ear hears it. Ultimately, playing is an integration of mind and muscles in which

hear tone		hear touch
and	becomes	and
feel touch		feel tone.

The content of the present chapter and the four that follow is not intended as a discussion of performance practice. For that, the reader is referred to Sandra Rosenblum's monumental *Performance Practices in Classic Piano Music.*[1] The examples have two purposes, to illustrate the subtlety of Classic scores and to speculate on the role of that subtlety in interpretation. Exx. 2.1 through 2.27 illustrate this notational precision in single notes; of these, Exx. 2.1 through 2.14 relate to intensity and the remainder to duration.

The *fp* over the opening chord of the *Pathétique* (Ex. 2.1), separating a single sound into two dynamic levels, is an orchestral effect, as befits a piano sonata with symphonic pretensions. (The subtitle is, after all, *Grande Sonate Pathétique.*) Since piano sound, once produced, cannot be altered, the effect is comparable to splitting a musical atom to release its emotional force. No other sonata of the thirty-two begins in just this manner, the *fp* chord like the reeling of consciousness before a tragic situation. Although possible with an immediate release of the chord synchronized with a quick pedal change, the effect is also risky. Instead of a diminished C-minor chord, the player may be left with no sound at all. We cannot be certain that the composer himself would have tried to produce this explosive/muffled effect, although, if Schindler's memory was accurate, Beethoven held the chord until it had all but died away before continuing.[2]

Ex. 2.1. Beethoven, Sonata Op. 13, I, m. 1.

A *crescendo* over a held note, an orchestral effect that is impossible on the piano, resembles straining to enunciate a thought for which there are no words. The sole means of conveying this to the listener is a slight delaying of the louder note (as in Exx. 2.2 and 2.3). Stressing single notes that would otherwise be weak likewise holds back the tempo in Exx. 2.4 and 2.5. With so few notes to make the musical statement, underplaying the individual stresses reduces the passage to interpretive meaninglessness.

Ex. 2.2. Beethoven, Sonata Op. 7, IV, mm. 62–64.

Ex. 2.3. Beethoven, Sonata Op. 81a, I, mm. 252–53.

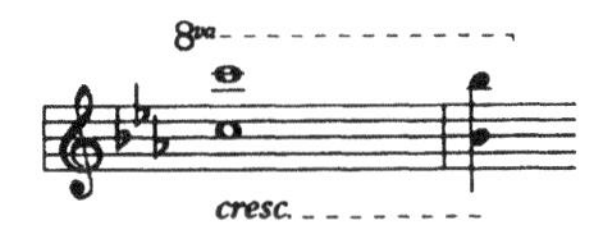

Ex. 2.4. Haydn, Sonata No. 33, I, mm. 13–14.

Ex. 2.5. Mozart, Sonata K. 457, II, m. 21.

In Ex. 2.6, a single *f* would have sufficed for the four staccato quarter notes; however, Beethoven indicated a strong, separate attack on each, in effect cancelling the sighing character of the two-note slurs. His intent may also have been a resumption of tempo, following a natural inclination to stretch the two-note slurs. In Exx. 2.7 and 2.8, the staccato becomes an accent marking a melodic line in what would otherwise be an empty chatter of broken chords.

Ex. 2.6. Beethoven, Sonata Op. 31 No. 3, I, mm. 43–45.

Ex. 2.7. Beethoven, Sonata Op. 14 No. 1, III, mm. 47–49.

Ex. 2.8. Beethoven, Sonata Op. 13, I, m. 93.

The staccato dots in the *leggiermente* passage near the beginning of Op. 110, by contrast, are a color-image suggesting elevation and distance, as though one were watching the sparkling of sunlight on a far-away lake (Ex. 2.9). Like the preceding eight measures, the passage is a variation of the opening four bars, the pitches marked staccato corresponding now and then with the important pitches in the first four measures of the movement. The effect is to transport the listener from the here-and-now of the first four measures of the movement to the rarefied sound of the two-voice melodic passage beginning in m. 20.

Ex. 2.9. Beethoven, Sonata Op. 110, I, m. 12.

In other instances, one would not interpret the staccato as an accent or permit a noticeable clipping of the note; instead, the staccato indicates lightness and lifting (Exx. 2.10–2.12). Finally, Czerny points out that *leggiermente* indicates non legato,[3] an observation supported by the absence of a slur in Exx. 2.13 and 2.14.

Ex. 2.10. Beethoven, Sonata Op. 26, I, mm. 1–4.

Ex. 2.11. Beethoven, Sonata Op. 26, I, mm. 34–37.

Ex. 2.12. Beethoven, Sonata Op. 31 No. 2, III, mm. 1–2.

Ex. 2.13. Beethoven, Sonata Op. 31 No. 1, II, m. 10.

Ex. 2.14. Beethoven, Sonata Op. 78, I, mm. 8–9.

Exx. 2.15–2.27 illustrate the use of touch to determine precise duration, which in turn creates character, defines formal structure, underlines dynamic levels, and promotes clarity of voice lines and orchestral effects. Varying note lengths in Ex. 2.15 transform a structural corner into a gradual return to the character of the opening. The non legato in the sixteenth notes in the second bar could indicate slackening the pace and lessening the intensity in preparation for the reentry of the theme.

Ex. 2.15. Beethoven, Rondo Op. 51 No. 1, mm. 12–14.

The measures quoted in Ex. 2.16 occur within the second half of the exposition of the first movement of the A-minor Sonata of Mozart, the character of which is difficult to piece together. The uninterrupted sixteenths and the repetitive patterns beginning in m. 22, although continuing the Baroque-like motoric quality of the first 21 bars, seem ear-tickling within the tragic cast of the piece. How does the strange laughter of this section fit the character of the movement as a whole? One answer involves the interchange of slurred and unslurred writing. Slurs appear in mm. 28 and 29, simultaneously with the sustained two-voice writing in the left hand. For two measures, the pattern of the figuration in the right hand changes, becoming warmer—one might say, almost heart-felt—for a moment. When the melodic pattern in m. 35 is repeated unslurred in m. 36, the interpreter must read between the lines. Within the rhythmic sameness, character may change subtly from one brace of sixteenths to another. The absence of a slur in m. 36 is much like a return to lighter thoughts, just as the slurred thirds in the left hand in the parallel section in the reprise (m. 104) reinforce the mysterious character. It is easy to speak of Mozart as a genius; what is difficult is revealing the genius when realizing the score. In Exx. 2.17 and 2.18 a shift from legato to non legato is coordinated with a change in dynamic level.

Ex. 2.16. Mozart, Sonata K. 310, I, mm. 35–38.

Ex. 2.17. Beethoven, Sonata Op. 22, I, mm. 108–109.

Ex. 2.18. Beethoven, Sonata Op. 31 No. 3, IV, mm. 274–75.

Because of the *crescendo* in the parallel measures of the more assertive answering phrase, the peculiar separation of the half notes in Ex. 2.19 seems to imply hesitation, perhaps also a *decrescendo.* The same indication of separation in Ex. 2.20 may be exploited to increase the force of the *crescendo.*

Ex. 2.19. Beethoven, Sonata Op. 13, III, mm. 45–50.

Ex. 2.20. Beethoven, Sonata Op. 14 No. 1, I, m. 15.

In the Rondo Op. 51 No. 1, differentiation between sixteenth note and staccato eighth note may indicate voicing the thirds in the left hand through a crisper touch, again an orchestration of piano sound (Ex. 2.21). The even sharper differentiation in Ex. 2.25 affords the interpreter the opportunity to exploit the conflict between the staccato thirds and the tenuto offbeat melody notes as a written *rubato*. Nothing could be further from the truth than to treat this variation note-literally, without revealing its deeply troubled character. In fact, in the autograph of Op. 26, the left-hand staccato is indicated with dashes that are not uniform but increase in length throughout the *crescendo*, expressing the increasing tension within the phrase.[4] The detached notes of the moving bass line in Ex. 2.22 and of the accompaniment figure in Ex. 2.23 train the listener's ears to the held notes of the principal melodic line in the right hand. In the contrast between held notes and moving lines in Ex. 2.24, the sound of the piano is enriched by the imitation of orchestral colors, the held thirds sounding like winds and the moving lines like strings. Making these touch indications unmistakably audible reveals the self-conscious nature of the music.

Ex. 2.21. Beethoven, Rondo Op. 51 No. 1, mm. 25–26.

Ex. 2.22. Beethoven, Sonata Op. 2 No. 2, II, m. 1.

Ex. 2.23. Beethoven, Sonata Op. 7, II, m. 25.

Ex. 2.24. Beethoven, Sonata Op. 10 No. 3, II, m. 23.

Ex. 2.25. Beethoven, Sonata Op. 26, I, mm. 102–103.

The duration of a note also indicates how a phrase is to be ended; a staccato dot is absent where it would result in clipping the end of the phrase (Exx. 2.26 and 2.27). In the passage from the *Pathétique* the absence of a staccato on the first beat of m. 55 tempers the pace of the Allegro, in order that the last note of the phrase is not lost before the leap back to the bass.

With respect to touch as it applies to slurred groups of notes, the dropping and lifting of the arm is one of the first movements learned at the piano and is basic to natural musicianship. As subtle as the difference is, extending the two-note slurs in Exx. 2.28 and 2.29 over the bar lessens the melodic importance of the sixteenth (or eighth respectively) and the natural lift of the upbeat into the downbeat, an oversight encountered often in teaching.

Ex. 2.26. Beethoven, Sonata Op. 13, I, mm. 51–56.

Ex. 2.27. Beethoven, Bagatelle Op. 119 No. 1, mm. 1–2.

Ex. 2.28. Mozart, Sonata K. 283, I, mm. 1–2.

Ex. 2.29. Beethoven, Sonata Op. 2 No. 1, I, mm. 41–43.

In the theme of the Rondo of Op. 13, the upbeat eighths must be lifted as written and separated from the appoggiaturas that follow (Ex. 2.30), if the figure is not to become 𝅗𝅥. ♬♬ | 𝅗𝅥., thus detracting from the integrity of the motive of sequential descending fifths. Haydn's original slur (Ex. 2.31) places equal stress on the beginning of the two-note slur and the eighth-note downbeat; extending the slur across the barline causes the downbeat to feel too light, too long, or too early. Haydn explicitly notated the pairs of sixteenths in Ex. 2.32 to be separated. Combining the two short slurs into one slur extending over the barline ( ) robs the theme of its individuality. Like a clay fragment with inscriptions of an ancient tongue, Haydn's separation of the four sixteenths into two two-note slurs must be read carefully, as though one were looking for a clue, in one instance to understanding an extinct language, in the other to penetrating a pattern of thought. The separation prevents the music from sounding slick or glib. Within the separation shown in Ex. 2.32 there is a peculiar childlike charm that will unfold throughout the movement in its playfulness tinged with melancholy. In music that says so much with so little, the interpreter always faces the probability that so few will understand the so-much. In Exx. 2.33 and 2.34, the stress-lift relationship within a two-note slur is reversed.

Ex. 2.30. Beethoven, Sonata Op. 13, III, mm. 4–6.

Ex. 2.31. Haydn, Sonata No. 53, I, mm. 1–2.

Ex. 2.32. Haydn, Sonata No. 59, I, mm. 1–2.

Ex. 2.33. Beethoven, Sonata Op. 31 No. 3, IV, mm. 127–29.

Ex. 2.34. Beethoven, Bagatelle Op. 33 No. 2, m. 1.

Another group of articulation slurs (shown in Exx. 2.35 and 2.36) could be called uniquely expressive slur figures. A quality of pleading or pulling away becomes more realistic in the purposefulness of the separation. The dramatic entry of the left-hand octaves in Ex. 2.36—*forte, allegro,* and slurred so forcibly in two-note groups—is reminiscent of Don Giovanni resisting being dragged off to hell and encourages one to play the passage with the same sense of terror. In the passage from the second movement of Op. 10 No. 3 (Ex. 2.37), the visual impression of complex rhythm and articulation itself suggests great anxiety; the actual realization of the articulation slurs will be no less physically uncomfortable.

Ex. 2.35. Haydn, Sonata No. 33, I, mm. 1–2.

Ex. 2.36. Mozart, Fantasie K. 475, mm. 36, 40.

Ex. 2.37. Beethoven, Sonata Op. 10 No. 3, II, mm. 9–11.

The articulation in the slow movement of the Mozart D-major Sonata K. 311 produces a similar held-back quality (Ex. 2.38), consistent with the marking *con espressione*. However, because of the smoother subdivision and the one important pitch around which the phrase moves, the uncomfortable feel of the Beethoven phrase (in Ex. 2.37) is missing in Mozart's melodic line. Interpretively, the physical pulling away of the two-note slur from the quarter note (separating between the two-note slur and the quarter note) links the phrasing to the extramusical idea of parting in Op. 81a (Ex. 2.39). In the slow movement of the same sonata, the repetition of the dotted motive becomes progressively more earnest through modifications of the articulation (Ex. 2.40).

Ex. 2.38. Mozart, Sonata K. 311, II, mm. 1–2.

Ex. 2.39. Beethoven, Sonata Op. 81a, I, mm. 17–19.

Ex. 2.40. Beethoven, Sonata Op. 81a, II, mm. 1, 5, 11–12.

The expressive climax of the Recitativo in the third movement of Op. 110 occurs with two-note slurs on the same pitch (Ex. 2.41). The speaking quality of the passage is supported by a cluster of expressive directions: the 4–3 fingering (indicating that the second note is to be played), the long pedal, and the *crescendo* to *tutte le corde*, followed by *decrescendo* back to *una corda*. In an instance where no fingering is given (Ex. 2.42), musical sense tells one that the staccato over the tied note indicates a precise release and not a re-striking of the note.

Ex. 2.41. Beethoven, Sonata Op. 110, III, m. 5.

Ex. 2.42. Beethoven, Sonata Op. 28, I, mm. 141–43.

A slur figure in the first movement of Op. 101 (Ex. 2.43), another effort figure, presents the problem of a two-note slur beneath a slur extending over all three eighths. Since it is impossible for both slurs to be articulated, it would seem reasonable that the first eighth, with which both slurs begin, should receive additional stress, less than *sforzando* but heavier than a single slur would produce. The lower two-note slur, if stretched, conveys the yearning quality of the particular phrase. This figure, especially with the addition of *sforzando*, is as effortful as the contortion in Michelangelo's figures of *Night* and *Day* in the Medici tombs. Like the twisted posture, the complexity of the slurs and the unnatural stress on a weak beat represent a physical distortion of the norm. The notated shortening of the second note of the two-note slur in Ex. 2.44 isolates the expressiveness of the long melodic leap downward and encourages one to stretch the beat. The same notated shortening of note values defines the character of weakening and complaining (Beethoven's words: *Ermattet, klagend*) in the second *Arioso* in Op. 110.

Ex. 2.43. Beethoven, Sonata Op. 101, I, mm. 14, 49.

Ex. 2.44. Beethoven, Sonata Op. 2 No. 2, IV, mm. 2–3.

Ex. 2.45. Beethoven, Sonata Op. 110, III, mm. 120–21.

Exx. 2.46–2.51 illustrate the singular musical character created by a two-note slurred figure that is either unusually abrupt or clipped. In Exx. 2.46 and 2.47 an exaggerated separation is necessary for the full effect of the *sforzando* to be heard. A two-note slur that is to be treated as a grace-note figure is mentioned on at least four occasions in Czerny: "The 2 eighths sharply broken off without being connected with the quarter that follows [Ex. 2.48]."[5] "The separated sixteenths are to be played quickly, almost like grace notes [Ex. 2.49]."[6]

Ex. 2.46. Beethoven, Sonata Op. 2 No. 1, III, mm. 12–14.

Ex. 2.47. Beethoven, Sonata Op. 26, II, mm. 1–2.

Ex. 2.48. Beethoven, Sonata Op. 28, III, mm. 5–8.

Ex. 2.49. Beethoven, Sonata Op. 78, II, m. 12.

Ex. 2.50. Beethoven, Concerto Op. 15, III, m. 1.

"In this theme, [Ex. 2.50], the 2 sixteenths are separated in such manner that the second of the two is torn off and in no way slurred together with the eighth that follows. Therefore more in this fashion: than this . The left hand in the same manner."[7] Ex. 2.51 "is to be played softly and lightly, but at the same time the second sixteenth in [mm. 123–24] short and broken quickly, somewhat like this":[8]

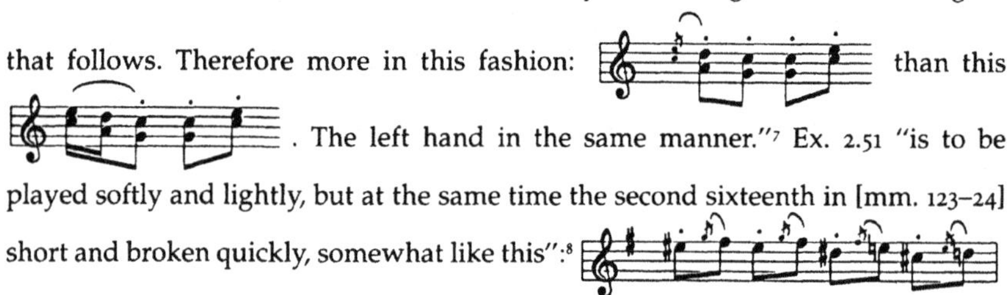

Ex. 2.51. Beethoven, Concerto Op. 58, I, m. 123.

Curiously, Czerny's slurs in m. 125 depart from the pattern of the previous two measures and from the original edition. Other passages of two-note slurs that might be treated similarly are shown in Exx. 2.52 and 2.53.

Ex. 2.52. Beethoven, Sonata Op. 49 No. 2, II, mm. 28–29.

Ex. 2.53. Beethoven, Sonata Op. 81a, III, mm. 9–10.

If not as grace-note figures, the slurred seconds in the first movement of the "Tempest" (Ex. 2.54) are reportedly to be played as though one were dusting off the keys.[9] Not only is the movement built on three ideas (the broken chord, slurred seconds, and turn figure), but themes have been reduced to their basic raw material—sound—in this instance, sound that moves and sound that does not, the sound of stillness and rustling sounds, and sounds that either ascend or descend versus sounds that whine in circling movements. A tune-theme may please the senses, but a theme that is a sound effect intrigues the imagination. Other slurs seem more strongly associated with structure. The G-major Sonata, Op. 49 No. 2, begins with a chord and a flourish, followed by a slurred phrase; it is the latter which begets the second theme of the movement, as well as the theme of the *Tempo di Menuetto*. The tetrachord is an important building block in the outer movements of Op. 27 No. 2; the articulation slurs and dynamic swells in the second theme of the finale mark off the melodic patterns that trace the stepwise ascent of four notes (Ex. 2.55).

Ex. 2.54. Beethoven, Sonata Op. 31 No. 2, I, mm. 2–3.

Ex. 2.55. Beethoven, Sonata Op. 27 No. 2, III, mm. 21–25.

In Op. 78, thematic material in both movements is related to an ascending second that should be clearly distinguishable to the listener through the articulation (Ex. 2.56).

Ex. 2.56. Beethoven, Sonata Op. 78, I, mm. 31–32; II, mm. 1–2, 22.

In Op. 109, the tetrachord is again an important compositional building block, which Beethoven marked, in this instance, not only with a slur but also with the indication legato (Ex. 2.57).

Ex. 2.57. Beethoven, Sonata Op. 109, I, mm. 67–69.

While all the important themes of Op. 110 lie within the compass of a hexachord, the exposition of the first movement is built on a stepwise descent through four structural pitches, the same pitches as the four slurred notes with which the second movement opens (Ex. 2.58); for this reason the slur should not be extended over the bar into the third measure. In the Bagatelle Op. 126 No. 1, the melodic tag in m. 20 is repeated in ever-shorter note values; the three-note pattern is kept intact by means of rests, articulation slurs, and dynamic markings (Ex. 2.59).

Ex. 2.58. Beethoven, Sonata Op. 110, II, mm. 1–4.

Ex. 2.59. Beethoven, Bagatelle Op. 126 No. 1, mm. 16–28.

The phrasing of the original is clear and unambiguous, a fact that can be appreciated if compared with excerpts from a 1913 article entitled "Secrets of Artistic Phrasing."[10] The author, theorist and historian Hugo Riemann, was at that time professor of music at the University of Leipzig. To support his argument, he quotes Jerome Joseph de Momigny, a French theorist and composer who lived from 1762 until 1838: "All unaccented beats stand in the relation of upbeats to the next succeeding accented beats." Riemann then proceeds to add slurs to the opening of the Sonata Op. 7, in which the original lacks any slurs whatsoever until the fifth measure.

> In the first case [Beethoven's original] there would be increased depth of expression such as painful sighing; while in the latter, the widely separated notes of the upbeat and the long leap are full of bold energy. It is at once clear that only the latter form of interpretation corresponds to the character of the whole movement . . . .

Editing of this sort is fortunately harmless, since it is impossible to make a listener actually hear (1) a nonexistent upbeat to such a definite beginning on a downbeat or (2) the chord in the second measure as melodically disassociated from the first measure and instead melodically connected, over rests, to the beginning of m. 3. The author continues,

> Like possibilities of false reading could be found in hundreds of examples selected from the works of this same composer. For instance, the fervently tender, and almost mischievous, opening measures of Beethoven's E-flat major Pianoforte Sonata, Op. 27, No. 1:

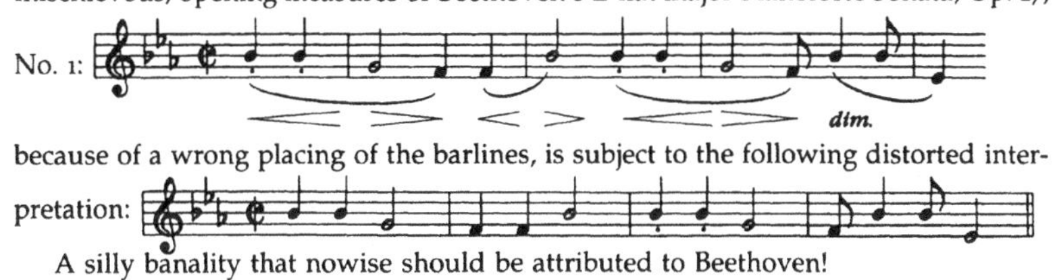

> because of a wrong placing of the barlines, is subject to the following distorted interpretation:
>
> A silly banality that nowise should be attributed to Beethoven!

Even allowing for the preceding century's creative attitude toward the score, the naked fact that the "distorted interpretation" is Beethoven's own barring of the passage recalls José Iturbi's remark that the floor of hell will be paved with the skulls of editors. Beethoven manipulated the stress in the opening of Op. 27 No. 1 by placing the longer notes on weak beats, resulting in an impression of harmonies that stand still like colors on the page. Riemann, in his improved version, assigned stresses, ensuring that the harmonic content would go somewhere. Ironically, what was originally simple and understated is, after improvement, still simple but overstated and truly banal. The article continues with a warning that rests and notes of long value should not always be regarded as marking the end of a motive: "Some of the most intense and forceful effects rest upon the writing of rests within a motive (*Innenpausen*), and also upon an emphasized lengthening of an upbeat through the placing of a rest even at the beginning of a motive." Riemann then quotes the Bagatelle, Op. 126 No. 1, maintaining that it

> would convince even the most doubting Thomas of the need of deepening his faculty of comprehension by the serious study of the theory of phrasing. Instead of:
>
> 
>
>
> Beethoven writes the passage with rests scattered throughout:
>
> 
>
>
> and these rests easily cause a mistaken way of reading. He who accepts the long *a* (♩.) in the fourth measure, as also the rests in the fifth measure, and those following, as motive endings, as boundaries of motives, will hardly take much pleasure in this truly wonderful composition; but rather he will wonder at the crinkled stuff the great master has written.

If the player cannot get "the simple form whose principle is shown above" straight, he should either use a phrased edition or study a book on phrasing in order to learn how to deal with obstacles such as that posed by the Bagatelle.

> On the other hand, he who pays attention to the proper phrasing finds the passage to be exquisite and very finely wrought and very far from being confused and meaningless:

The feminine ending, a–f♯, in the fourth measure should be clearly understood, a matter made difficult by the length of the a; but when the meaning of this feminine ending is grasped, then the still more complicated feminine endings caused by the rest and appended notes are somewhat simplified.

If there is a lesson to be learned from "Secrets of Artistic Phrasing" it is that academic zeal must be tempered by common sense. There are no secrets regarding musical phrasing in Beethoven's notation; once one has learned the meaning of the lines and dots, the realization of the composer's intent should be as instinctive as the spoken inflections of one's native language.

Philip Emanuel Bach's statement that the notes of a slurred broken chord should be held down[11] is yet another device for releasing the expressive potential of the simplest idea. Since Beethoven advised Czerny's father to purchase a copy of Bach's *Essay* for his son, the practice just described could presumably be applied to appropriate passages in his own music. For example, holding the slurred broken chords at the beginning of the Rondo of the *Pathétique* makes possible the use of shorter pedals, so that details of articulation in the theme are not lost in either washes of sound or dry, seemingly unattached sounds (Ex. 2.60).

Ex. 2.60. Beethoven, Sonata Op. 13, III, m. 1.

Czerny advised that each bar of the second movement (the A-section and its repetition) of Op. 27 No. 1 should be separated from the following bar at the barline, so that the third quarter note would always sound somewhat staccato and torn off.[12] Holding the three quarter notes under the slur produces a dynamic swell within each C-minor broken chord, a breathless, gasping effect (Ex. 2.61). The same swelling of sound resulting from holding down slurred broken chords follows six measures of non legato sixteenth notes with which the finale of Op. 27 No. 2 begins. Beethoven undoubtedly intended the device as an intensification leading to the *forte* in m. 9 (Ex. 2.62). Czerny's comment that consonant notes within a *legatissimo* could be held down parallels Bach's statement.[13] As shown in Exx. 2.63 and 2.64, Beethoven on occasion added a verbal direction to such slurs. In the finale of Op. 31 No. 2, however, Beethoven specified which broken chords were to be held down (Ex. 2.65).

Ex. 2.61. Beethoven, Sonata Op. 27 No. 1, II, mm. 1–2, 89–90.

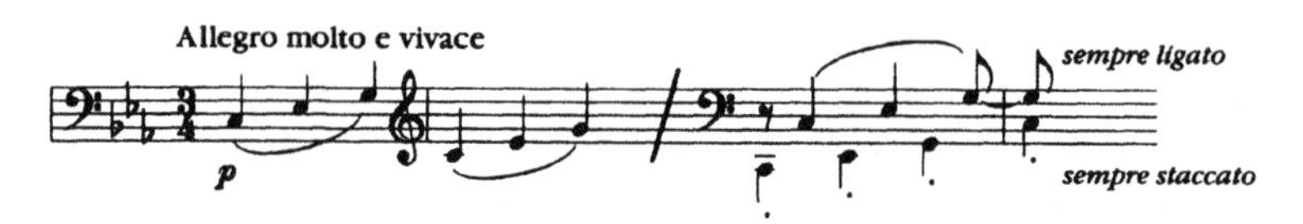

Ex. 2.62. Beethoven, Sonata Op. 27 No. 2, III, m. 7.

Ex. 2.63. Beethoven, Sonata Op. 28, IV, m. 17.

Ex. 2.64. Beethoven, Rondo Op. 51 No. 1, m. 110.

Ex. 2.65. Beethoven, Sonata Op. 31 No. 2, III, mm. 322–27.

Like the passage from the Beethoven E♭ Sonata in Ex. 2.61, the beginning of the Mozart B♭ Sonata K. 570 is also slurred from barline to barline. Musical instinct will naturally express its preference for an unbroken line, since, unlike the Beethoven, the character is anything but dramatic, and a noticeable break between measures would sound contrived. In Ex. 2.66 we may presume that Mozart gave the broken chord individuality by notating within it the sensation of stress and lift, producing, instead of a bland sameness, a gentle rocking motion and an elasticity within the line that stretches downward and then floats upward.

Ex. 2.66. Mozart, Sonata K. 570, I, mm. 1–7.

Depending upon the extent he wished to emphasize the change of harmony, Beethoven might have separated the first three measures in Ex. 2.67, following which an uninterrupted line would have been effective. A definite separation at the barline before the *sforzando* on f♭ in the second theme of Op. 2 No. 1 makes clear the tonal ambiguity of a key that is A♭ major/minor, as well as the relationship to the opening theme, of which the second theme is an inversion (Ex. 2.68). A phrasing break just preceding the ascending scale beginning with the *forte* in the third measure in Ex. 2.69 is musically convincing, principally because a regular 6/8 grouping is being reestablished, following the 2/8 grouping of the sixteenths in the previous measures.

Ex. 2.67. Beethoven, Sonata Op. 14 No. 1, II, mm. 1–8.

Ex. 2.68. Beethoven, Sonata Op. 2 No. 1, I, mm. 20–22.

Ex. 2.69. Beethoven, Sonata Op. 27 No. 1, I, mm. 59–62.

Words such as "lift," "stress," "pressure," "release," "connection," and "separation," although inadequate to indicate precise nuances of articulation, describe the muscular sensation by which the mind makes very exact calculations regarding duration and intensity. Just as the units of length in the English system of measurement, such as inch, foot, yard, and mile, were derived from the members and performance of the human body, technique as touch implies that the dimensions of the spiritual are known by the measure of the physical.

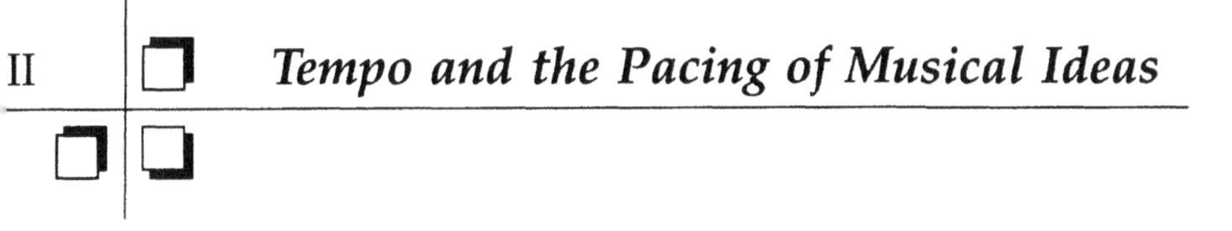

II Tempo and the Pacing of Musical Ideas

The notes I handle no better than many pianists. But the pauses between the notes—ah, that is where the art resides!

ARTUR SCHNABEL

A score, like a map, is a visual representation of an abstract idea, the one a design in time, the other a location in space. To be meaningful, each must be experienced. A highway map indicates the exact distance between Denver and Salt Lake City, but driving a certain number of hours over mountain highways, through traffic, or while hungry or thirsty or tired will indicate the *conscious* distance between the two cities.

The indicated tempo for a piece may be conceived as an absolute, exact and unchanging, like the movement of a clock by which one keeps daily appointments. Pacing, as in "pacing oneself," is the tempo of the moment, the time it takes to make musical ideas intelligible. Like the words we speak, not every musical idea is of equal importance, taking more or less time to be introduced, thought about, and left. The metronome marking merely indicates a mean, as Beethoven noted in a sketchbook: "100 according to Maelzel, but this is valid only for the first measures, since feeling also has its beat, which however cannot be expressed completely by this tempo (namely, 100)."[1]

Keyboardists function relatively detached from the biological act of living. We can continue physical breathing while playing, and, for that matter, can play *prestissimo* for hours without panting. We must be reminded that instruments of multiple pitches or variable pitch derive their expressive power from emulating the original instrument, the human voice. "Why limit the piano to the limitations of the human voice?" a student once asked. The question illustrates the importance of teaching that the pacing of a phrase should be decided by imagining a singer's breath control, and that of leaps and intricate subdivisions by the time required to sing through the notes.

If technique is knowing where one is going to be when, the usefulness of the metronome in coordinating muscles, ears, and mind is evident. Just as important, however, is explaining how musical content pulls against this inflexible beat, whether within phrases or between formal sections. Expressive playing is much like pulling on a rubber band, feeling it stretch and then return to its original shape. The teacher who wishes to be indispensable by becoming dispensable will share with the student a basis for judgment, beginning with tempo modifications already indicated by the composer and the reason for these indications.

In the exposition of the first movement of Op. 2 No. 2, a *rallentando* is indicated at m. 48, the point where a neighboring-tone pattern appears (Ex. 3.1). It follows what has been predominantly linear writing, alternately rising and falling in a sustained direction. When the motive is expanded to a theme in m. 58, the *espressivo* turns aside the exuberant thrust of the opening forty-odd measures by indicating that the tempo be held back, a musical signpost pointing to an important moment in the continuation of the movement: the emergence of the twisting motive that strains upward, probing for a stable tonal center. The long lines that have covered a wide expanse of keyboard space are superceded by brief circular units that occupy, by comparison, the smallest possible space. The markings *rallentando* and *espressivo* occur at a musical intersection of freedom and confinement, of effortless play and straining toward the "somewhere" of a diminished seventh chord.

Ex. 3.1. Beethoven, Sonata Op. 2 No. 2, I, mm. 47–49, 58–60.

The *espressivo* over the second theme in the first movement of Op. 81a draws attention not only to the motivic derivation (Ex. 3.2) but also to the programmatic significance of the original *Lebewohl* inscription. The *espressivo* placed over this particular theme and its recurrence recalls Beethoven's remark that "feeling also has its beat." Tempo modifications not specifically indicated by the composer but done at the discretion of the player ought to have a similar logical basis. The examples below have to do with the corners of a musical building—introducing a new section and defining its boundary, a new tonality, subdivision, dynamic level, character, articulation, melodic line, or modulation. To overlook the arrival of a different idea, because of playing like a robot or like a libertine, is as inexcusable as carelessness with respect to correct notes, dynamics, or articulation.

Ex. 3.2. Beethoven, Sonata Op. 81a, I, mm. 1–2, 50–52.

Concerning the finale of the *Waldstein*, Czerny wrote, "As peaceful as the beginning must be, with the entrance of the *ff* and the triplet passages that follow, the liveliness will be increased somewhat, which however returns to the earlier calm at the re-entry of the theme."[2] The quickening subdivision and the dynamic intensity in the development of the second movement of the Mozart A-minor Sonata (Ex. 3.3) likewise ominously hasten the pace of the movement to the point at which the sextuplet repeated notes burst forth. The repeated notes sound faster than the preceding broken chord sextuplets, since we become aware of *each* note.

Ex. 3.3. Mozart, Sonata K. 310, II, mm. 31–32, 37–38, 43.

Similarly, the eight measures of slurred eighth-note pairs opening the development of the first movement of K. 311 sound held back, followed by a return to the original tempo with the sixteenths in m. 48 (Ex. 3.4). In the middle movement of the same sonata, the sixteenth-note accompaniment and generally longer note values in the melody line beginning in m. 8 sound "released" following the unsmooth rhythm and fragmented articulation of the previous bars (Ex. 3.5).

Ex. 3.4. Mozart, Sonata K. 311, I, mm. 40–41, 48.

Ex. 3.5. Mozart, Sonata K. 311, II, mm. 7–10.

In Ex. 3.6, the pauses, the change from legato to non legato, and the position of the *f* encourage one to avoid a mechanical beat. At first hesitating and then moving forward sounds improvisatory, as though the piece were at that point taking shape in Haydn's mind. The development section of the same movement opens with a quiet half cadence in C minor/major that, after some twenty measures of working out, recurs *forte*. Broadening the tempo approaching the second cadence lends a grandeur to the painting-like perspective between these two points (Ex. 3.7).

Ex. 3.6. Haydn, Sonata No. 62, I, mm. 3–5.

Ex. 3.7. Haydn, Sonata No. 62, I, mm. 44–45, 66–67.

Delaying the *pianissimo* chord in Ex. 3.8 would likewise underscore the pivotal effect of the diminished seventh chord, appearing somewhat hesitantly as one idea ends in a distant key and another begins in the expected key. The movement is as impulsive tonally as it is in its keyboard style; the rests surrounding the diminished seventh constitute a pause preceding still another impulsive sally. Although the unvocal leaps in Ex. 3.9 pose no difficulty on the keyboard, it would seem musically right to stretch the phrase as would a singer adjusting to awkward intervals. Following the dreamy E-major section, the *ffp* in Ex. 3.10 arrests the tempo and jars the listener's attention to the sudden shift back to E♭ major, marked with no fewer than three *pianissimos.*

Ex. 3.8. Beethoven, Sonata Op. 10 No. 2, I, mm. 44–47.

Ex. 3.9. Beethoven, Sonata Op. 14 No. 2, I, mm. 6–8.

Ex. 3.10. Beethoven Sonata Op. 7, IV, mm. 161–62.

Pacing relates also to character. The *ritardando* in Ex. 3.11, again the composer's own indication of tempo modification, deepens the seriousness of the heavy repeated chords, only for us to discover, at the *a tempo*, that it was a ruse. A tempo modification may be nothing more than treating a dynamic stress *tenuto*, as in Ex. 3.12, where the *sf* on the third beat makes the melodic ascent sound as though it strained one's strength. As foreign as it may be to an ideal of facile playing that our training often instills, the experience of struggle is part of the musical structure in Beethoven. The pedalled recitatives in the first movement of Op. 31 No. 2 are the only melodic phrases of any length in the movement. The mysterious character will be lost if the Allegro is resumed too abruptly (Ex. 3.13).

Ex. 3.11. Beethoven, Sonata Op. 31 No. 3, I, mm. 91–92, 96.

Ex. 3.12. Beethoven, Sonata Op. 28, I, mm. 122–25.

Ex. 3.13. Beethoven, Sonata Op. 31 No. 2, I, mm. 158–60.

Dwelling on the heaviness of the offbeats in the melodic line of the third variation of Op. 26 sets up a contrast with the rhythmic lightness of the variation that follows, which then sounds as though it had been set free to move ahead (Ex. 3.14). Holding back the tempo at the end of mm. 46 and 47 in Ex. 3.15 suggests reflection followed by action.

Ex. 3.14. Beethoven, Sonata Op. 26, I, Variations III and IV.

Ex. 3.15. Mozart, Sonata K. 284, I, mm. 46–48.

The student who believed the music was "too sacred" to expand a phrase at a climatic moment in Op. 111 exemplifies a pervasive reluctance to respond to an idea in the score, if such response involves elasticity of tempo: "If you play Mozart that way, it will be too romantic." In reality, the character, and therefore the rightness of the interpretation, is written in the score. We cannot alter it; we can only reveal it or ignore it. What is in the score to be revealed is Mozart, the person, speaking about what it is like to be alive. Would the man who wrote his father that he had never prayed as fervently or received communion as devoutly as when Constanze was by his side deny subjective response when he sat down at the instrument or put his pen to the paper at his desk? On the contrary, there is so much of life in a Mozart sonata that one is hard pressed to reveal the whole of it.

One might imagine an age when time was not conceived as the price of a Superbowl commercial but was measured by the passing of thoughts across the sky of the mind. That which is sacred is not the ticking of the metronome but meaning, which is our response to character. The interpreter who breathes between phrases or stretches intensity is not distorting "Classic" style. Instead, there is no higher discipline than intelligently obeying the spirit within the music.

IV Dynamic Nuance and Musical Line

The worn faces and figures dressed in black in family photo albums from past generations, when placed next to the glamorous model in the cigarette ad who has "come a long way," illustrate how far the reality of the one world lay from the illusions of the other. There was little to distract the one from the fact of tomorrow's labor: no thoughts of "overnight to London" or "live via satellite from Tokyo," no cars, no radio, no labor-saving appliances, and no wonder drugs. However, the figure in black and the model, each in her time, had in common the biological capability to pass on to the next generation life and physical characteristics.

A Bach fugue subject is for a fugue what human genes are for heredity. If the subject moves stepwise, the writing of the fugue will be smooth; if leaps predominate, the fugue will sound more instrumental than vocal. Like the average person living in the year 1722, who accepted more readily than we the social and occupational boundaries inherited through birth, a Bach fugue subject is less important in and for itself than as the genetic blueprint for the piece.

The piano, offering a control of nuance unavailable on instruments of fixed dynamic levels and the capacity to project sound far beyond that of the clavichord, became an aesthetic watershed that would alter forever the way Bach's keyboard works would be heard. Then also, things must have seemed to have come a long way. It is inconceivable that the musician playing the preludes and figures on a fortepiano in the year 1800 would have been distracted by considerations such as terrace dynamics or whether "bringing out" a particular voice was appropriate.

When playing music of the past, making music with whatever means available was undoubtedly more important than a concern for what has become known as performance practice. Czerny's editing of the *Well-Tempered Clavier* was based on a healthy confidence in his own creativity. In the preface he states:

> It has been my endeavor to indicate tempo and interpretation:
> First, according to the unmistakable character of each movement;
> Secondly, according to the well-remembered impression made on me by Beethoven's rendering of a great number of these fugues;
> Thirdly, according to convictions matured by more than thirty years' study of this work.[1]

Significantly, one finds in almost every subject an accent placed over the note at the turning point of the phrase, indicating dynamic direction toward some point of stress.

Ex. 4.1. Bach, *Well-Tempered Clavier*, Book I, fugue subjects (according to Czerny).

Because all dynamic inflection is realized through touch, Czerny's edition of the *Well-Tempered Clavier* is a kind of touch recording enabling us to imagine Beethoven's aesthetic ideal through our fingertips and muscles, as well as our ears. For Bach there were other devices to project the ebb and flow of intensity and a sense of climax: the direction of lines, contrapuntal devices, harmonic rhythm, the density of the writing, a particular area in the compass of the keyboard. Czerny's editing speaks for the musical thinking of his generation, namely, interpretation shaped by the dynamic qualities of the piano, on which a spirit of insecurity, searching, and striving for fulfillment found its true element. Whether or not it would have seemed alien to the thinking of Bach and his contemporaries, what was for him an important pitch in the phrase became, under the hands of Beethoven and Czerny, the focal point of the phrase through dynamic level as well. Since dynamic contrast evokes the listener's immediate response, goose pimples had now become part of the structure of the piece.

Unlike pitch, which is the same from one day to the next, dynamic level is subject to the tides of the player's psychological state. Walter Georgii's characterization of the Baroque as music of "being" and that of the Classic era as music of "happening"[2] applies also to performance. In part because of the nature of their respective instruments, a work that the keyboardist/interpreter of 1722 heard in terms of the oneness of the affection of the piece would have been "brought up to date" by pianists of Beethoven's day and habit of thinking with the unbounded tonal fantasy of the player. The greater availability of sensuous sound must have been intoxicating, leading to an increased subjectivity and sense of aloneness in the nineteenth century. Thomas Mann developed this theme in *Tod in Venedig*, in which Aschenbach speaks to the Polish boy in his imagination as he sits delirious on the seashore:

> For beauty, Phaidros, bear this in mind, only beauty is at the same time divine and visible, and thus it is the way of the sensuous, it is, little Phaidros, the way of the artist to the spirit. But do you believe, my dear fellow, that he can ever acquire wisdom and manly dignity, for whom the way to the spiritual leads through the senses? Or do you believe on the contrary (I leave the choice to you) that this is a dangerous-charming way, in truth a way of error and sin, that impels us to wander? . . . We poets . . . are not able to soar upwards, we are only able to yield to excess.[3]

While this may seem a circuitous approach to the treatment of dynamics in Beethoven and the Classic period generally, the heart of the matter is the momentary coordination of dynamic levels and expressive intent. How much of the former does it take to make the listener pay attention to the latter? The question makes every performance a new undertaking. A reviewer may refer to a particular recording as the "definitive performance," but who can predict attitudes two generations hence toward a performance that has been stilled for fifty years in plastic?

The repertoire of the Classic period consists of a fabric of relatively few notes, in which the physical energy directed into an individual note produces a result that may be both more sensitively shaded or more intense. Exx. 4.2–4.5 show an increasing intensity in the association of dynamic and line, from an appoggiatura (Ex. 4.2) to an *fp* over a single note (Ex. 4.3) to the voicing of a melody line in chords and octaves that naturally calls for greater exertion and produces more sound (Ex. 4.4). Then, as now, diverging lines symbolize increasing tension. Add the force of octaves and full chords, *forte* to *fortissimo*, and the effect can be overwhelming (Ex. 4.5).

Ex. 4.2. Mozart, Sonata K. 284, I, mm. 17–19.

Ex. 4.3. Mozart, Sonata K. 309, II, m. 1.

Ex. 4.4. Beethoven, Sonata Op. 10 No. 2, I, mm. 18–22.

Ex. 4.5. Beethoven, Sonata Op. 2 No. 2, II, mm. 16–18.

In the cadential refrain from the first movement of Op. 90, the precise point to which a *crescendo* leads determines character. The ending of the *crescendo* on the supertonic seventh chord, when previously it had continued to the dominant seventh, suggests a shift from resolve to resignation (Ex. 4.6). A dynamic marking may be a signpost for an important structural pattern. The indications of *ff* and *sf* in the final measures of the first movement of Op. 2 No. 1 are the physical marking of an intellectual construction, the descending hexachord motive that appears throughout the sonata. That a cerebral concept should be made intelligible through physical violence will remain a revolutionary idea as long as the sonata is played (Ex. 4.7).

Ex. 4.6. Beethoven, Sonata Op. 90, I, mm. 16–24.

Ex. 4.7. Beethoven, Sonata Op. 2 No. 1, I, mm. 146–52.

For Beethoven, the upper limit of the keyboard presented another limitation to be challenged. The second half of Ex. 4.8 is an exact transposition, a fourth higher, of the first half. With the highest pitch approaching the top of the piano's compass, Beethoven places the dynamic swell at *that* point, earlier in the phrase than previously, defying the weak-sounding register in his piano.

Ex. 4.8. Beethoven, Sonata Op. 10 No. 1, I, mm. 118–33.

Like Czerny's interpretive markings in the *Well-Tempered Clavier* "according to the unmistakable character" of the movement, a *subito piano* or a similar sharp contrast, as in Exx. 4.9–4.12, is responsible for the impression of vacillation and self-consciousness. A *subito piano* seems musically and muscularly unnatural because it disturbs the shape of a phrase. Just as unnatural is an extended passage in which there is no dynamic change at all, such as the sequential writing, *forte,* beginning in m. 110 in the development section of the finale of Op. 31 No. 2 and continuing for forty measures. Similar passages are found in the development section of other Beethoven sonata-allegro movements, such as the first movements of the Fourth and Fifth Concertos and the first movement of the Sonata Op. 53. Dramatically, one might imagine the effect of a tantrum played out on stage while action having to do with the plot is suspended (Ex. 4.13). A dynamic marking over a held note also suspends movement (Ex. 4.14).

Ex. 4.9. Beethoven, Sonata Op. 10 No. 3, IV, mm. 53–55.

Ex. 4.10. Beethoven, Sonata Op. 26, I, mm. 24–25.

Ex. 4.11. Beethoven, Sonata Op. 27 No. 1, III, mm. 11–12.

Ex. 4.12. Mozart, Sonata K. 279, II, mm. 18–19.

Ex. 4.13. Beethoven, Sonata Op. 31 No. 2, III, mm. 110–11.

Ex. 4.14. Beethoven, Sonata Op. 10 No. 1, I, mm. 28–34.

Mention should be made of those instances in which a dynamic marking is repeated although not preceded by any indication of a change in dynamic level. For example, the *piano* indicated in m. 14 of the Menuetto of Op. 2 No. 1 is followed five measures later by another *piano*. The melodic/harmonic sequence in the four intervening measures rises, in observance of which one instinctively wants to insert a *crescendo*. In the finale of the same sonata, there is no dynamic indication between the *piano* in m. 34 and the *fortissimo* in m. 50, while, in the parallel passage in the recapitulation, *piano* is indicated again at the repeat of the melodic line midway through the section. Was this intentional? Was it a mistake that occurred during engraving? Perhaps there is an interpretive basis for a *crescendo* that falls back and rises again, as though the character of the piece at that point were so impatient to reach the fury of the final eight measures that it could not be contained.

Other examples invite similar speculation. In the Scherzo of Op. 2 No. 3, *piano* is repeated in m. 8. Was this because the gradually increasing density of the writing produced in practice a *crescendo*? If so, the same reason could be advanced for the repetition of the *piano* in m. 8 of the second movement of Op. 10 No. 2. Two examples from the second movement of Op. 10 No. 3 occur (mm. 17 and 78) at a point at which one might wish to move to a higher dynamic level. In the Rondo of the same sonata, was the *pianissimo* repeated in m. 76 because one might be inclined to play a *crescendo* in the motivic descent into the bass in the two preceding measures? Should the latter be avoided in deference to the indicated *crescendo* in m. 77? Might the repeated *pianissimo* in m. 25 of the first movement of Op. 27 No. 1 be a similar caution to avoid playing the repeated eighth-note chords louder? Or does it reestablish the earlier dynamic level following the accent and expanding lines of the preceding measure? (The *pianissimo* is similarly repeated in m. 5.) At other times, the reason for the re-indication of *piano* seems to have been the introduction of a subsection and new material, as in m. 25 of the first movement of Op. 31 No. 3 and m. 153 of the second movement of Op. 49 No. 1. In the Prestissimo of the Rondo of Op. 53, *pianissimo* is indicated anew at each restatement of the theme in a new key—in mm. 493, 497, and 501—possibly, and one must emphasize the adverb, because the long pedal causes sonority to accumulate.

Dynamic level being an immediate determinant of response, it follows that extremes of dynamics should be essential to Beethoven's musical speech and no doubt were his stock in trade when improvising. At such moments, the transcendent impression of the music was no doubt due to an attempt to communicate unbounded dynamic dimensions. Playing that reflects that attempt reveals that dynamic nuance and contrast is the most telling musical device the pianist of the twentieth century has in common with the living Beethoven's improvisation. As such, it is the interpreter's door to the spirit of the music, the beginning point for realizing the composer's intent.

V The Role of Silence

Speech after long silence; it is right.

WILLIAM BUTLER YEATS

Whether a jazz band playing *sempre fortissimo*, or electronic nothings piped into our ear when phoning or swathing our consciousness when shopping or dining, we become accustomed to decibels and white noise and become uneasy when we have to listen to silence. Silence is the sound of aloneness, when we become conscious of unhappiness or boredom. For the musician, silence is the sound of the inner self, the sound of concentration. As shown by the following table, Beethoven frequently notated an extended silence at the conclusion of a movement, creating a frame for the listening experience. The sonatas listed are those in which one or more movements end with a fermata over a final rest (marked *) or with a fermata over a complete measure of rest (marked **).

	Tempo	Meter	Dynamic Level
Op. 2/1	*Allegro	¢	*ff*
	*Adagio	3/4	*pp*
	Menuetto	3/4	*pp*
	*Prestissimo	¢	*ff*
Op. 2/2	**Allegro vivace	2/4	*pp*
	Largo appassionato	3/4	*pp*
	Scherzo: Allegretto	3/4	*ff*
	Rondo: Grazioso	c	*p*
Op. 2/3	*Allegro con brio	c	*ff*

	Adagio	2/4	*pp*
	*Scherzo: Allegro	3/4	*pp*
	*Allegro assai	6/8	*ff*
Op. 7	**Allegro molto e con brio	6/8	*ff*
	*Largo, con gran espressione	3/4	*pp*
	Allegro	3/4	*f*
	*Rondo: Poco Allegretto e grazioso	2/4	*pp*
Op. 10/1	**Allegro molto e con brio	3/4	*ff*
	Adagio molto	2/4	*pp*
	*Prestissimo	¢	*p*
Op. 10/2	*Allegro	2/4	*ff*
	**Allegretto	3/4	*f*
	**Presto	2/4	*ff*
Op. 10/3	**Presto	¢	*ff*
	*Largo e mesto	6/8	*pp*
	Menuetto: Allegro	3/4	*pp*
	*Rondo: Allegro	c	*p*
Op. 13	**Grave—Allegro molto e con brio	c/¢	*ff*
	Adagio cantabile	2/4	*pp*
	*Rondo: Allegro	¢	*ff*
Op. 14/1	Allegro	c	*pp*
	**Allegretto	3/4	*pp*
	Rondo: Allegro comodo	¢	*f*
Op. 28	**Allegro	3/4	*pp*
	Andante	2/4	*pp*
	Scherzo: Allegro vivace	3/4	*ff*
	Rondo: Allegro, ma non troppo	6/8	*ff*
Op. 31/1	**Allegro vivace	2/4	*p*
	Adagio	9/8	*pp*
	**Allegretto	¢	*pp*
Op. 31/3	Allegro	3/4	*f*
	Scherzo: Allegretto vivace	2/4	*pp*
	Menuetto: Moderato e grazioso	3/4	*pp*
	*Presto con fuoco	6/8	*ff*
Op. 49/1	Andante	2/4	*pp*
	*Rondo: Allegro	6/8	*ff*
Op. 49/2	*Allegro, ma non troppo	¢	
	Tempo di Menuetto	3/4	
Op. 53	Allegro con brio	c	*ff*
	*Adagio molto—Allegretto	2/4	*f*
Op. 54	In Tempo d'un Menuetto	3/4	*pp*
	*Allegretto	2/4	*ff*

Op. 57	Allegro assai	12/8	*ppp*
	Andante con moto	2/4	*ff*
	*Allegro ma non troppo	2/4	*ff*
Op. 79	*Presto alla tedesca	3/4	*p*
	Andante	9/8	*p*
	Vivace	2/4	*p*
Op. 90	*Mit Lebhaftigkeit	3/4	*pp*
	Nicht zu geschwind	2/4	*pp*
Op. 101	Etwas lebhaft	6/8	*p*
	*Lebhaft	c	*f*
	Langsam	2/4	
	*Geschwinde	2/4	*ff*

In the sonatas following Op. 14 No. 1, the complete measure of rest with fermata occurs much less frequently.

Silence, then, is the blackboard on which the Classic repertoire is written. Whether or not Mozart actually said that the rests were as important in his music as the notes, the remark is excellent advice. Listening to silence promotes the clarity of partwriting and articulation and the significance of individual notes (Exx. 5.1–5.3). Silence acts as a psychological buffer zone between dramatic outbursts (Ex. 5.4) and as a means of separating formal sections (Ex. 5.5).

Ex. 5.1. Beethoven, Sonata Op. 2 No. 1, I, mm. 11–16.

Ex. 5.2. Beethoven, Sonata Op. 2 No. 2, II, mm. 1–2.

Ex. 5.3. Beethoven, Sonata Op. 2 No. 3, IV, mm. 111–12.

Ex. 5.4. Mozart, Sonata K. 457, III, mm. 269–75.

Ex. 5.5. Haydn, Sonata No. 31, I, mm. 16–18.

The importance of silence in these examples can be appreciated by comparing the clangorous background of the E♭-minor Étude Tableau of Rachmaninoff, in which the melody line competes with the repeated-chord accompaniment. The relatively transparent writing of Classic keyboard repertoire has a speaking quality of one-to-one conversation that is made intelligible through silence (Ex. 5.6).

The indication *con una certa espressione parlante* in Ex. 5.6 depends upon recurring silences: the separation following the staccato upbeat, the rests in the left hand following the eighth-note chords, and the numerous rests in mm. 27–29. In contrast to the speaking-quality of the Classic period, it is the sensuousness of the Romantic piano's voice that becomes the vehicle for projecting the piece, with the sonority of the instrument its own accompaniment.

Ex. 5.6. Beethoven, Bagatelle Op. 33 No. 6, mm. 1–4, 26–30.

Listening to silence means listening to one's own playing—precise pedaling, an appropriate tempo, the separateness of each note within a chord, and sensitivity for nuance within a melodic line. Listening to silence is listening to clarity of detail. Clarity, in the music of this period, is not dry objectivity but the ability to express thoughts exactly. Clarity is warmth and the revelation of perspective and depth. The distinction between the background of Classic and Romantic keyboard literature is important when playing the late sonatas of Beethoven, where the complete work is wrapped in the silence of the within, beyond the reach of any disturbance from without. Alfred Einstein wrote that the Beethoven sonatas fall into two categories: works to be heard and works that, like soliloquies, are to be overheard.[1]

An article by Edmund Carpenter, entitled *"Silent Music and Invisible Art,"* deals with attitudes of primitive cultures, offering the interpreter a helpful analogy. The author refers to the common purpose shared by prehistoric cave paintings, the mounds and designs on the earth's surface recognizable only from the sky, and the secret chant of the North American Indian warrior: to allude to the individual's innermost beliefs and most treasured fantasies without, however, revealing them. If he possessed the right qualities, the American Indian boy, who at puberty was made to live alone in the wilderness for a period of time, might receive from the Great Spirit a chant for his personal source of strength throughout life. So private was this divine message that it was never shared with anyone, except perhaps at the point of death. A grotesque facial mask such as those found in collections of the art of early peoples may have represented for its maker the enunciation of only one syllable from his personal chant, so strong was the impulse to keep it secret. By contrast, we in the West "treat art as public property. We display it with maximum clarity, in every possible medium, hoping for the largest possible audience. Our museums boast of crowds who come to see art and buy reproductions to take home."[2]

If the variation theme of Op. 109, or the opening of Op. 110 or its Recitativo, or the Arietta theme of Op. 111—each a personal, secret chant—is played with a "big singing tone" in order to project the tune to the farthest listener in the hall, what that listener would otherwise perceive as inward-peering, spiritual contemplation becomes good, traditionally acceptable piano playing, solid and singing, but dull and unimaginative. The student who remarked that the late Beethoven sonatas were intended to be thought about rather than played had never read about the secret chant of the American Indian, but, in a moment of great "in-sight," he had listened to the silence within himself.

VI Sound as Color

Those who knew Beethoven as a child remembered his being held spellbound by unusual sounds, such as the whirring of the shutters in the wind, recalling Czerny's remark that, with Beethoven, "every sound and every movement became music and rhythm." Color goes beyond pleasing sonority or bell-like "singing tone" to the unique timbre of a particular sound that is only one step removed from the whirring of the shutters. Imagination for color is finding character in harmony that is tonally nonfunctional, in chromaticism, in a particular interval, register, accompaniment figure, or detail of articulation, in a character piece, in the contrast of major and minor, and in the indication of long pedals.

"Tonally nonfunctional" describes a suspension of harmonic movement during which sound is heard for its intrinsic property to draw the listener's attention to itself (Exx. 6.1 and 6.2). In Ex. 6.1, the extended dominant-seventh harmony and the chromatic play within it introduce a few moments of stillness and reflection following the intensity of the first half of the exposition. This passage also marks the first appearance of the triplet sixteenths, which provide a kind of rhythmic relief from the duple eighth and sixteenth subdivision that has gone before. One may suppose that, because of the *adagio* in m. 24, the *tenute* and longer note values in m. 25, and the fermata in m. 26, Haydn would have played the triplet sixteenths freely, perhaps with a *rallentando*, so that the tempo of the latter would have led naturally into the *adagio* cadenza. Treating the triplets freely establishes a basis for contrast with the triplets in the closing theme, which begins in m. 32.

Ex. 6.1. Haydn, Sonata No. 33, I, mm. 22–26.

Ex. 6.2. Haydn, Sonata No. 54, I, mm. 88–91.

The brightness of E major *is* the principal theme in Ex. 6.3, sustained by the vigor of the rhythm and the rising line. The movement ends with the same figure, one would imagine played *forte*, in tempo. In the second part of the example, the repeated E-major broken chord becomes an ostinato against a rising bass line.

Ex. 6.3. Haydn, Sonata No. 15, III, mm. 1–6, 80–82.

In character, the first movement of the G-major Sonata of Haydn (Ex. 6.4), marked *Allegretto innocente,* combines the playfulness of the child with the knowingness of the adult. (Schumann might have written an inscription over the movement, similar to that in the final piece of the *Davidsbündlertänze.*) In part, the charm of the movement lies in its touches of chromaticism.

Ex. 6.4. Haydn, Sonata No. 54, I, mm. 37–38.

In the closing measures of the finale of the C-minor Sonata of Haydn (Ex. 6.5), the c's are tied over the playing-out of chromatic coloring. The articulation separating the five eighth notes in each measure illustrates how the smallest detail adds, in this movement, to the musical delirium.

Ex. 6.5. Haydn, Sonata No. 33, III, mm. 146–50.

In the chromatic approach to the six-four chord in Ex. 6.6 (Nathan Broder attributes the dynamic markings to the Breitkopf & Härtel edition of 1799), the altered chords are marked *forte* and the neutral harmony *piano.* Whether or not the dynamics are Mozart's, the extension of the chromatic idea indicates that the composer was momentarily fascinated with the sound.

Ex. 6.6. Mozart, Sonata K. 533, I, mm. 82–87.

A good composer knows when to say something and when to permit the listener to reflect upon what has been said. In Ex. 6.7, color in the form of a repeated half-step pattern supports the melodic spinning-out lasting fourteen measures before resolving. In Ex. 6.8, the play with the dominant seventh of C♯ major extends the harmonic daydreaming over four measures. In Exx. 6.9 and 6.10 a sequence continuing at the interval of a whole step has little if anything to do with harmonic progression, creating instead a moment of aural relaxation in which the listener can enjoy the sound of the harmony in and for itself. In the finale of the Sonata K. 310 (Ex. 6.11), the restricted range and dwelling on the third of the parallel major gives the melodic line in thirds—a strong color component—a whining quality. In this instance, the sound of major is anything but happy.

Ex. 6.7. Beethoven, Sonata Op. 28, I, mm. 77–79.

Ex. 6.8. Beethoven, Sonata Op. 78, I, m. 20.

Ex. 6.9. Beethoven, Sonata Op. 2 No. 3, IV, mm. 45, 47, 49, 269.

Ex. 6.10. Mozart, Sonata K. 533, II, mm. 19–20.

Ex. 6.11. Mozart, Sonata K. 310, III, mm. 143–46.

Chords of the sixth, extended for two measures and rising through a range of an octave and a half, comprise the theme of the finale of Op. 2 No. 3—a technical figure that may be regarded as a color device (Ex. 6.12). Since a Beethoven theme foretells the nature of the movement, it is not surprising to find many repetitive patterns throughout the movement, for instance, the G-major theme that introduces the B-section (and its parallel section) and the sequential passages in mm. 45–55 and 87–96.

Ex. 6.12. Beethoven, Sonata Op. 2 No. 3, IV, m. 1.

By placing the hands in widely separated registers and doubling the third in the chords in Ex. 6.13, Haydn achieved a ringing sort of clarity and magnificence, a brilliant display of keyboard color.

Ex. 6.13. Haydn, Sonata No. 60, III, mm. 94–99.

The neighboring tones in the broken-chord accompaniment in Ex. 6.14 surround, aura-like, the tender and intimate quality of the appoggiaturas in the melody line.

Ex. 6.14. Beethoven, Sonata Op. 2 No. 3, II, m. 19.

The staccato marks in Ex. 6.15 are a particularity of color added to the second variation of the opening phrase of the movement. Like flecks of light in a painting, the pitches so marked direct the ear to a harmonic relationship with preceding material.

Ex. 6.15. Beethoven, Sonata Op. 110, I, m. 12.

In the *Marcia funebre* from Op. 26, a character piece, the lower register of the piano, depending upon one's imagination, becomes brasses, more thinly spaced writing woodwinds, and the pedaled tremolo the roll of drums. For that matter, the Mozart *Rondo alla turca*, when heard on a Viennese piano with a Janizary stop, is a far more extravagant example of color, a precursor of twentieth-century pieces for prepared piano. A turn to major or minor is an obvious color change (Ex. 6.16), as are, most important of all and immediate in effect, long pedals.

Ex. 6.16. Mozart, Sonata K. 330, II, mm. 20–21, 60–61.

The chief shortcoming of all stringed keyboard instruments is the immediate decay of the sound. The solution to the problem lent the particular instruments their own unique character. Thus, *Bebung* is the soul of the clavichord, *stile brisé*

the glory of the harpsichord, and undamped strings the mystique of the piano. Beethoven indicated the pedal only for specific effects, for which reason alone these indications are not to be ignored at the whim of the player. Neither should the long pedals be attributed to deafness—if Beethoven was able to hear in his mind the pitch he wanted, he could certainly have heard the quality as well—nor solely to the lack of sonority in the piano of the period. On an early piano in a good state of restoration, the brighter, often more pungent sound makes the control of the blurring as much a problem as on a modern piano. However, Czerny's description of Beethoven's playing of the theme of the slow movement of the Third Concerto (1803) indicates that he might not have agreed with the preceding statement.

> Beethoven . . . permitted the *pedal* to continue through the complete theme, which went very well on the weak sounding *pianos* of the time, especially if the Verschiebung was used also. But now that the tone has become much stronger, we would recommend that the damper pedal be taken anew with each more important change of harmony, however, in a manner that no break in the sound is noticeable. For the complete theme must sound like a distant, holy, and unearthly harmony.[1]

The concluding sentence could only have been written by one who possessed imagination for character—and we think of Czerny as a writer of exercises. How one imagines a "distant, holy, and unearthly harmony" will determine whether to pedal through new harmonies, half-pedal, or merely pedal to avoid any break in the sound. Sounds on a fortepiano decay rather suddenly and then sustain on a lower level. Czerny's recommendation implies that Beethoven's intent was not primarily to produce a blur but to overcome the natural decay and to produce a generally more sensuous sound. One's success in painting character is the important consideration, not, in this case, whether one is able to hold the pedal down literally, as the score indicates.

Not all long pedals have the same purpose. Only three or four of Beethoven's long pedals produce blurring of more than one harmony or of adjacent pitches in a melodic line. In most instances, the sustaining of sound is neither controversial nor problematic. A long pedal sustains a single harmony at a specified dynamic level that would otherwise decay too rapidly and lose its base of sonority (Exx. 6.17 and 6.18). Long pedals serving the same purpose may be found in Opp. 53, 78, 81a, 101, 106, 109, 110, and 111. A pedal may also be used to augment the force of a dynamic marking (Ex. 6.19), in this instance pointing up parallels with the first movement, or to sustain sound at the end of a movement (Ex. 6.20). Similar examples are found in the third and fourth movements of Op. 26, and in Opp. 57, 106, 109, and 110. A long pedal may connect the end of one movement to the beginning of the next (Ex. 6.21).

Ex. 6.17. Beethoven, Sonata Op. 57, I, mm. 123, 131–32.

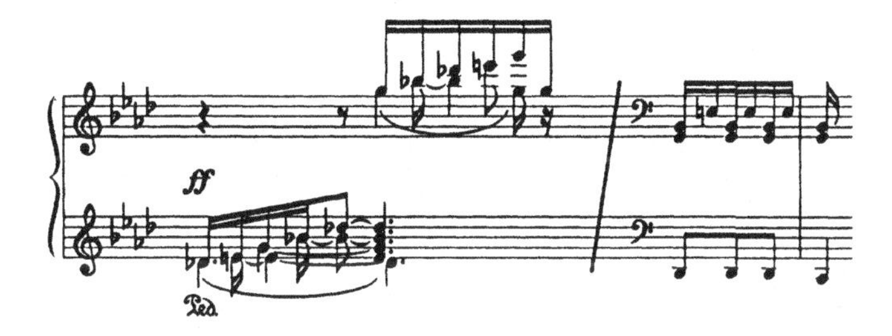

Ex. 6.18. Beethoven, Sonata Op. 57, III, mm. 192–93, 195–96, 200–204.

Ex. 6.19. Beethoven, Sonata Op. 27 No. 2, III, mm. 1–2.

Ex. 6.20. Beethoven, Sonata Op. 26, I, mm. 216–19.

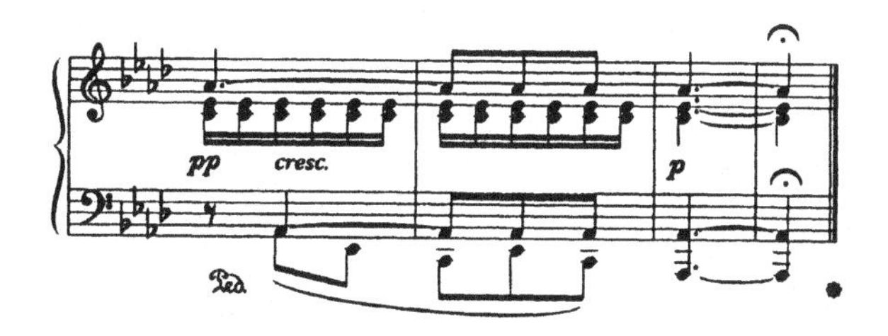

Ex. 6.21. Beethoven, Sonata Op. 27 No. 1, I, m. 86; II, m. 1.

On one level, the long pedal in Ex. 6.22 amplifies the legato; on another, it creates perspective by making the passage sound as though it were being heard in the distance—in contrast with the immediate presence of the dotted rhythm that prevails throughout the main section of the movement.

Ex. 6.22. Beethoven, Sonata Op. 101, II, mm. 30–34.

Finally, there are those few examples of long pedals over which pianists are always fretting, the recitatives in the first movement of Op. 31 No. 2 and the theme of the Rondo of Op. 53, mentioned above. By means of the recitative, Beethoven asks us to imagine the piano as a human voice singing an actual narrative. Moreover, he is supposed to have said that these recitatives, the only melodic writing of any length in the entire movement, should sound like a voice within a vault.[2] Whatever extramusical thoughts the individual may entertain when listening to the passage, to ignore Beethoven's long pedals and play the single-line melody with a buxom sound is as disturbingly illogical as it would be to turn up the house lights during Lady Macbeth's sleepwalking scene. With respect to the finale of the *Waldstein*, Czerny remarks that the movement is based upon the use of the pedal, which he reproduces in the brief excerpt from the theme exactly as given in Urtext editions. The argument for a literal observation of Beethoven's long pedals in this movement has to do with the impression of arrested time; Beethoven stacks harmonies and pitches atop one another, as a result of which the music, instead of progressing somewhere, stands still.

In the seclusion of the practice room, the score, like the keyboard, may remain black and white. Through imagined color, notes become sounds associated with images outside the four walls. Color takes the flat surface and gives it perspective; it shows what is near or far, within or without, active or still, spoken or thought, more important or less important. Color is to the keyboard music of this period what imagery is to poetry, enabling us to comprehend a world of thought beyond the spoken word.

The Sonatas

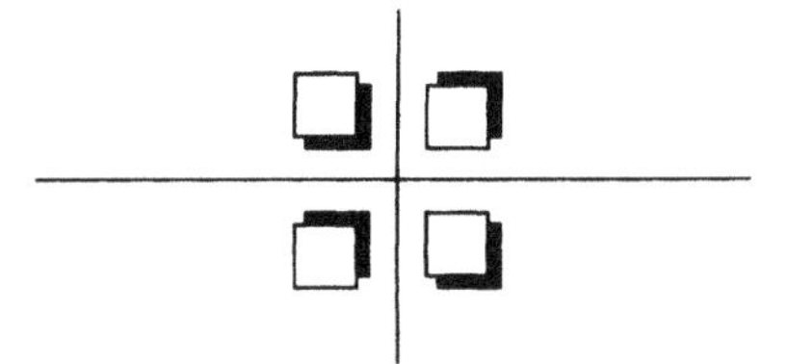

A piece of music is a meaningful construction, at once sensuous and logical, fashioned and sustained by the need of the mind to explain itself to itself. Lacking a fixed physical dimension but existing in time on a tangible instrument, the playing of a piece is the embodiment of subjectivity. In this meeting of self and ideal in which the support of tradition and reputation is insufficient, the player is forced to look for musical meaning. If that search is successful, the result is a oneness with the music that confers upon the player a new, spiritual identity.

To achieve this oneness, the sole reliable, if sometimes perplexing, guide is the composer's score. Through the discipline of analysis, perceptions compared become judgments made, as a result of which a larger and more complex piece emerges, requiring new perceptions and judgments. Thus the playing of a piece presupposes, within fulfillment, the possibility of unfulfillment, as it was for the composer in the moment of creation.

The listener's understanding of the depth and richness of a piece depends upon the player's perceptions and judgments. Nevertheless, just as the player, in attempting to define the indefinable, may never fully comprehend the composer's own concept of the music, the listener may be only dimly aware of what the player comprehends during performance. Ultimately, all that can be communicated is an awareness of a spiritual presence. That the conjuring up of this presence should be effected by an insecure human being in a state of unfulfillment remains the mysterious irony of our profession.

VII

Descriptive Music

Op. 81a, Op. 13

If a music appreciation class were to listen to the Sonata Op. 81a, without being aware of the programmatic titles, and another class were to listen to the same sonata but after being told the titles of the three movements, the second group would almost certainly remember the piece in greater detail. The historical background alone is like a fabric of fantasy woven of threads of a variety of colors—the Archduke who later became an Archbishop, Beethoven's gifted student and patron, the relationship of a Hapsburg royal to a composer who once felt the need to insist that the "van" in his name indicated nobility, the approach of the French armies, the flight of the Archduke—making a pattern we know as the *Les Adieux* Sonata. Descriptive or programmatic music will be taken seriously or not according to the associations established in the mind. If they are too literal, the piece will seem more entertaining than serious. However, imagining the sentiments that were exchanged between these two flesh-and-blood human beings coming from two widely separated levels of society and meeting in a kind of temple of the spirit, musician and nonmusician alike will hear the music as an "immortal sign" of a human experience. Life *does* lend significance to the act of making music.

Since Beethoven rigorously subjected everything he created to the test of musical reason before it reached final form, he would not have capriciously added a descriptive title to a piece of music without having in mind a purpose of which he himself was convinced. When studying Opp. 81a and 13, the only sonatas to which

Beethoven gave titles, one should ask why he used titles at all and what they have to do with the music.

Op. 81a

Another time, walking in the fields near Baden, Neate spoke of the "Pastoral" Symphony and of Beethoven's power of painting pictures in music. Beethoven said: "I have always a picture in my mind, when I am composing, and work up to it."[1]

The following anecdote in Wiedemann's *Musikalische Effectmittel und Tonmalerei* was told by Beethoven's friend Karl Amenda: "After Beethoven had composed his well-known String Quartet in F major he played for his friend [Amenda, on the pianoforte?] the glorious Adagio [D minor, 9/8 time] and asked him what thought had been awakened by it. "It pictured for me the parting of two lovers," was the answer. "Good!" remarked Beethoven, "I thought of the scene in the burial vault in *Romeo and Juliet*."[2]

A remark of Ries . . . will bear repetition: "Beethoven in composing his pieces often thought of a particular thing, although he frequently laughed at musical paintings and scolded particularly about trivialities of this sort. Haydn's 'Creation' and 'The Seasons' were frequently ridiculed, though Beethoven never failed to recognize Haydn's high deserts. . . ."[3]

Among the sketches to the [Pastoral] Symphony are to be found several remarks that in part are directed toward comprehending the titles, in part of a general nature. We do not learn much more from these than what is said in the printed titles. These [the remarks] always prove that Beethoven, in the writing of the titles, approached [his] work with deliberation. The remarks are as follows.

one permits the listener to discover the situations
Sinfonia caracteristica—or recollections of life in the country
a recollection of life in the country
Every sort of painting, after it has been pushed too far in instrumental music, suffers loss—
Sinfonia pastorella. He who has ever obtained an idea of life in the country can imagine for himself what the composer intended without lots of titles—
Also without description one will recognize the whole more as feeling than tone painting.[4]

Plainly, extramusical stimulus played an important role in Beethoven's creative process. Nevertheless, as Nottebohm remarked, "Tones learned by listening to nature and those that flow forth from the human soul are fundamentally different things."[5] As for the reason for the titles for the separate movements of Op. 81a, the only sonata among the "32" to be "explained" in such a manner, the most credible answer is that the sonata was an acknowledgment of personal affection on the occasion of the Archduke's enforced departure. (In a letter to Breitkopf & Härtel dated October 9, 1811, Beethoven asks why the publisher had brought out the sonata with both French and German titles; *Lebewohl*, he insisted, would be said "in a warm-hearted manner to one person," *Les Adieux* "to entire towns—."[6]) Perhaps

Beethoven felt that the work had such a clear ring, such a directness and brilliance, that the listener would miss the sentiment that gave it birth—that it was a soul-painting, as Nottebohm described it. Or, he may have thought that the one-line and two-line voice parts would sound merely thin and strange if the title *Das Lebewohl* were not added above the motive. As a matter of fact, the stretto that produces a superimposition of tonic and dominant (Ex. 7.1) in which the farewells overlap *was* misunderstood, as Marx points out:

> Fétis, the learned director of the conservatory in Brussels, expressed it accurately: "If that is called music, it is not what I call music." It is not the music of Fétis and the French nor of the majority of musicians; it is poetry, or, more precisely, the transcending of music that naturally always lives only in a very few and is understood only by a very few.
>
> If the player has grasped Beethoven's thought, the listeners let themselves be led where he [the composer] wishes. And eventually we say with Goethe:
>
> Und wer mich nicht verstehen kann,
> Der lerne besser lesen!
>
> (And whoever cannot understand me,
> Let him learn better to read!)[7]

Therefore, the titles were intended to help the listener read in the score "the transcending of the music."

Ex. 7.1. Op. 81a, I, mm. 229–35.

Studying the parallels between this sonata and Bach's *Capriccio on the Departure of His Beloved Brother* points to the universality of programmatic symbols. The inscription in Beethoven's handwriting reads: "The Farewell. Vienna, 4th May 1809 on the departure of H. R. H., the esteemed Archduke Rudolf." Over the first movement of the *Capriccio* one reads, "This describes the affectionate attempt of his friend to deter him from embarking on his journey." In the examples below, melodic continuity and harmonic movement are held back, display vacillation, and are postponed, linking these, especially in the light of the programmatic titles, to human experience.

Appoggiaturas. Appoggiaturas, especially those that repeat the preceding pitch, delay the direction of the line (Ex. 7.2). The principal theme of the Allegro begins with an appoggiatura *chord* followed by an even stronger appoggiatura in m. 19 (Ex. 7.3). The suspensions (prepared appoggiaturas) in mm. 46–49 encourage holding back the tempo, delaying the entrance of the second theme (Ex. 7.4). The appoggiaturas in the first two measures of the second theme give practical effect to the indication of *espressivo,* i.e., holding back the tempo (Ex. 7.5). The appoggiatura g♭, in Ex. 7.6 delays a full resolution to the B♭ chord. Finally, the *crescendo* over the last appoggiatura in the movement can only be suggested by playing the note of resolution louder and delaying it (Ex. 7.7).

Ex. 7.2. Bach, Capriccio, I, mm. 1–2; Beethoven, Op. 81a, I, m. 6–7, 11–13.

Ex. 7.3. Op. 81a, I, mm. 16–18, 18–21.

Ex. 7.4. Op. 81a, I, mm. 46–47.

Ex. 7.5. Op. 81a, I, m. 50.

Ex. 7.6. Op. 81a, I, m. 58.

Ex. 7.7. Op. 81a, I, mm. 247–53.

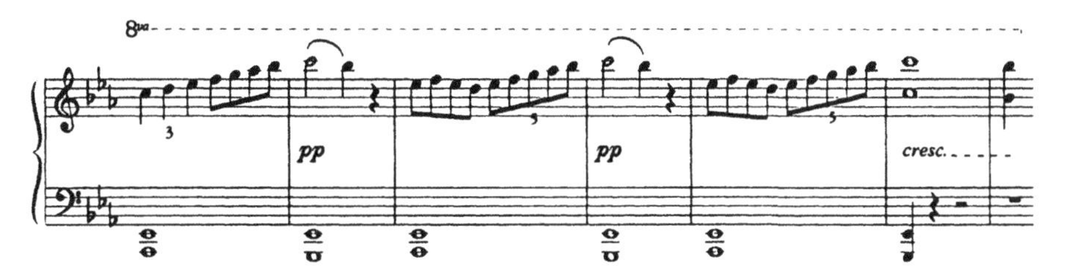

Harmonic Extension and Repetition. In the Arioso of the *Capriccio*, a cadential chord of resolution may include repeated notes that sound redundant, weakening the conclusion. The resolution of the cadence reached in m. 5 is extended one full measure to resolve once more in m. 6 (Ex. 7.8). Following the cadence in m. 12, B♭ harmony is prolonged a full measure using the repeated-note figure exclusively, the half cadence is repeated in m. 13, and the three-note figure is repeated over a descending bass (Ex. 7.9).

Ex. 7.8. Bach, Capriccio, I, mm. 4–6.

Ex. 7.9. Bach, Capriccio, I, mm. 13–15.

Consistent with detaining and delaying, separating the two-note slur from the quarter note in the theme of the Allegro of the sonata impedes what would otherwise be a forward-thrusting tempo. The delayed resolution on the tonic of B♭ major (Ex. 7.6), which is immediately repeated, is another example of diverting the progress of the piece and filling time harmonically, as is the play with a B♭ scale in mm. 62–65.

Vacillation between Major and Minor. In the Bach, the repeated-note pattern vacillates chromatically, just as the repeated patterns in Ex. 7.10 from the sonata alternate between minor and major. In the sonata, rests and articulation slurs isolate the sounds of major and minor respectively.

Ex. 7.10. Bach, Capriccio, I, mm. 8–9; Beethoven, Op. 81a, I, mm. 14–16, 35–39.

Sequential Treatment. In the second movement of the *Capriccio,* in a fugato with the inscription "This is a description of the misfortunes which could befall his friend in a sojourn in distant climes," each exposition begins a whole step lower than the preceding one (Ex. 7.11). The resolution first to a diminished seventh chord and then to a half cadence in F minor amounts to a musical portrayal of uncertainty. The generally downward melodic direction also suggests a negative prospect for the traveler's fortunes. A similar downward-tending sequence occupies the development section of the first movement of the sonata (Ex. 7.12). The second half of the second movement of the sonata is, for the most part, a repeat of the first half a whole step lower. However, since the range between the hands has been widened, the expressive effect is likewise more compelling—the yearning becomes more earnest.

Ex. 7.11. Bach, Capriccio, II, mm. 1–2, 6–7, 11–12.

Ex. 7.12. Op. 81a, I, mm. 73–74, 77–78, 81–82, 85–86, 94–103.

Harmonic Immobility. In the third movement of the Bach, "a mutual lamentation of both friends," the decision is now definite, hence the "unavoidable" repeated bass line of the passacaglia, while the treble melodic line comments upon it with sigh figures. The second movement of Op. 81a seems motionless at its opening, the C-minor chord slipping into a diminished seventh the way a person would peer into the unknown, its repetition suggesting the monotony of aloneness. The anxiety intensifies with the shortening of the articulation slur and the adding of *sforzandos* six measures later (Ex. 7.13).

Ex. 7.13. Op. 81a, II, mm. 1, 5, 11–12.

Immediately repeated and ornamented (not unlike the Bach passacaglia) and harmonically stationary, the two-measure phrase, mm. 15–16, beginning and ending on the dominant, has the stillness of a picture, the more florid repetition like a daydream about the picture. The two-note slurs in mm. 17 and 33 are evidently to be separated clearly up to the point at which the quickness of the subdivision prevents it. The extended E♭ harmony beginning in m. 181 of the last movement and the manner in which the lines cling to one another is likewise suggestive, perhaps of inseparable reunion.

Imitative Writing. In the fourth movement of the *Capriccio,* "the friends bid each other farewell, since they see that the departure cannot be avoided." By a curious coincidence, the descending thirds in m. 4 are the same pitches as the double thirds in the sonata. Aside from this, a true parallel exists between the imitation in the Bach and the conversation between the hands in the coda of the sonata (Ex. 7.14).

Ex. 7.14. Bach, Capriccio, IV, mm. 4–5; Beethoven, Op. 81a, I, mm. 30–31, 181–85.

The two works have in common the stimulus of a similar situation, although we may take the Bach less seriously, as something clever and entertaining. There are works of a more profound content than Op. 81a among the sonatas, but we hear it at its face value, occasioned by an actual historical figure who also happened to have been close to Beethoven personally. According to Nottebohm, approximately half a year separated work on the first movement from the sketches for the second and third. Among the sketches for the first movement are the words "The Departure [crossed out: The Farewell]—on the 4th of May—dedicated and written from the heart H. R. H." As Marx writes, Beethoven did not "exaggerate the parting to convulsions of sorrow, but clothed it with the moderation and grace of amiable personalities . . . "[8] We accept its regal sound as genuine.

On a musical level, the 3–2–1 scale-step descent of the *Le-be-wohl* motto is the basic pattern for the first movement, embedded in the principal theme of the first movement, in the passage of thirds (Ex. 7.14), in the opposing lines of mm. 35–38 (Ex. 7.10), in the inner voice of mm. 41–46 (Ex. 7.15), in the measures leading to the second theme (Ex. 7.4), in the second theme, and in the last measures of the exposition.

Ex. 7.15. Op. 81a, I, mm. 41–43.

The individual interpreter must decide whether the opening of the second movement is related to the opening of the first movement and the significance such a connection might have. Features supporting this relationship include the time signature (2/4), the opening pitches (g/e♭), and the similarity of rhythmic movement beginning in the second measure of each passage. If these similarities seem convincing, one may hear the two-note slurs in the second movement as derived from the *Lebewohl* theme, as are the slurred two-note groups in the finale (Ex. 7.16). Convincing the listener of this relationship would necessitate holding back these two-note slurs, making them more explicit and forceful. Separating the two-note slurs, *vivacissimamente,* would be letting the difficulty show through using it for an expressive purpose. As Stanley Fletcher advised, "When in trouble, interpret." Hearing the imposing passage beginning in m. 37 as a huge expansion of a two-note slur provides a glorious moment in performance (Ex. 7.17).

Ex. 7.16. Op. 81a, III, mm. 9–10, 69–74.

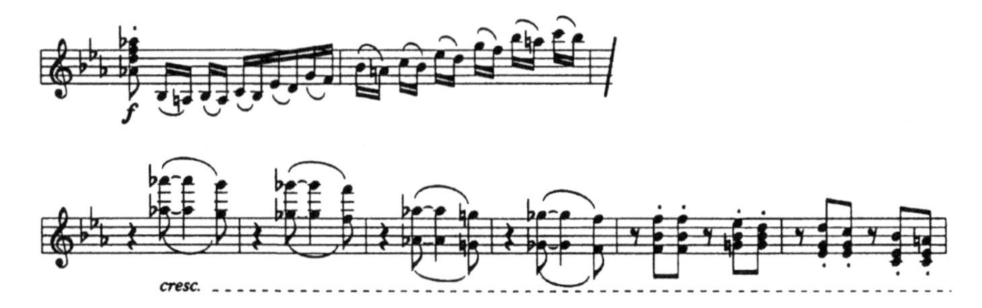

Ex. 7.17. Op. 81a, III, mm. 37–44.

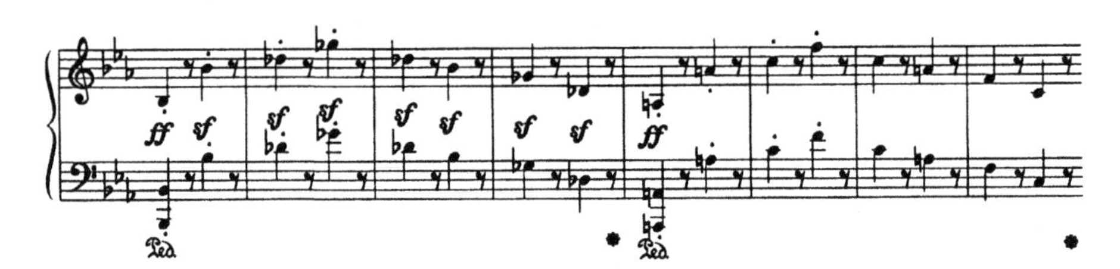

The lower voice of the *Lebewohl* motive, forming a broken chord, is the generating motive for the finale, again a programmatic element—the closely spaced, stepwise pattern of the first movement contrasts with the open, broken-chord pattern of the finale—from restraint to a release from it. Another feature tying the outer movements together is the prominence of b♭ through dynamic emphasis and repetition. The pitch is marked with a *sforzando* in m. 6 (Ex. 7.2), mm. 22 and 26 (Ex. 7.18), and other parallel passages in the first movement. B♭ is the pitch to which the eighth-note counterpoint is attached in the coda of the first movement; it is repeated in mm. 239–42 (Ex. 7.18) and is the note of resolution after an appoggiatura in mm. 248, 250, and 253 (Ex. 7.7). In the finale, b♭ is the pitch from which the principal theme sways; the pitch is also marked by a strange *sforzando* in m. 176, at the beginning of the *Poco Andante* (Ex. 7.18).

Ex. 7.18. Op. 81a, I, mm. 21–23, 239–42; III, mm. 11–12, 176–77.

Surely anyone who has played this sonata would question this willful accent near the close of the finale. Thinking back through the work, the emphasis on the pitch B♭, colored first as dominant and then as tonic harmony, may be yet another "descriptive" detail. From a programmatic standpoint, b♭ as the dominant, harmonized with dominant harmony in first theme of the *Allegro* in the first movement (m.22), is much like a fixed point of unresolved tension. F, the respective dominant of B♭ major in mm. 40–50, is, by extension, the "fixed point of unresolved tension" at that point. In the second movement, the lyrical theme, mm. 15–19 and 31–35, also drapes from the dominant. B♭ is harmonized as the fifth of the tonic chord in the theme of the *Wiedersehen* finale and also at the *poco andante*. What has been unresolved in the first two movements is now resolved in the third.

If, as Beethoven said, he always composed with a picture in mind, by publishing extramusical titles for Op. 81a, he shared the initiating impulse preceding the movement of creation.

Op. 13

No historical event, only definitions, can be associated with the word *Pathétique:* affecting, moving, exciting emotion, expressing pathos or suffering—terms that mark the sonata as program music of the soul. Conversely, the qualities of this music define the adjective *pathétique* more clearly than the dictionary. Mendelssohn, as Alfred Einstein points out, was correct in maintaining that "the thoughts which good compositions express are not too vague to be contained in words, but too definite."[9]

The *Pathétique* is, first of all, music of the will. If the Op. 13 is compared on a philosophical level with the C-minor Sonatas of Mozart and Haydn, each of the latter is more fatalistic, like a commentary by an observer who is reacting to a circumstance. By contrast, the *Pathétique* represents the reaction of one who will engage the circumstance by associating the emotional force released in exploiting raw sound with the intellectual intensity of the network of motivic relationships. Instead of thinking notes, it would be nearer the spirit of the piece to think, when marveling at the tight construction, of roaring and howling and throbbing, the sounds of passion with which the composer burns his musical logic into one's consciousness (Ex. 7.19).

Ex. 7.19. Op. 13. I: a. 1; b. mm. 5–6; c. m. 11; d. m. 51; e. m. 89; II: f. mm. 41–42; III: g. m. 107; h. mm. 182–83; i. mm. 198–201.

That the *Grande Sonata Pathétique* has always appealed to the young is not remarkable. The piece had only recently been published when Czerny, not yet ten years old, played it for the composer. Moscheles also learned the sonata at approximately the same age, only to be advised by his teacher, Dionysius Weber, to put it aside, because Beethoven wrote "lots of crazy stuff" and did not know what he wanted.[10] Weber obviously did not see Beethoven as a Gargantuan figure, but as a controversial contemporary. He recognized "crazy stuff" when he heard it. We, on the other hand, are unlikely to perceive anything controversial in it, preoccupied as we are with our standards of piano playing.

Beethoven himself appears to have been drawn to a youthful idea in the writing of the sonata, the first movement of which resembles the early Bonn Sonata in F minor of 1782–83, WoO 47, although, compared with the Op. 13, the keyboard writing and the musical ideas are far less advanced. The earlier sonata also opens with a slow introduction that recurs, and the theme of the *Allegro assai* is similar to the principal theme of the first movement of Op. 13 (Ex. 7.20) in the ascending line and noise-making bass.

7.20. SONATA IN F MINOR WoO 47, I, MM. 10–13.

Perhaps only the young or those who rediscover the vividness of youthful impressions can realize the primitivism of the living *Grande Sonata Pathétique,* for an understanding of the piece begins on the threshold of intelligibility, the least-sophisticated level of musical speech: the suddenness of dynamic shifts in reaction to psychological explosions; the sound of tremolos, repeated chords, and broken chords; and the dynamic forcing of the top of the compass of Beethoven's piano. The impact of these devices cannot be measured or calculated; the "how much" is a decision of the moment, nearer the composer's initial motivation than prepared performance. These are devices that are deceptively uncomplicated and yet potentially awesome, as though one's equilibrium were threatened by a crisis never before encountered. The keyboard devices of the *Pathétique* symbolize the common denominator of Beethoven's humanness and our own, the frustration of reaching without ever being satisfied.

Secondly, the sonata is music of youth, although Beethoven was almost thirty years old when he wrote the *Pathétique,* comparatively late in life for an outburst one associates with adolescence. By age thirty, most pianists are less likely to be drawn to the piece. The technical challenges of the writing have by now been more than adequately met, and the pianist has gone on to repertoire that is outwardly more difficult. However, this is also a time of readjustment to reality, a second adolescence and period of searching, when the dreams of youth have blanched. The sound of primitivism in this work is the language of someone reaching into the unknown.

Beyond its outward primitivism, Op. 13 is anything but primitive music. Throughout its four-measure ascent, the principal theme of the *Allegro di molto* dwells on F minor. One could maintain that F minor here is parenthetical and that the key is still C minor, except that Beethoven resolves in C minor/major in m. 13

(Ex. 7.21a). Perhaps, for the moment, the key is C major, or the dominant of F minor (Ex. 7.21c).

Ex. 7.21. Op. 13, I: a. mm. 11–15; b. 134–35; c. m. 197; d. m. 4; e. mm. 137–38; f. mm. 150–51; g. mm. 167–69; h. mm. 181–83; i. II, mm. 1–8; j. III, mm. 208–10.

Next, one may notice that the development begins in E minor with a change of key signature and preceded by a return to Tempo I, in which e♭ is respelled d♯ (Ex. 7.21b). This, in turn, may focus the player's attention on the strangely forced group of four notes that first appears in m. 3 of the *Grave* (a gesture of incompleteness deserving of the adjective *grande*), again involving e♭ and e♮. Over this motive the composer has written a slur, a staccato (indicating a separation, relatively abrupt), and three dynamic marks (Ex. 7.21d).

The interpretive indicators just mentioned should signal that the four-note group is a statement of considerable importance. The e♭ and e♮ pull in opposing directions, the former downward to the dominant and the latter upward to the subdominant. The harmonic effect is strangely inconclusive, as though one were to take four words from the middle of a sentence consisting of two clauses: "If I were to go to Rome I would learn Italian"—"to Rome, I would." Following the three statements with which the *Grave* opens, each closing with a falling second, the four-note motive emerges, breaking away from the pattern, although still sounding confined in range. Like two impulses leading in opposing directions, it mirrors a mind frustrated by indecision.

There are three peaks of intensity in the Allegro, the first and third of which are produced by the expanding lines of broken chords in mm. 93–98, 105–10, and the parallel passage in the recapitulation. The second such peak is found in the second half of the development, between mm. 167 and 187 (Exx. 7.21g–h), its writing leaner and constructed from the four-note motive. Because of the unusually forceful manner with which it is repeated, the ear comes to regard it as perhaps the most important motive, from which other thematic material is derived.

Paradoxically, the writing in the climax of the development sounds more effective on a fortepiano, where its forcefulness strains the capacity of the instrument. The working out of the four-note motive at the height of the drama (mm. 181–87) in the extreme treble of the contemporary piano, regardless of whether the sound was satisfying or wooden, represents another affront to the tastes of the Dionysius Webers of the day, who could not accept music as realism—in this case, as the experience of insufficiency and frustration.

The tonal ambiguity within the principal theme is derived from the four-note motive, just as this motive forms the balancing point for the duality of C minor/major and its composing out in the first movement. The e♭/e♮ polarity sets apart the darkness of the exposition from the brighter sound of the opening of the development. The shift to E minor and emphasis on *e*♮ may be the reason for the *sforzando* over the C-major chord in mm. 197 and 205 (Ex. 7.21c). Beethoven was using dynamic intensity—again a less-sophisticated communicator of musical meaning—to manipulate the uncertain balance between light and darkness in chord "color" throughout the movement.

The shape of the motive appears in other passages throughout the sonata: the jagged ascending lines in mm. 137–38 of the first movement (Ex. 7.21e), the left-hand line in mm. 149–58 (Ex. 7.21f), and, in a general way, in the direction of the melodic line in the theme of the second movement (Ex. 7.21i), that descends e♭–d♭–c in m. 2 and ascends to f in m. 4. In a general way also, the theme of the rondo follows the same plan, first descending e♭–d–c, then ascending to g. One could also point to the forced reach for the high f in mm. 182–85 of the rondo, as well as the final reach for the same pitch in the last three measures of the movement.

The web of motivic connections between the three movements extends to other patterns and derivations. The three ascending scale steps in m. 1 of the first movement reappear with an appended upbeat in the E♭ minor theme (Ex. 7.22a), as descending scale steps in the second movement (Ex. 7.22b, c), and in the theme of the rondo (Ex. 7.22d); beginning the rondo with a cadence and a 3–2–1 descending melodic line (the theme of the G-minor Ballade of Chopin follows the same pattern) is another touch of musical fatalism, as though an unalterable decision had been made at the very outset. That each of these should point to the first three steps of the minor scale and that the g♭ dotted half notes in the E♭-minor theme should be marked with *sforzandos* indicates an absorption with minorness and with the descending half of the polarity between e♭ and e.

The principal theme of the Allegro of the first movement is, in effect, restated in the closing material (Ex. 7.22e), giving the nervous quality of the theme a triumphant character. The pattern of fifths and fourths that begins to emerge in the exposition of the first movement (Ex. 7.22f), but is most clearly stated in the reprise (Ex. 7.22g), forms the second half of the theme of the Adagio and occurs in a like position in the theme of the rondo, one spacious and warm, the other breaking into sigh figures. The sequential fifths are treated in invertible double counterpoint in the middle section of the rondo (the legato lines recalling for a moment the Adagio). The scale descent of two and a half octaves in mm. 58–61 (and its repetitions) in the last movement is in reality one of these fifths, expanded and filled in (Ex. 7.22h), like a sigh become a scream; near the close of the movement it sweeps downward through three octaves and a third (Ex. 7.19i). The filled-in fifth closes the sonata with a strangely willful reach for the f at the top of the piano's range (Ex. 7.21j). Following the pattern of fifths and fourths from its emergence in the exposition of the first movement to the spaciousness of the *Adagio* theme to the sigh figures in the rondo theme to the precipitous filled-in falling fifth illustrates how carefully Beethoven planned the consummation of dramatic force with one last reach for the f at the top of the keyboard.

The phrase "familiarity breeds contempt" unfortunately applies to works such as Op. 13, Op. 27 No. 2, Op. 53, and Op. 57, whose very popularity conceals their individuality. Real familiarity raises questions that challenge the security of a pedantic concept of performance. Merely identifying motives has no purpose except for academic analysis. Only when such study shapes interpretation by revealing what is interpretively significant is real familiarity achieved.

It is the unnatural and the bizarre, principally in the dynamic exaggeration, that

Ex. 7.22. Op. 13, a. I, mm. 51–52; b. II, mm. 16–20; c. II, mm. 36–40; d. III, mm. 1–8; e. I, mm. 257–62; f. I, mm. 51–83; g. I, mm. 244–49; h. III, mm. 58–61.

moves us, so that we empathize with being overpowered and ruled by the force of feelings that lead us to irrational acts. Each time we compromise by subduing the assault of a *subito* dynamic, or attenuating the breadth of a *crescendo,* or narrowing the extremes of *pp* and *ff* or the extremes of tempo—to avoid marring a "beautiful" work of art—we diminish its kinship with the reality of life. Beethoven did not "free music." Mozart is infinitely "freer" in that he does not need to depend upon dynamic exaggeration—visceral force—to make the structure of the piece believable. The interpreter of a Beethoven sonata, on the contrary, is constantly forced to look into the face of life and ask, in all insecurity, "Is this your true likeness?"

VIII *Motivic Development*

Op. 2 N. 1, op. 57, Op. 110

Armed with our urtext editions, scholarly studies of performance practice, and doctorates, we may think that our performances represent a more accurate reading of the printed page than any in the past. However indispensable reliable editions and an understanding of performance practices may be, to realize literally and irreproachably the printed page is no feat at all, compared with the "original interpretation" of the Fourth Concerto when it was still a blank page in the sketchbook. Like the composer, with every performance a true interpreter mentally faces a blank page of manuscript paper. The muscles know the notes; the intelligence and fantasy of the player must decide what to do with them.

Grouping particular sonatas under various headings should not be regarded as excluding other sonatas that illustrate the same procedure, in this case, motivic development. Op. 2 Nos. 2 and 3, Op. 13, Op. 27 Nos. 1 and 2, Op. 28, Op. 49 No. 2, Op. 78, Op. 106, and Op. 109 all contain one or more motives that reappear, playing new roles and wearing new guises throughout the sonata. The three sonatas grouped together under the heading "Motivic Development"—Op. 2 No. 1, Op. 57, and Op. 110—have been chosen because the motivic pattern is *the* vehicle for developing the singular character of each sonata; and because they are works that span a lifetime, one may follow Beethoven's growing sophistication in the use of simple patterns to develop character.

Op. 2 No. 1

In at least three aspects, the F-minor Sonata contrasts with the other two sonatas in Op. 2 and with later sonatas of a tragic, intense nature. It is the only sonata of its opus in a minor key. The concentration on the tonal color of the minor mode extends to the darkening of A♭ major in the first movement with c♭ and f♭ (Ex. 8.1), and to the use of the minor sixth scale step in major in the slow movement and the Menuetto (Ex. 8.2).

Ex. 8.1. Op. 2 No. 1, I, mm. 20–22, 29–30, 41–42.

Ex. 8.2. Op. 2 No. 1, II, mm. 59–60; III, mm. 14–16.

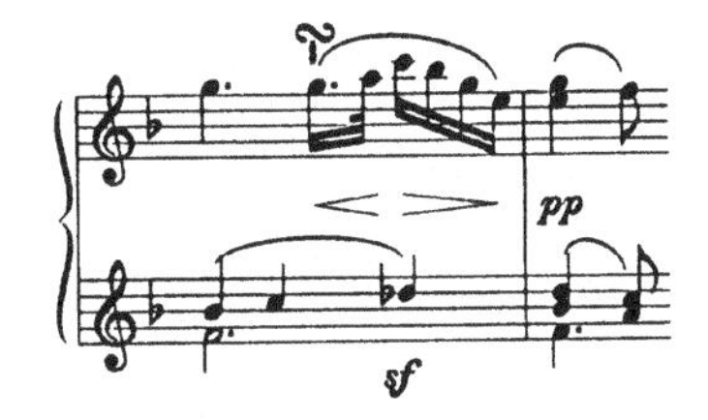

The F-minor Sonata is also unique among the sonatas in Op. 2 in that the drama is sustained to the very end. By comparison, the final movement of the A-major Sonata is graceful and pleasant, its two outbursts notwithstanding, while the effect of the C-major Sonata depends on a technical muscularity that has less to do with emotional depth. Finally, in contrast with both these sonatas and with movements from other tragic sonatas, such as Op. 13, Op. 27 No. 2, and Op. 57, the keyboard writing of the F-minor Sonata sounds somewhat bare. Considering the passion one expects from so serious a piece, the eighth-note broken octave accompaniment and the passages of basically linear, two-part writing give the first movement a bony sound. The sonata, with its self-confident, if gangling stride, moves like a youthful body possessed by a rebellious, indomitable spirit.

From the sketch for the exposition of the first movement (Ex. 8.3), as reproduced in Nottebohm,[1] one would expect more notes and a more fluent manner in the completed work. The obvious change in the printed score was the discarding of the triplets in favor of a subdivision in quarters and eighths. As Nottebohm remarks, "In the printed version the melodic nature is predominant, in the sketch, passagework."[2] Considering the tragic character, Beethoven may have thought the triplet passages too facile compared with square-shouldered quarters and eighths. He may also have thought it better drama to save the triplet subdivision for the finale, where it is used for broken-chord figures, in contrast with the scales in the sketch of the first movement.

Ex. 8.3. Op. 2 No. 1, sketch of exposition.

The piece as we know it (Ex. 8.4) shows changes of momentous importance in the first eight measures of the exposition, which, like the last eight measures, are much nearer the final form than the remainder of the sketch. These changes include:

adding the upbeat in the right hand and the rest on the first beat in the left hand, increasing the forward movement;
unifying the eight-measure section by continuing the repeated chords in the left hand in mm. 5 and 6;
impeding the tempo in measures 7 and 8 with the arpeggiated chord, *fortissimo*, and the appoggiatura, an inverted turn;
replacing the clipped dotted figure in m. 7 with even eighths;
omitting the return to c³, simplifying the direction of the line;
adding a fermata to create a pause separating the half cadence in F minor from the continuation in C minor.

Ex. 8.4. Op. 2 No. 1, I, mm. 1–8.

At the peak of the intensity in mm. 7 and 8, Beethoven made his most telling alteration, replacing the sprightly dotted figure with a new motive, dissociated from the foregoing dotted rhythms and melodic leaps. How does one know that this motive is important? In contrast with the indications of a *piano* and two *sforzandos* in the six measures preceding, the six-note descending figure has been lavished with expressive detail: an *arpeggiando* sign, a *fortissimo*, a *decrescendo*, a compound appoggiatura, a *piano*, a two-note slur, and a fermata over the quarter rest—a crowding of expressive directions equivalent to the notation of physical strain. The six-note motive, furthermore, turns out to be the structural scaffolding of the piece, the entity that moves through all four movements like the principal character in a play (Ex. 8.5).

Ex. 8.5. Op. 2 No. 1, I: a. mm. 7–8; b. mm. 16–18; c. mm. 26–28; d. mm. 33–35; e. mm. 69–81; f. mm. 146–52; II: g. mm. 1–2; h. mm. 8–11; i. mm. 21–23; j. mm. 29–30; k. mm. 54–55; l. mm. 56–57; III: m. mm. 10–14; n. mm. 30–36; o. mm. 45–50; IV: p. mm. 1–3; q. mm. 7–9; r. mm. 12–13; s. mm. 26–29; t. mm. 34–42; u. mm. 61–68; v. mm. 111–27.

h
i
sf
j
sfp
k
sf
l
sf
m
p
sf
n
tr
sf
sf
sf
sf p
o
p
Prestissimo
p
f
q
r

No finer coach exists for playing the sonata than the score itself, specifically the association of dynamics and motive in the preceding examples. In Ex. 8.5e, once the six-note descent begins to take definite shape, the *sf* is placed only above pitches belonging to the six-note motive. In Ex. 8.5f, the *fortissimo* is repeated in m. 148, even though it is still in effect from m. 146, and the *sforzandos* are again placed over motive pitches. Were this music of a hundred years earlier, the composer would have relied on other devices—perhaps stretto, augmentation, diminution, or a particular register—to indicate musical importance. Even a Classical sonata-allegro such as the Mozart Sonata K. 333 relies on pitch and rhythm for the impact of its opening lines, which lack any dynamic marking. The identifying motive is an appoggiatura, and the increasing excitement derives from hastening its recurrence and from rising to a higher point on the keyboard. To breathe into this piece the spirit of Op. 2 No. 1, dynamic indications such as those in Ex. 8.6 would have to be added. The added dynamics include those used in mm. 8–17 of the first movement of the Beethoven Op. 106, a passage similar to the Mozart, plus accent marks over pairs of notes and a *sforzando*. Continuing with Op. 2 No. 1, Exx. 8.5e and f illustrate an intellectual construction given dynamic intensity. That the comprehending of the intellectual statement should depend on bodily force—demonstrating the interdependence of brain and flesh and of intellect and emotions—makes Op. 2 No. 1 once and for always revolutionary.

Ex. 8.6. Mozart, Sonata K. 333, I, mm. 1–10.

As pianists we do not meet Beethoven the revolutionary until we must decide how much dynamic stress, or bodily force, is required to make the intellectual statement compelling—instead of tragic, utterly tragic. How much is *utterly*? The answer, if there is one, is that anything less than utterly will sound trivial. The effect of the music has been made subject to the judgment of feeling, which knows no scale or boundary. To make matters more difficult, Beethoven has not written great numbers of notes on which to exert bodily force. The composer seems to be our antagonist (and perhaps his own, as well) by insisting that the conflict be carried out on a barren terrain, where there is little behind which to hide. The warning of Moscheles' teacher, so pertinent here, has already been mentioned. Instead of the Op. 13, the young Moscheles was to be learning Bach and Mozart—Beethoven only "leads the student astray."[3]

With respect to mm. 7 and 8, what happens psychologically between the arpeggiated F-minor chord, *fortissimo*, and the half cadence, *piano*? One can imagine that an actor playing Hamlet never utters "To be, or not to be, that is the question" without wondering whether there might be a still more convincing inflection and pacing for these words, on which the plot of the play turns. The measures in question are just such a line for the sonata and just as challenging for the interpreter. Are we talking about defiance, certainty, instability, vacillation, unfulfillment? A comparison with the parallel passage at the reprise is helpful. In mm. 101–104, what had earlier been a probing question has now become—with the immediate *forte*, the beginning on the downbeat, and the *sforzandos*—a determined, self-confident act. After all that has happened thus far in the movement, the complete passage, mm. 101–108, seems now more knowing than the beginning of the movement and the half cadence far more yearning in relation to the inevitable continuation in F minor.

The same uncertainty surrounds the fermata in m. 8, where the length of the silence may determine how seriously the listener takes the sonata. A fermata is a psychological indication. Ironically, only an inexact measure of time can indicate the exact moment to begin anew with the offhand, detached statement in C minor, making the difference between sounding profound or perfunctory.

The serviceability of the six-note motive for development of character lies in its simplicity: a stepwise scale. The flexibility of Beethoven's imagination in creating new material from the original motive may be summarized in general procedures, in considering which it may be helpful to refer again to Ex. 8.5:

1. Neither the direction nor the exact intervallic pattern is inviolable; dynamics, articulation slurs, and character provide the interpreter with proof of derivation.
2. The motive may be disassembled by articulation slurs or by rests.
3. The motive may be extended, note by note, to form a scaffolding for lengthy sections of the music.
4. The motive is nonresolving, and thus any use of it avoids a complete stop, although the composer does not restrict himself to a half cadence ending.
5. The motive may be transposed.

To a certain extent, public performance is an exercise in futility. Some will only see the performance. Some will hear only notes. A large number will be broadly aware of character, while a remaining handful will understand the significance of dimensions and relationships within the piece. To communicate with such a variety of listener, the pianist who understands the piece has no choice but to assume the same of the listener. It must be a sobering thought for a composer to realize that a lifetime of musical thinking rests with fallible fingers and an often lazy mind.

Among these relationships and dimensions, the re-assembling of the six-note motive just preceding the second theme in the first movement will be intelligible only through clear articulation of the slurs (Ex. 8.7). The ascent and descent beginning in m. 26 and ending in m. 41 is an event of greater proportions (Ex. 8.5c and d). The fragmentation in the ascending six-note pattern (g^1 to $e\flat^2$) makes the line sound tentative. The descent in eighth notes is also an extension of the motive, marked off by the sudden *piano* at the beginning of m. 35. Compared with the ascent, the descent is sweeping and bold, and the composer does it twice—it should be heard against the original statement in mm. 7 and 8 as one would hear a shout of confidence after a wail of complaint.

Ex. 8.7. Op. 2 No. 1, I, mm. 15–18.

Throughout the movement, Beethoven has used only two statements of the six-note motive, the original one in F minor and the other transposed to A♭ major. In fact, the complete movement, except for brief passages in B♭ minor and C minor at the beginning of the development, remains in the tonic key and its relative major. That Beethoven found this possible is attributable in part to the unresolved nature of the motive. Its extended reintroduction in m. 69 (Ex. 8.5e) is followed by a further extension of fourteen measures of dominant pedal. In the parallel section in the finale, the same six notes support the musical discourse from m. 109 to m. 127, followed by eleven measures of play with the dominant of F minor (Ex. 8.5v).

Beethoven's self-imposed restriction in using only two intact forms of the six-note motive enabled his setting up large-scale relationships similar to blocking the movement of actors on the stage. Beginning with the abrupt entrance of the theme in C minor in m. 8, e♭ is imprinted upon our consciousness throughout the exposition: It is the starting pitch for the transposed motive (Ex. 8.5b), the pitch on which the second theme turns, the goal of the melodic ascent in mm. 26–33, and finally, e♭ is marked by *sforzandos* and a *fortissimo* in mm. 43, 45, and 47. In the development, after twenty measures of tonal wandering, the thirteen measures that follow reintroduce and confirm the preeminence of the original motive. The breadth of a performance depends on one's grasp of the scope of this statement compared with the original one in mm. 7 and 8. The movement, in addition to its three-part sonata-allegro form, is divided in half by the grandeur of this huge descent and its resolution in m. 93, enabling it to be viewed from more than one angle, like a piece of plastic art.

There is a duality also in the first phrase of the theme (Ex. 8.8). It ascends as a broken chord and descends stepwise; it ascends staccato and descends legato; it ascends in a rhythmically even manner and descends in an uneven manner. Therefore, it is a matter of speculation whether these measures may not contain the seed of the vacillation between purposefulness (in the sense of *making* something happen) and passivism (in the sense of *letting* it happen). In mm. 5 and 6, the purposefulness becomes more impatient, as five, and then four, ascending quarter notes are condensed into the appoggiatura from c♮ to a♭ and then to b♭.

Ex. 8.8. Op. 2 No. 1, I, mm. 1–2.

The six-note motive is incorporated in the opening phrase of the second movement (Ex. 8.5g). For the sake of argument, it would be gratifying to claim that it was for this very reason that the appoggiatura c² was included in the melodic line. However, the theme was borrowed from the slow movement (in the same key) of the Piano Quartet in C major, WoO 36, of 1785, perhaps specifically because of the presence of the descending six notes (Ex. 8.9).

Ex. 8.9. Piano Quartet WoO 36, II, mm. 8–9.

The Adagio is shaped melodically by this motive. Except for the huge leaps crossing hands in the D-minor section, stepwise melodic movement predominates, resulting in an overall manner of smoothness, suavity, and grace. The falling second, a segment of the motive, is present in thirty-eight of the sixty-one measures (not counting seconds in the form of accented appoggiaturas within stepwise lines), giving the music generally a sighing quality (Ex. 8.10). It is in the rest separations (Exx. 8.10b, j, and m), dynamic stress (Exx. 8.10f, h, j, l, m, and n), and pitch repetition (Ex. 8.10h and derivations) that the emotional kinship with the passion of the other movements is revealed. Within the *Adagio* itself, an intense pleading quality is set against the sighing character mentioned above.

Ex. 8.10. Op. 2 No. 1, II: a. m. 2; b. m. 3; c. mm. 6–7; d. mm. 8–9; e. m. 12; f. mm. 14–15; g. mm. 17–18; h. mm. 21–23; i. m. 24; j. mm. 29–30; k. mm. 34–35; l. mm. 54–55; m. mm. 56–57; n. m. 48; o. m. 60; p. m. 61.

Because of the sustained motivic development, there is no formal development section, merely an exposition and its repetition. To enumerate the differences, the D-minor section does not return in the recapitulation, embellishment becomes more florid, and the dynamic markings indicate a generally lower level of sound, shown by the numerous indications of *pianissimo* and the absence of a *crescendo* to a *sforzando* in mm. 40–41. The second half of the movement thereby becomes more reflective, like a memory of the past. In any event, the interpreter who opts to exaggerate the expressive effects for a darker delineation of character has solid reasons for so doing, not the least of which is the most obvious; the movement is marked *Adagio* not *Andante*.

The minor key of the Menuetto and the seriousness of the music do not fit the character of a courtly dance. The minor tonality becomes more affective through the sixths and thirds, the drooping quality of the line and its manner of clinging to the third of the triad, the repetition of the cadences, the suddenness of dynamic contrast, the *sforzandi*, the unison passages, and the contrast with the smoothness and longer breathed phrases of the trio. Instead of permitting the movement to sound merely nicely longing, the two-note slurs, the rests, and the brusqueness of *subito* dynamics need to be exaggerated to reveal the antisocial, untamed side of the music.

Outwardly, the finale occurs on two planes, the triplets in the exposition and recapitulation defining one plane, and the seemingly new theme in A♭ major and the repeated chords defining another. However, because of the interweaving of motivic material throughout the movement and the sonata as a whole, the division is more apparent than real, as Ex. 8.5 illustrates. The finale opens with the same cadence figure with which the first movement ended. It continues with another I–V^7–I in a position emphasizing c, the beginning note of the original descending hexachord. The entry of the six notes, or hexachord, in quarters (Ex. 8.5s) owes its moving quality to the resolution to a tonic (in contrast with its previous open-endedness), to the sudden calm in the sameness of dynamic level, and to the repetition of the phrase, all of which suggest the opposite end of the emotional spectrum from that of the first and third movements and the beginning and end of the exposition of the finale. The interaction of themes continues in the development, where the theme in A♭ major has the same identifying characteristics as the opening theme of the first movement: the ascending broken-chord melodic line, the repeated chords, and the six-note stepwise descent. The extended appearance of the hexachord as a structural framework in mm. 109–27 has already been mentioned.

The piano writing in much of the development is subdued, unlike the physically demanding nature of the opening of the movement and, as such, less likely to make pianists' fingers happy; one may assume that the composer's priority was relating the section in question to the first movement. The necessity to rationalize cerebral elements in Beethoven's craft without regard for the treatment of the instrument arises repeatedly. It was apparent to a contemporary critic, writing about the sonatas for piano and violin, Op. 12, in the *Allgemeine musikalische Zeitung:* To read through "these curious, extraordinarily difficult sonatas" required great effort. He could not deny that Beethoven was "going his own way, but what an eccentric, tortuous way it is! Intellect, intellect, and more intellect, but without nature, without song! . . . [nothing] but a mass of learning without even a good method of conveying it."[4]

The question of gratification versus meaning becomes more perplexing in the outer movements of the sonata, where Beethoven indicates a repeat at the end of each movement. If either movement is to be heard as a dramatic act, the repetition of the latter two-thirds of the act is anticlimactic. If Beethoven had an expressive reason (as opposed to a traditional one) for the second repeat, perhaps it had to do with a concept of the music as an expression of one or more psychological states, as opposed to a dramatic narrative. Walter Georgii's description of the Baroque and Classic periods as music of *to be* and *to happen* respectively does not exclude the possibility of traces of earlier thinking lingering on.

Op. 57

The principal interpretive challenge in Op. 2 No. 1 is that of credibility. Is the realization of the dynamic indications, those signposts of musical importance, intense enough to direct the listener's attention to the structure of the piece? Op. 57 presents a different challenge in its technical difficulty. One might play the sonata for years as a piece of bravura writing without being aware of the motivic cell that determines the true character of the work.

The plot of Op. 57 is summarized in the three notes of a neighboring-tone figure. The brevity of the figure, its simplicity, and the thread of musical sense it weaves from one idea to another throughout the work defines genius as no verbal explanation can. The structure of Op. 57, as the following pages will argue, is built around peaks of frustration. What better musical symbol of frustration could one devise than a stepwise figure that rises and falls, or departs and returns, back to the same pitch? To find this figure embedded within the second theme of the first movement, a passage that in no way sounds frustrated, is the dramatist's way of saying that in life, success and failure, pleasure and pain, fulfillment and disillusionment are all interwoven. When one has identified with the real *Appassionata*, the work exerts an even stronger appeal, in which technical difficulty becomes the tragedian's vehicle for recreating character.

A nickname becomes a problem when it calls up an image created by decades of traditional performance, obscuring the real piece within the score. The popular title, *Appassionata*, becomes synonymous with that which is technically overwhelming in power and sonority. Does the recital need a piece that will bring the audience to its feet? The big moments in the first movement and the final pages of the sonata are pianistic stagecraft of the first order, whether the listener has heard the sonata before or not. Is Op. 57 on the repertoire list for a competition? The sonata is a keyboard monument with which the contestant can demonstrate technical skills and "show" depth. By its very reputation, the sonata is sure to make an effect.

Large sections in the first movement, however, are less than heaven storming, the music lapsing at times into a spell, as though waiting for something to happen. How can one rationalize the preconceived image of a pianistic nightmare of passion and fury with the remark by Czerny that the finale should be "only rarely stormy"?[5] Czerny was a musician of solid achievement, a serious, thinking pianist who understood the spirit of his age. He enjoyed—as none of us has—the favor of fate in being able to speak with and play for Beethoven in life.

The *Appassionata* raises questions that lead one to want to rewrite the score in order to indulge in poses of pathos. How does the fixed quality of the A♭-minor section beginning in m. 24 or the strangeness of the single-line descending scale, *pp*, in mm. 47–50 fit the popular image of the piece? Ought one hurry the tempo to sound "in character"? Should one not immediately play *ff* upon beginning the A♭-minor closing theme (m. 51), or the transition beginning in E minor (m. 78)? Following the five g♭s, *sf*, in mm. 91–92, does the D♭ section not sound directionless, even uninteresting? If the pianist does not "do something" with it, will an audience sit on the edge of its seats listening to an inactive passage that returns to the same chord and pitch (m. 103, Ex. 8.11) with which it began a dozen measures earlier? How can the force of the climax just preceding the recapitulation be credible when the broken diminished seventh chord constantly halts? Is it not the privilege of staged passion to ignore the rhythmic pattern and the beat and treat the broken chords like a wild and free cadenza? How can the monotone quality of the theme of the Andante be kept from sounding boring? Are the variations really satisfying, considering the strangeness of the first variation and the blandness of the second? Is *ma non troppo* what one would expect in the tempo marking of an Allegro finale to a sonata such as this?

Ex. 8.11. Op. 57, I, mm. 94–105.

Op. 57 has the qualities of a heroic epic, its breadth derived from the expressive importance of details. The first sixteen measures contain four important clues for forming a concept—not of the *Appassionata*—but of the Sonata in F minor, Op. 57, as the composer must have conceived it.

1. *The basic rhythmic cell.* In the first sketches, as given in Nottebohm, the rhythmic form of the theme is in duple subdivision (Ex. 8.12). The sketch would seem to indicate that Beethoven had not yet decided on the meter, whether common time, or, following the "fate" motive and sextuplet sixteenths, a subdivision of three. If the sixteenth in the opening rhythmic cell as it was finally written is not to sound clipped and meaningless, the tempo will have to be held back; thus, the 12/8 rhythmic cell determines the tempo of the first movement, just as the appearance of the fate motive may have determined the choice of time signature. It would seem that, as Beethoven thought about the rhythm in its present form, the movement became more expansive and more complex in the sense of sounding hesitant and uncertain.

Ex. 8.12. From Nottebohm.[6]

The concentration that the rhythmic cell requires emphasizes the importance of small units and, specifically, the eighth note as the unit of counting, preventing any feel of a 4/4 subdivided in triplets. Counting eighth notes changes one's perception of the F-minor chords, *ff*, in m. 17, which are not triplet eighths alternating between the hands (Ex. 8.13) but a conflict between 12/8 and a hemiola 6/4, in which the syncopation of the right-hand chords makes it difficult to hear which meter is dominant. Played as in Ex. 8.13, the passage reveals no mark of genius. Played as Beethoven actually notated it, the same passage is equivalent to a willful rhythmic reordering. If one counts eighth-note beats, the repeated e♭s in the A♭-minor episode beginning in m. 24 fix the listener's attention on a stationary point, much as one's eyes would be trained on the flickering of a single candle on an otherwise dark stage. Counting eighths exposes the strangeness of the scale descent in mm. 47–50, which Czerny writes must be played absolutely evenly and in strict tempo. In 12/8, the individual sixteenth notes in the closing theme (m. 51) crackle like flames, instead of never seeming fast enough. For this reason, a realization such as should be avoided out of preference for even sixteenths. The integrity of the eighth note guarantees also that certain rhythmic quirks will be heard, such as the frustrating abbreviation of the left-hand segments in mm. 123–24 and the halting on each third beat in mm. 126–29, where the effect is that of thwarted rage that can only utter irrational sounds. If one counts eighths, the sixteenths in mm. 130–33 are not crowded into an unintelligible muddle; and, finally, the rhythmic hitch in mm. 219–23 (Ex. 8.14) becomes a willful act. Beethoven's indication of the pedal release coincides, significantly, with the beginning of the delayed figure in the right hand.

Ex. 8.13. Op. 57, I, mm. 17–18.

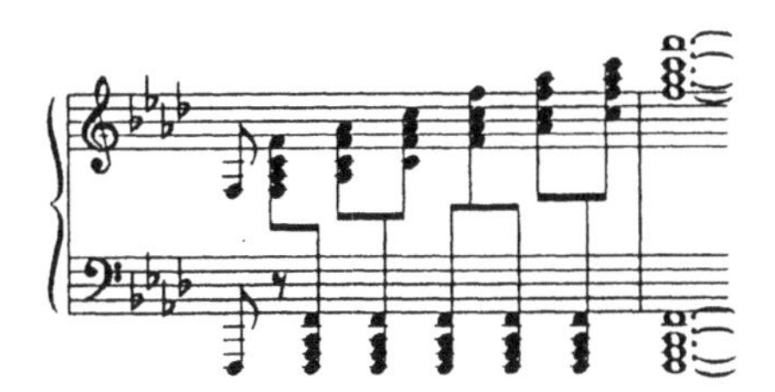

Ex. 8.14. Op. 57, I, m. 219.

The 12/8 rhythmic cell determines that the movement will be not so much a piece of fast-paced action as the contemplation of a tragic personal flaw. The long measures complement the long lines of the music, much as long lines and stanzas are fitting for a narrative poem of grand dimensions. An idea so colossal, to use

Czerny's adjective, requires time to unfold. Such may also be the most convincing explanation for the long repeat of the development and recapitulation in the last movement—to quote Czerny once more:

> The Finale cannot be played too quickly. The passages are to be played with a clear evenness and lightness, little *legato*, and only seldom stormy. Not until the repeat of the second part and toward the end does the agitation and the unfolding of strength become always more powerful, and the *Presto* concludes the *Sonata* with all the force that can be elicited from the *Fortepiano* through all one's means.[7]

With respect to an epic quality, the lyrical second theme in A♭ major in the first movement strangely does not appear in the earliest sketches. As Nottebohm remarks, "The parallel major [i.e., the relative major] is not touched at all. The sketch does not come out of the minor tonality. The stormy and dark predominate. The tender is missing, and with it the contrast."[8]

2. *Broken chord writing at the unison,* legato, pianissimo, *spaced two octaves apart.* The physical space between the hands and the resulting range of the opening broken chord are more than physical distance, representing also a psychic dimension. (A comparison with the beginning of the development, where the theme at the octave sounds warmer and more personal, confirms the importance of the spacing.) Upon further reflection, the impression becomes stronger that the keyboard style of the sonata is essentially two-voice writing and that much of the epic breadth of the sonata derives from lines which drift apart or cross. This wide spacing occurs in I, mm. 10–14, 17–18, 51–54, 61–65, 78–93, 105–109, 203–10, and 257–62 (where the theme covers a compass of six octaves); II, mm. 9–14; and III, mm. 50–62; 168–76, and 349–59. Other lines extend over a wide expanse of keyboard space: I, mm. 14–15, 30–35, 47–50, 109–30, and 218–35; II, where the range ascends through the three variations, to a peak in mm. 79–80; and III, mm. 5–20, 76–96 (left hand), 112–16, 164–67, and 176–206.

3. *A neighboring tone, one scalestep up and back.* Three notes, c–d(♭)–c, form an organic unit from which the features of the entire sonata derive. This three-note unit is distinguished by differences between the opening two measures—where there is unison writing, tonic harmony, a melodic line constructed from a broken chord, and simplicity—and mm. 3–4, which contain part writing, dominant harmony, a melodic line in scale steps, and greater complexity.

One may in fact hear the C-major chord in m. 4 as an independent key, instead of the dominant of F minor. In addition to the harmonic significance of the diminished seventh chord in m. 3, Beethoven has incorporated much melodic detail in the three-note cell. In a sense, the latter is a trill figure, so that mm. 3 and 4 contain a trill with a prefix and an ornate suffix as a part of and placed above another trill in augmentation. If the slow-moving, vacillating manner of the first movement is reminiscent of *Hamlet*, the writing of a trill within a trill is analogous to writing a play within a play.

The analogy with Shakespeare is not that far-fetched. The harmonic and melodic movement turns in a tight circle, its resolution uncertain; like a momentary facial expression, these measures, in microcosm, mirror the waxing and waning of tension throughout the piece, which culminates in climaxes of frustration. It is a symbol of frustration

> that the resolution to the dominant in m. 16 of the first movement is marked with a sudden *piano*;
> that the termination of the closing theme is marked with a sudden *piano*, following the *fortissimo* in the preceding measure;
> that the prolonged dominant seventh in mm. 91–92 resolves on the same chord, *piano*;
> that the same harmony in mm. 105–108 also resolves *piano*;
> that the awesome climax in the development is nine measures of diminished seventh harmony, *fortissimo*—when singing no longer suffices, shouting, or, after music, noise;
> and that the twenty-one measures of broken-chord writing beginning in m. 218 ends on the dominant, *piano*.

It is probably also significant that, like the diminished seventh in the three-note cell, diminished seventh harmony in the first movement and the finale (mm. 123–31 and 184–205 respectively) occurs at important junctions in the score.

Ex. 8.15 illustrates the many musical ideas related to the stepwise neighboring-tone pattern. The individual passages are self-explanatory, although particular mention should be made of the pitch relationship between c and a♭ at the close of the first movement and the superposed melody in thirds played by the left hand in the finale (Ex. 8.15s), which Czerny points out. Merely noticing the many instances of motivic relationship as an academic assignment will not by itself make a performance of Op. 57 more convincing. Only by asking what these relationships may have meant to the composer himself will the piece become a part of performer's self. Playing the F♭-major broken chord in m. 52 (Ex. 8.15h) should awaken an aural afterimage of the same chord from the earlier A♭-minor section (Ex. 8.15d); associating the two sounds connects the "now" with the "having been," the "here" with the "back there." Associating the principal theme of the first movement with that of the finale (Exx. 8.15a and r) places the restless against the ghostly, and one could go on, connecting Exx. 8.15i and v, or 8.15n and the theme in thirds in the finale (Ex. 8.16).

Ex. 8.15. Op. 57, I: a. mm. 1–9; b. m. 12; c. mm. 15–16; d. mm. 24–27; e. m. 35; f. mm. 35–39; g. m. 44; h. mm. 51–54; i. mm. 59–60; j. mm. 61–62; k. m. 91; l. mm. 105–106; m. mm. 243–44; n. mm. 249–52; II: o. mm. 1–2; p. m. 58, 73; III: q. mm. 5–7; r. mm. 22–28; s. mm. 30–34; t. mm. 38–39; u. m. 81; v. mm. 76–77; w. mm. 134–36; x. mm. 142–45.

b
c
d
e
f
g
h
i
j
k
l
m
n
o
Andante con moto
p
q
r
s
t
u
p e dolce

Ex. 8.16. Op. 57, III, mm. 36–43.

In the theme of the slow movement, the neighboring tone occurs within the melody line in its normal form and inverted, severely restricting the range of the line. The theme is more timbre than pitches, more atmosphere than substance. Attempting to project a healthy singing line is to ignore the point that it may have been intended only as a mysterious, understated, inward quality. In the finale, the short neighboring tones, if held back sufficiently so as to be heard as having motivic importance, help exercise control of the tempo (Ex. 8.15u).

If one accepts that the c–d–c figure is a slow trill, its relationship to other trill figures represents another element of perspective: the slow-moving against that which moves more quickly. The question of whether the three notes technically constitute a trill is relatively unimportant. The melodic characteristic of a trill is the alternation of two adjacent pitches; remove the adjective "adjacent," and the common denominator between the many such patterns becomes evident. The relationship of the neighboring tone to subsequent patterns illustrates the total integration of a dramatic element—confinement, vacillation, frustration, inability to escape—in the fabric of the entire work. The accompaniment in the A♭-major second theme is thus related to a trill figure (Ex. 8.15e), as are the alternating chords in the first movement (mm. 17, 152, and 251). In that sense, the writing of the A♭-minor closing theme is also related. The third variation in the second movement contains written-out trills (Ex. 8.15p).

The embedding of the neighboring tone, inverted, in the second theme of the first movement (Ex. 8.15f) unites both segments of the principal theme: The rhythm and broken-chord line of the latter have been adapted to the circular movement of the neighboring tone, and the impersonal nature of the opening is exchanged for a more human, tender quality. Finally, there are the two-note figures still related to the neighboring tone, such as the "fate" motive (Ex. 8.15b) and adjacent pitches marked with a *sforzando* (Ex. 8.15m).

4. *A procedure of growth by adding in layers*. Taking the trill within a trill in

mm. 3–4 as a cue, one notices notes and particularly dynamic markings added as intensification of a particular repeated feature, again a symbol of contemplation rather than action. For example, a dynamic layer is added to the neighboring tone motive in mm. 9 and 11 of the first movement. In m. 17, F minor *pianissimo* is interrupted by F minor *fortissimo*. The addition of the f♭^{3} *sf* in m. 26 is a subtle adding-in-layers of notes and dynamics (Ex. 8.15d). In the A♭-minor closing theme, the sudden *ff* in mm. 53–54 is similar in effect to the examples just mentioned.

In the slow movement, the writing of the three variations progresses upward, as though through the layers of the piano's compass, just as the phrase segments in the second half of the theme itself rise progressively through the compass of an octave. As the movement ends, a diminished seventh chord *pp* is followed by the same chord *ff*, and again by the same chord hammered in a dotted rhythm. The theme in thirds (Ex. 8.15s) is added above the principal theme of the finale, as is the melodic fragment in eighths in the recapitulation beginning in m. 220. The intensity of the finale is increased through contrapuntal means, including canon and the simple adding of voices (mm. 13, 28, 38, and 134–35). In the *Presto*, there is a connection between the broken chord in eighths and the more intense sixteenth-note figuration beginning in m. 341 (Ex. 8.17).

Ex. 8.17. Op. 57, III, mm. 308–11, 341–43.

Op. 110

Moderato cantabile molto espressivo—the fullness of the tempo marking itself suggests an image of floating, unfolding, and expanding. "Take time to play singingly, greatly holding back the tempo" does not mean to draw out each melodic unit until the overall train of thought is lost. Even worse would be to play in step with a metronomic beat. The teenage student who said of the second theme of the Chopin E-minor Concerto, "This music should sound as though it were always beginning" had the understanding to follow the elusive nature of Beethoven's thought in clothing the same idea in one new keyboard pattern after another.

The opening movement displays a clear-cut exposition, development, recapitulation, and coda. In this sonata form, however, there seem to be two distinguishable principal themes stated at the very beginning. Unless one decides which is *the* principal theme, the continuity of the movement will be lost at the very outset

(Ex. 8.18). The melodic line and part of the bass line in m. 10 correspond exactly with m. 3. There are harmonic parallels, including the bass line, between mm. 5 and 6 and mm. 1 and 2 and between mm. 7 and 8 and mm. 2 and 3. In addition to the melodic parallel between mm. 10 and 3, and "first" principal theme begins on c and comes to rest on b♭ in m. 2, just as the "second" principal theme (mm. 5–12) begins on c and continues (with d♭ in the bass) from b♭.

Ex. 8.18. Op. 110, I, mm. 1–12.

Obviously, mm. 5–12 constitute a variation of mm. 1–4, the true principal theme, although the cadenza-like features in m. 4—the fermata over the trill, the hairpin *crescendo-decrescendo* sign, and the crowding of notes—will always mislead one to believe that the preceding has been an introduction to the actual beginning of the movement, in m. 5. Measures 5–12 occur on a new plane of consciousness, just as the writing begins in a new, higher range of the keyboard. Also, instead of four-part writing, there is now melody and accompaniment. Furthermore, the first dynamic marking in m. 4 is a *subito piano*, while in the parallel measure (m. 11) it is a *sforzando*. The music thereby makes a point of saying what earlier was left unsaid.

Measures such as this in late Beethoven especially require a piano sound that is at once inward and intense. Those who, as a matter of habit or necessity, calculate their sound for effect in huge halls may not find the door to the inner world of Op. 110. This is not music to be projected to an audience. Immediately, with the sound of the first two-note slur—with the pull between the dotted quarter and the eighth—the player must believe that the piano can communicate a welcome to regions of the soul so intimately that even spectators in the audience will follow.

For this music is always beckoning the listener to its train of thought. Thus, mm. 12–20 constitute a variation of the preceding variation, based on harmonic likenesses and the occasional hint of a melodic parallel, such as the G in m. 13 with the g^2 in m. 6, or the B♭ in m. 15 with the $b\flat^2$ in m. 7. The impression is that of having passed through yet another door leading further inward, a still higher level of consciousness (and a higher range of the keyboard reaching $a\flat^3$), still more remote from the place at which the movement began. The challenge to the fingers is not the same as playing an étude. The problem is finding how feathery light the thirty-seconds can sound, whether one drifts into them instead of playing metronomically, and whether the staccato notes can ring and yet sound distant—all of this with the help of the pedal.

Measures 20–21 sound like new material although they are actually derived from mm. 1 and 2 harmonically and progress melodically from c to b♭. Notice that the variation of these two measures in mm. 22–23 emphasizes a descending second, which is then repeated insistently through m. 24 (Ex. 8.19).

Ex. 8.19. Op. 110, I, mm. 20–24.

The *sforzandos* in mm. 27 and 31 mark b♭ and c respectively as important pitches, of which b♭ will become predominant and then descend to g. The bass line in mm. 28–30 outlines a hexachord, e♭ down to G. The same hexachord is mirrored in the ascending slurred seconds in the right hand of mm. 28 and 29 (Ex. 8.20) and repeated on different pitches in mm. 29 and 30. The stepwise descending line of trills in the left hand in mm. 25–27 also encompasses a hexachord, as does the melodic line of the principal theme in the opening measures of the movement.

Ex. 8.20. Op. 110, I, mm. 28–29.

The development section, mm. 40–56, is unique in consisting solely of a two-measure sequence, all but two statements of which carry identical dynamic markings. As a result, actual development is more evident in the exposition and recapitulation than in the development proper. Pitch-wise the sixteen-measure section descends stepwise from c^3 to c^2. One may assume that Beethoven regarded a straightforward, sequential development section as a necessary relief to the diverse keyboard patterns of the exposition and outlined a descending D♭ scale as preparation for the digression to D♭ major and E major in mm. 63–77. As Ex. 8.21 illustrates, the treatment of pitch structure gives the movement a circular direction, a kind of pitch enclosure within which the piece expands upon the *amabilitá* character of the opening.

Ex. 8.21. Op. 110, I.

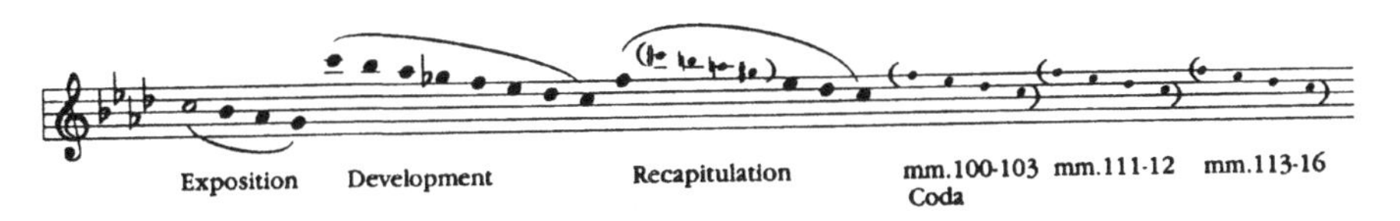

The rhythmic structure of mm. 100–103 sets the descending tetrachord in relief, as does the *subito piano* in mm. 111 and 113. The reiteration of the same descending pitches proves that the same descending pattern noticed in the exposition is real, not imaginary. Placing the first variation of the principal theme in the recapitulation in the key of the subdominant (beginning on f) strengthens the association with the descending pitch pattern beginning in mm. 79, 100, 111, and 113, and tightens the cohesiveness of the recapitulation. Although Schubert's purpose when beginning the recapitulation in the subdominant was to avoid disturbing the original key relationships of the exposition, Beethoven's seems to have been to *disturb* that relationship, leading further to E major, the most distant key in the movement and a still more remote area of the mind within the music.

How does one communicate the significance of the harmonic digression that is established in m. 63? To feel oneself bound by an obsessive obedience to the metronome at this point in Beethoven's soliloquy is to diminish the musical effect of the digression. Only a tempo adjustment—beginning more slowly, as though more thoughtfully—in m. 63 will project the impression of beginning again somewhere off to the side of the main action, much as if an actor were to walk to another part of the stage as he began a new paragraph in the script. Returning in virtually one remarkable measure to the same pitch (f) in m. 79 with which the section began in m. 63 makes the passage through E major sound like an aberration (Ex. 8.22).

Ex. 8.22. Op. 110, I, mm. 77–79.

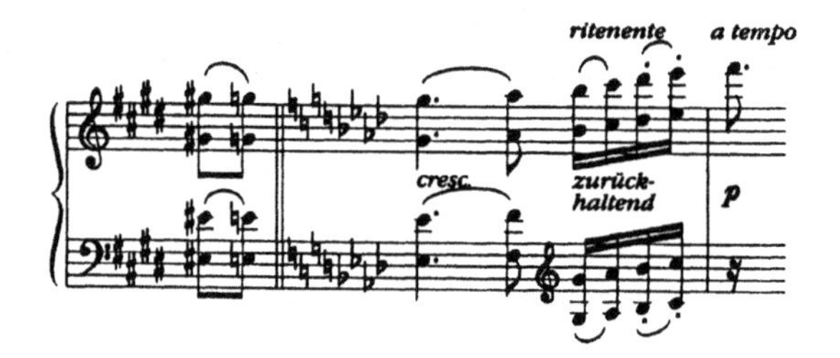

The imagination to conceive planes of consciousness and the craft to project the same through musical means make this movement one of the most thought-provoking and absorbing pieces in the repertoire. There is the symmetry of the plan of structural pitches, the pervasive appearance of the hexachord pattern, the tetrachord, the two-note slurs, the harmonic diversion in the recapitulation, the lingering over the tetrachord in the coda, and *molto expressivo* pacing throughout the movement, all of which, separately and interacting, create a multidimensional image similar to computer drawings that can be moved to be studied from any angle.

The opening phrase of the *Allegro molto* beings on c (and the movement ends on c) and descends stepwise the distance of a hexachord (Ex. 8.23). It is important not to overlook the ending of the slur with the second quarter in m. 2, setting apart the same group of four descending pitches on which the exposition of the first movement was based. That in itself disputes the idea that the first measure must be played as an upbeat to the following one in order that the dominant chord in m. 4 sound like a downbeat in a contrived 4/4. Far more worthy of speculation is the derivation of the opening phrase from a Viennese popular song, quoted by Martin Cooper (Ex. 8.24.[9] Beethoven wrote an accompaniment for this folk song and submitted it to Simrock in March 1820. It begins, "Our cat has had kittens," and gives the number and their markings. The theme in mm. 17–24 bears an equally strong resemblance to another folk song, whose words "Ich bin lüdelich, du bist lüdelich, wir sind alle lüdelich," may be translated, "I'm loose, you're loose, we're all loose"

(Ex. 8.24b). Like the four-note grouping in the theme, the brace of four eighths within each bar of the middle section also spans a tetrachord, as do the series of beginnings on f^3, $b\flat^3$, $g\flat^3$, and again f^3 (Ex. 8.25).

Ex. 8.23. Op. 110, II, mm. 1–4.

Ex. 8.24. a. From Cooper; b. Op. 110, II, mm. 120–27.

Ex. 8.25. Op. 110, II, mm. 41, 56–57, 72–75.

Even if one were not aware of the words to the popular tunes that Beethoven incorporated in the movement, the bumptious humor of the music would be difficult to misunderstand. The *forte* and *fortissimo* interruptions, the bass *sforzandos*

falling with an upbeat or the lifting of a two-note slur in the treble, the two-measure pause, the "unbuttoned" quality (a term once applied to one of Beethoven's moods) of the rather nonsensical trio, the trailing off of an idea into a fermata, the *ritardando* added to the opening phrase in the reprise, and the jolting of the separated, offbeat chords in the coda raise a question about the reason for following so tender an opening movement with one so bizarre and foreign to it. Just as strange is the transition from this scherzo to the mysterious aloneness of the Adagio, the sighs and yearning of the recitative, and the darkness of the *Klagender Gesang*.

Words such as "mysterious," "aloneness," "sighs," "yearning," and "darkness" are taken from the interpreter's imaginary lexicon of meaning. An experiment such as the following may be helpful in proving to oneself the validity of meaning: Play the right hand an octave lower and the left hand an octave higher for six beats, change the double-dotted eighth and thirty-second to a dotted eighth and sixteenth, and disregard the *una corda* (Ex. 8.26), and all hints of distance and aloneness will disappear. Play the recitative in as strict a time as possible, ignoring the changes of tempo, any inflection in the repeated a's and the dynamic indications, and no trace of a personal narrative will be heard. Keep the thick, repeated bass chords in the Arioso light and evenly flowing so that the voice leading within them does not obtrude, avoid stressing the tied-over upbeats or taking time for crowded subdivision, and the passage may sound acceptable, but hardly sorrowful. It may be that actors realize character more readily than we do, because they understand the language they are speaking; pianists tend to be trained in the diction of playing and less often in using their imaginations to read between the notes in the score. Listen to the effect of the return from the somewhere-sometime reflection of the widely spaced writing to the here and now of normal spacing in the opening of the Adagio (Ex. 8.27).

Ex. 8.26. Op. 110, III, mm. 1–2.

Ex. 8.27. Op. 110, III, m. 2.

The reader is referred to the detailed study of the third movement by John Cockshoot,[10] who subscribes to Schenker's thesis that Beethoven wanted to unify the Adagio and the fugue in one movement, avoiding a division between them and making the fugue the most important section. Since a fugue is a tripartite form—exposition, middle section, and a final return to the tonic key—Beethoven had to determine where to interrupt and resume the fugue. His solution was to repeat the Arioso after the exposition of the fugue, in actuality expanded into three expositions, closing with a stretto and a pedal point. The final E♭ seventh chord is treated as a German sixth leading to the second statement of the Arioso in G minor. Instead of resuming the fugue with three voices, Beethoven introduces one voice at a time, in inversion, as though the fugue were beginning all over.

Without disputing the logic of this explanation, many playings of the sonata lead one to regard the first fugue, whether or not in theory it is only an exposition, as an exposition and development interrupted at the point of the German sixth (mm. 110–14). This impression of "all-but-the-finish" arises from several aural landmarks in addition to the E♭ seventh chord, namely, the developmental nature of the second exposition (mm. 45–86)—its length, the *fortissimo* "giant's step" bass entrance in m. 73, and the development-like episodes—the entrance of the subject in D♭ and the closing pedal.

Why did the Arioso have to be introduced a second time? Would the sonata not have been more unified if Beethoven had expanded the Arioso the first time and left the fugue intact? In practical terms, the repetition of the Adagio is a worrisome point for the performer, who can hardly help being concerned about holding the listener's attention. The "weakening" direction must be realized as clearly as possible through the fragmentation of the melodic line and, perhaps, a suggestion of unsteadiness in the repeated chords.

The player must find an interpreter's reason for what can seem like an unwieldy repetition. If the first fugue (or, if one prefers, the exposition and development), is compared with the final fugue (or recapitulation), the former sounds smooth in its voice leading and rhythmically even, while the second merely begins in this manner and then proceeds in augmentation, diminution, double diminution, stretto, and rhythmic complexities, finally breaking into a sixteenth-note Alberti-like figure whose pattern is based on the original fugue subject. The ecstasy of the final lines of the movement, with the pedal point on a low A♭ and the high treble chords ascending in fourths, defies description.

The "interpreter's reason," therefore, is that the keyboard writing of the first fugue had to be broken apart rhythmically and reassembled using an ever-quickening subdivision to construct the sort of heroic conclusion that the sonata required. The repetition of the Arioso, weakened and more problematic in character, provides the interpretive reason for the re-entry of the fugue in inversion, its resigned character prepared by the pedaled G-major chords. If the sonata were to have ended with the first fugue, both the musical and the dramatic solution would have lacked credibility—one must face greater trials before strength can be tested and found sufficient. Whatever importance one attaches to the words of the street songs that Beethoven appropriated, the second movement is a wild, extravagant scherzo that knows no sense of propriety. As such, it is the untamed opposite of the *sanftness* of the first movement. The shift in character of the recitative and Arioso is much like sorrow after excess, and after sorrow, restoration. That the latter is achieved by reversing the melodic direction of the opening theme (rising fourths, as opposed to falling thirds) connects the outer movements dramatically.

Pitch relationships that bind the sections of the last movement together also strengthen the overall continuity from the first movement to the last: The Adagio opens on f, the Arioso on e♭ (and, not to be overlooked, the first phrase spans a hexachord), the first fugue ends on a d♭, and the movement concludes melodically in measure 209 on a c—an architectural expansion of the oft-repeated tetrachord in the first movement.

Motivic relationships and transformations provide food for thought for the playing of these sonatas throughout life. Without such study, there can be no basis for independent judgments in interpretation. The presence of the same motivic building block in the form of a hexachord in two sonatas as widely separated in time as Op. 2 No. 1 (1795) and Op. 110 (1821) gives one an appreciation for the creative intellect of the younger Beethoven. Constructing so lifelike a work as Op. 110 from so commonplace a pattern is like Shakespeare's basing a monument of the literature on a common human impulse, such as love, ambition, greed, vacillation, or naiveté. We listen to, we play, we interpretively weigh six notes, and we perceive that Beethoven has developed with this pattern a picture of human weaknesses and triumphs which we then associate with our own inner failures and victories.

X Quasi una Fantasia

Op. 27 Nos. 1 and 2, Op. 26

Fantasy, as in make-believe, the realm of dreams, is the safety valve of human consciousness, the drawing board of the architect, the curiosity of the inventor, the *raptus* of the composer. Beethoven seems to have used the term *quasi una fantasia* as an explanation for the departure from conventional form—beginning with a slow movement, joining movements, including a cyclic element—not to escape the restraint of the rational but to unify the sonata through rational means.

Op. 27 Nos. 1 and 2

> This sonata [Op. 27 No. 1], by its rather vague subtitle, "In the style of a Fantasy," would seem to imply that it is somewhat rambling and incoherent in plan. Such was doubtless the composer's intention, but at the period when he wrote it he had not discovered how to write rhapsodically. His composition persists in presenting itself in watertight compartments, and it is in vain that he writes "*attacca*" at the end of each movement (meaning "follow on") when he contradicts himself perpetually by making an emphatic cadence with a pause after it. The first movement, at any rate, is an ingenious attempt to get away from the discontinuity of a theme and variations by the agreeable expedient of breaking out into an *Andante* [?] and a *Scherzo*, yet relapsing into his variations again and again. This would make an excellent piece to play by itself, and the reason why it is not done can only be a disinclination to expose Beethoven's failure of plan.[1]

As the quotation indicates, "fantasy" has different meanings for different people. Why would a good composer set out to be "rambling and incoherent" or, for that matter, point to such an intent with a phrase such as "quasi una Fantasia"? Why would pianists in the twentieth century be concerned about "protecting" Beethoven's reputation? The fact that the author taught at an internationally known school unfortunately makes the remark that "Beethoven had a huge advantage over all of us—he never attended a school of music" sound less facetious.

Beethoven's reasons for using the term *quasi una fantasia* are to be found in the features, shared by both sonatas, that set them apart from his work up to that time. *Attacca subito l'Allegro* or *l'Adagio* or *il seguente* tells us that Beethoven considered the musical content too integrated and personal to permit any break in the listener's concentration. In the E♭ Sonata, the term occurs after each of the first three movements, while, in the C♯ Sonata, *Attacca il seguente* is found only at the end of the first movement. It appears that Beethoven wanted a conventional pause before the finale to set it apart as an independent movement. Perhaps his reason was that the second sonata is not a cyclic piece, and also that beginning anew draws attention to the motivic parallels with the first movement.

The direction *attacca* does not appear in any preceding sonata and, in the later sonatas, only preceding the finale in Opp. 53 and 57. In both of these instances, the finale is harmonically joined to the preceding movement. This statement should be qualified, however, by pointing out that the long pedal at the close of the first and third movements of Op. 26, by extending the musical "spell," implies somewhat the same effect as *attacca*. At other times, the absence of a double bar between movements, as, for example, in Opp. 81a, 101, and 109, is equivalent to *attacca*; the visual appearance of continuity is even stronger. In addition, the reader may wish to include Op. 106, in which, as in Op. 53, an introductory movement of some length is joined to the finale.

The two sonatas of Op. 27 are alike also in beginning with a slow movement, a peculiarity shared only with Op. 26. Again, the statement must be qualified. The Andante of Op. 27 No. 1 is interrupted by an *Allegro*, and there are other opening movements (Op. 13, Op. 31 No. 2, Op. 78, Op. 81a, and Op. 111) that begin with a slow section; in Op. 31 No. 2 and Op. 78, it is very brief but important. Also, the first movement of Op. 110, while marked *Moderato*, unfolds slowly because of its content and the marking *molto espressivo*, "very held back."

Beginning with a slow movement, especially if the dynamic level is *piano* or *pianissimo*, is less straightforward, luring the listener's attention away from immediate surroundings into a musical twilight in which images are less distinct but, in the quietness, perception is far keener. Both sonatas of Op. 27 begin *pp*, indicated seven times in the first thirty-six measures of the E♭ Sonata, while the C♯ Sonata is marked *sempre pp*, to which is added the direction, "This piece must be played as delicately as possible. . . ." Beginning with a slow movement in a quiet dynamic level and the marking *attacca* are qualities of intimate conversation. One is unlikely to interrupt a friend who is sharing his innermost feelings and secrets.

Another important similarity is the exploiting of chord color. The first movement of the E♭ Sonata exists for long periods of musical time on the tonic and dominant of E♭ major and of C major. The trio of the second movement consists of extended play with the tonic and dominant of A♭ major. Neither should the color effect of the tonic pedal at the beginning of the Adagio be overlooked. In the finale, color is the purpose of the lengthy *ritornello*, mm. 9–24 (the dominant seventh of E♭) and the twenty-six measures of B♭ and B♭ seventh harmony, mm. 56–81. The color effect of the repeated triplets in the Adagio of the C♯ Sonata is virtually *the* appeal of the piece.

A fourth similarity, one that is common to several other sonatas among the thirty-two, is the presence of motivic transformation throughout the work and, in the E♭ Sonata, cyclic form. The latter may be one of the reasons that Czerny considered the E♭ Sonata the more fantasy-like of the two. Also, the interruption of the Andante with an *Allegro* and the return of the Adagio near the end of the sonata make the E♭ Sonata sound less conventional. The three well-marked movements of the C♯ Sonata are fewer in number and consistent within themselves, developing character in longer chapters. Since the "Moonlight" is the more familiar, the E♭ Sonata is perhaps best studied through the C♯ minor.

A number of parallels between the outer movements of Op. 27 No. 2 cannot be dismissed as coincidental:

broken chords constitute the fabric of the writing;
a stepwise descent in the bass from tonic to dominant at the opening of each movement;
sonata-allegro form;
the dotted upbeat with which the melody begins in the first movement is paralleled by the eighth note chords, *ff*, on the fourth beat in the theme of the finale;
g♯ as a prominent pitch;
a four-note "twist" motive midway in the exposition of each movement (Ex. 9.1);
the development section of each movement begins in F♯ minor;
a long dominant pedal in the latter half of the development, twelve measures in the Adagio, thirteen in the Presto;
the same harmonic progression in the half cadence at the close of the development in each movement (Ex. 9.2);
thematic material placed in the left hand in the coda of each movement.

Ex. 9.1. Op. 27 No. 2, I, mm. 15–17; III, mm. 29–30.

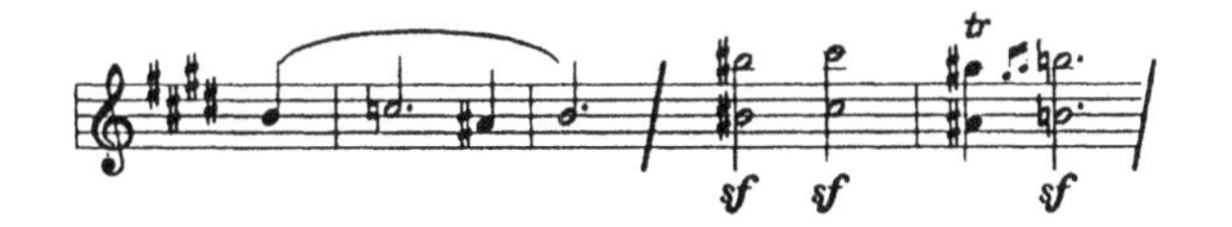

Ex. 9.2. Op. 27 No. 2, I, mm. 40–42; III, mm. 99–102.

However obvious, an awareness of these structural parallels is seldom considered as important as technical "polish." An architect's drawing of the exterior of a projected building must take into consideration the inner requirements of support and materials. If one thinks of the Presto, the complete movement, as one long character variation of the Adagio, or each of these movements as a variation of one unstated Ur-plan, the tightness of the form has a greater dramatic impact.

The interpretive possibilities are thought-provoking. The peaceful triplets, virtually the "theme song" of this popular sonata, not only determine its mood but emerge briefly as a kind of melodic whining at the high point in the Adagio. Czerny wrote of this passage, "In measures 32 through 35, a significant [bedeutend] *crescendo* and also *accelerando* to *forte,* which decreases again in measures 36 through 39."[2] They reappear as sixteenth-note broken chords in the finale, no longer an accompaniment figure but now, greatly accelerated and expanded, the thematic vehicle for agitation that dominates the movement, accompanied by drum beats and marked with *subito* dynamics. The mood figure of the first movement breaks through all restraints and becomes an uncontrollable rage in the Presto, resembling a dramatic scene in which a crazed character wails and screams, speaking only a few intelligible sentences. The link between the broken chords in the outer movements becomes clearer if one heeds Czerny's advice: "In accordance with the indication of *Alla breve,* the whole [first] movement is to be played in a moderate *Andante-tempo.*"[3]

From the first to the third movements there is another shift in importance, this time involving a tetrachord and the familiar right-hand melody. Although it is easily overlooked, the descending tetrachord at the beginning of the Adagio is the first melodic line to be heard, and it contains a circular three-note melodic cell from which the subsequent twisting and tightness of the melodic writing are derived (Ex. 9.3).

Ex. 9.3. Op. 27 No. 2, I, mm. 1–5, 7–9, 12–14, 15–17, 19–20, 25–27, 28, 40–41.

Only the upbeat of the melody line in the Adagio survives in the finale, now in the form of *subito fortissimo* chords on the fourth beat of the measure. The descending tetrachord bass line, which had only a clouded existence at the beginning of the Adagio, is now the sole melodic line in the first eight measures of the finale. The tetrachord also determines the shape of the second theme and occurs again in the closing section, where it is repeated, measure by measure, as the abbreviated, accelerated pattern of the second theme (Ex. 9.4).

Ex. 9.4. Op. 27 No. 2, III, mm. 21–25, 43–45.

Pitch, specifically, g♯, is an important unifying feature between the outer movements:

the opening tetrachord circles around g♯;
the treble melody dwells on g♯;
the pedal point in the development is a g♯ octave;
g♯ is the prominent pitch in the left hand in the coda;
much of the A-section of the Allegretto consists of the repetition of two alternating phrases, the first of which is in the key of the dominant, resolving on a♭;
at the close of the section, a♭ becomes more important, through the higher dynamic level, than the tonic note (Ex. 9.5);
g♯ is the highest pitch in the *fortissimo* chords in the theme of the finale;
after preparation by two measures built upon an a♮ in the bass, above which

there is chromaticism, a change in articulation, and an abbreviation of the preceding two-measure pattern, the half cadence on the dominant in m. 9 is then extended on a g♯ pedal for another six measures;

the g♯ pedal recurs in the development;

g♯ is the structural pitch heard in the recapitulation in the second theme and the closing theme (Ex. 9.6), as well as the approach to the dominant in mm. 188–89.

Because we have come to hear g♯ as an important pitch center, the tonic C♯-minor triad sounds less final, and the thematic material is generally suspended. It is as though, upon hearing the very beginning of the familiar melody in the first movement, there was already a prevailing restlessness, an incompleteness, and a searching manner.

Ex. 9.5. Op. 27 No. 2, II, mm. 33–36.

Ex. 9.6. Op. 27 No. 2, III, mm. 116–18, 151–53.

The opening measures of a Beethoven sonata often provide the key to the movement or even to the work as a whole. With respect to the E♭ Sonata, the first sounds heard are repeated pitches, a repeated rhythmic pattern, and an alternating between tonic and dominant harmony. Beethoven avoids beginning with a "theme." The sounds one hears do not so much form a melody as present harmonic colors, not harmonic progressions but a rocking back and forth for the pleasure of the sensation. As such, these measures are similar in musical purpose to the opening measures of Debussy's *Les cloches à travers les feuilles* or Webern's *Piano Variations.* The second four measures of the E♭ Sonata consist of extended dominant seventh harmony in the same rhythmic pattern, all eight measures of the piece thus far remaining in E♭.

A recurring "watertight compartment" and the variations into which the composer "relapses" again and again—Beethoven's "failure of plan"—have a single purpose, namely, to impress upon our memory a clearly defined formal and harmonic profile that we will be reminded of throughout the sonata. Counting repeats, the opening twenty-four measures of the Andante are in E♭ major; in fact, the dense eighth-note chords beginning in m. 9 (an abbreviation of mm. 1–8) sound like the tonic of the tonic, if there were such, in that the repeated notes in the melody blend into the chords, and the short contrapuntal phrase is absent in the left hand. Following this darker E♭ major, the cool clarity of the C-major chords is *the* harmonic effect of the movement that returns with great force in the Allegro. The care with which Beethoven isolated the sound of C major, a third relationship to E♭, had to be part of a master plan restricting all other key color to E♭ major. The variations provide the excuse for the prolonging of E♭-major sound and, as such, are variations of timbre. The most readily recognizable detail of this profile is the extension of dominant seventh harmony, including a *sforzando* on the fourth scale step (Ex. 9.7).

Ex. 9.7. Op. 27 No. 1, I, mm. 5–8.

Other details of this profile include the melodic interval of a third and the harmonic swaying between tonic and dominant. The extension of dominant seventh harmony in mm. 45–48 and 53–56 betrays the entire C-major section as a variation of the opening eight measures of the movement, further proof of which is the alternating of tonic and dominant harmony and melodic thirds. In the next movement (*Allegro molto e vivace*), the second half of the middle section (sixteen measures plus one beat) consists of dominant seventh harmony (or dominant ninth, depending upon how one explains the f). The chromaticism in the outer sections of the movement could also be described as coloristic, and the variation beginning in m. 89 as an excellent example of a variation of timbre (Ex. 9.8).

Ex. 9.8. Op. 27 No. 1, II, mm. 89–90.

The profile is found in the Adagio as well. The melodic line begins with an ornamented descent of a third from c to a♭ (Ex. 9.9a), and the fourth scale step, whether in A♭ or E♭ major, is always approached with a *crescendo* and marked, with one exception, with a *fp*, *sfp* (Exx. 9.9b–g), or *rf*.

Ex. 9.9. Op. 27 No. 1, III, mm. 1–2, 2–3, 4–5, 6–7, 18–19, 20–21, 22–23, 25–26.

With the Adagio and the finale, the keyboard style of the sonata changes. Long melodic lines prevail, and, in general, the writing is full-sounding. In the finale, also, the scoring is substantial, including a contrapuntal working-out of the theme in the development. Nonetheless, traces of the original profile can be found in the melodic thirds, the back-and-forth movement between tonic and dominant (Ex. 9.10a), and the extended passages of dominant seventh harmony (Exx. 9.10b and c).

Ex. 9.10. Op. 27 No. 1, IV, a. mm. 1–8; b. mm. 9–16; c. mm. 35–39.

Beneath the apparent simplicity of the opening lines of the sonata is a treatment of color and timbre as sophisticated as the depiction of a smile on the face of the *Mona Lisa*. The sonata is possibly a more purely "musical" work than the "Moonlight," lacking to a greater degree the dramatic realism of the latter, just as, in the same sense, the *Waldstein* might be considered a more musical work than the *Appassionata*.

Op. 26

Op. 26 would seem not to belong in the same category with the two Sonatas *quasi una fantasia*, although, in the sense that the fantasy element alters the traditional arrangement of movements and exaggerates the difference in character from one movement to another, Op. 26 is as much a fantasy sonata as Op. 27 No 1. According to Nottebohm, the two were being sketched at the same time.[4] That Op. 26 was to become a Joseph's coat of many colors seems to have been in Beethoven's mind from the very beginning. Nottebohm points out that the first sketch was for the finale, although, at that moment, it appears Beethoven did not even intend to use the material *in* a sonata (Ex. 9.11). Some thirty pages later, the same idea is

Ex. 9.11. Op. 26, IV, sketch, from Nottebohm.

reworked in a form that begins like the present finale. Two pages further, the theme of the first movement appears, much as in its present form (Ex. 9.12), followed by

Ex. 9.12. Op. 26, I, sketch, from Nottebohm.

the words "varied at once—then Menuetto or some other character piece like for example a March in A♭ minor and then this:"

The first sketch (Ex. 9.11) was only later chosen as the finale. Nottebohm asks, "How is one to interpret the juxtaposition of two so contrasting pieces as the projected Funeral March—for one cannot take the March in A♭ minor as anything else—and the sketched hurdy-gurdy [*bärenleierische*] finale?"[5] The same question might be raised regarding the juxtaposition of the Largo of Op. 10 No. 3 with a Menuetto, the passionate *Largo, con gran espressione* of Op. 7 with a bland *Allegro* (itself interrupted by a violent trio), and the *Largo appassionato* of Op. 2 No. 2 with an unburdened Scherzo.

Like the Mozart A-major Sonata K. 331, the Op. 26 lacks a sonata-allegro movement. Like the Mozart also, it begins with a set of variations—in effect with a closed statement, an announcement that the work is not beginning in a musically problematic way. Op. 26 and K. 331 are also alike in including a character piece not found in any of the other piano sonatas of either composer. Both sonatas exhibit a newness that is relevant to the moment for which it was fashioned.

The lyricism of the theme of the variations conceals its individuality. Yet the individual variations, based on various qualities within segments of the theme, are each unique and, in the importance of timbre in Variations II, III, and V, provide another similarity with the color element of the Op. 27 Sonatas. The six measures of unison writing in the theme are marked with one dynamic, *piano;* the non-unison writing, containing independent voice lines that at times move chromatically, bears frequent markings of *sforzando, crescendo* to *sforzando,* and *crescendo* to *subito piano.* Understated features are easily overlooked, such as the expanding lines in mm. 3–4, the zigzag line and *subito* dynamics in mm. 5–8, and the *sforzandos* on tied upbeats and on appoggiaturas in mm. 16–24. These become, within the balanced quality of the theme, marks of recognition that are then exploited in the variations. In a sense, the theme is given a sharper profile by its variations.

One of these marks of recognition is the feeling of lift in the two-note slurs and the lightening and/or shortening of phrase endings (Ex. 9.13). Another such mark is the suspended quality of the common tone, e♭, in the theme and the placing of a *sforzando* over a tied upbeat (Ex. 9.14), already mentioned. A third mark of recognition involves appoggiaturas, especially those marked with a *sforzando*.

Ex. 9.13. Op. 26, I, mm. 1–4, 7–8.

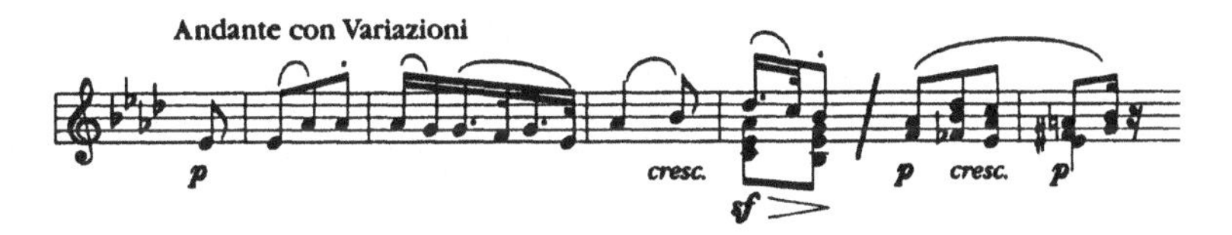

Ex. 9.14. Op. 26, I, mm. 16–18.

Each variation emphasizes one or more details of profile. In Variation I, that detail is the feeling of lift; instead of a suspension in the second measure, the downbeat is released (Ex. 9.15). The zigzag line of the second strain of the theme has been separated into short figures, the last note of which is shortened (Ex. 9.16). Short thirty-second note groups similarly suggest lift (Ex. 9.17). Throughout this variation the downbeat is consistently lightened, and stress is generally shared by the second and third beats.

Ex. 9.15. Op. 26, I, mm. 34–36.

Ex. 9.16. Op. 26, I, mm. 39–40.

Ex. 9.17. Op. 26, I, mm. 54–55, 60.

In Variation II, the harmonic structure of the theme is broken into a shimmer of sound. According to the score, the variation is to be played almost entirely on one dynamic level. The even patter of the rhythm, the placing of the melody in one register (except for the B-section of the theme), and the even dynamic level may be interpreted as derived from the suspended quality mentioned earlier.

The melody line of Variation III is always detained. Like a throbbing, continuing appoggiatura, the syncopated eighths accumulate an always greater burden of weight, the suspensions so formed resolving with little release of tension, because of the ongoing, unbroken melodic line in off-beats. The two brief phrases, mm. 118–22, that interrupt the ongoing syncopation set the droning quality of the remainder of the variation in relief.

Unlike the previous variation, Variation IV exploits lift. Except for six or seven measures, it moves in a two-note slur pattern anticipated by a tied upbeat. It contrasts with the preceding variation; here the player is constantly *releasing* weight, especially when the tied upbeat is marked with a *sforzando*. Beyond this, the writing enlarges upon the chromaticism of the original theme (Ex. 9.18).

Ex. 9.18. Op. 26, I, mm. 142–44, 152–56.

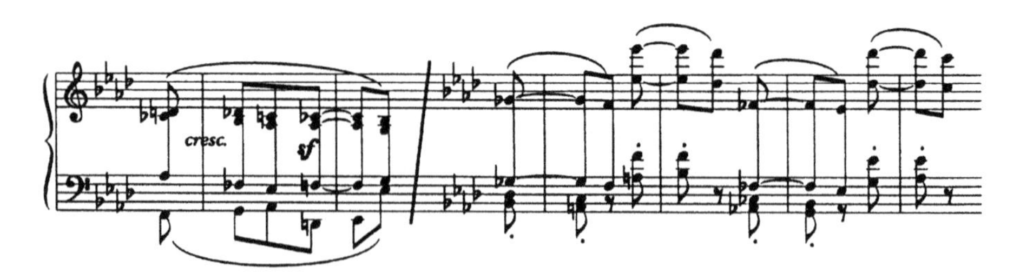

Variation V utilizes appoggiaturas that are eventually transformed into written trills, a transformation of a melodic element into a quality of color. The "new" theme in the coda of Variation V is reminiscent of the original theme: the suspension a♭–g in m. 206 reminds one of the same suspension in m. 2 of the theme, while the stretch of a ninth over the same pitches in m. 209 naturally has the same feel as the chord in m. 4 of the theme. Taken as a whole, the variations are like a discussion with the composer concerning what he found important when playing the theme itself.

In spite of the similarity of this sonata to a suite of widely differing movements, there are resemblances between the first movement and the rest of the sonata, such as the A♭-minor tonality, the register, the intense character, and the prominence of the pitch e♭ in Variation III and the funeral march. The dramatic diminished seventh in mm. 118–22, which is similar in effect to the diminished seventh in mm. 18–19 in the march (Ex. 9.19), tightens the connection. In like manner, the lightness of Variation II and IV corresponds to the character of the finale, as does the long pedal at the end of Variation V (the first pedal marking to be found in the sonatas) to the pedal in the last two measures of the march and the last four measures of the finale.

Ex. 9.19. Op. 26, III, mm. 18–20.

In contrast with the harmonic calm of the first movement, the Scherzo emphasizes keys other than its tonic. As in the middle movement of Op. 27 No. 2, the first phrase is in the key of the dominant. Midway through the A-section, twenty-one consecutive measures are spent establishing the dominant of F minor, which becomes the supertonic of the dominant of A♭, because the reprise of the theme must begin again in E♭ major. In fact, of sixty-seven measures in the A-section, only twenty-three are in A♭ major—by m. 60 (before the codetta) only sixteen measures out of sixty. The effect of the diversionary tonal plan is exaggerated by placing *sforzandos* on nontonic harmony (Ex. 9.20).

The *Marcia funebre*, already an incongruous link in this suite of diverse movements, bears the inscription "on the death of a hero"—an imaginary hero, so far as we are aware. The music is as mechanically solemn as one would expect to accompany the cortège of such a personage. With the B-minor section and the beating of the dotted diminished seventh *ff*, however, character becomes personal, giving the march greater relevance to the occasion. Unlike the trio of the Chopin Funeral March, this trio, which is less than one-fourth the length of the movement, is purely ceremonial. Also unlike the Chopin, Beethoven's march ends in the tonic major, its

Ex. 9.20. Op. 26, II, mm. 1–4, 18–20, 26–29, 44–48, 73–75, 88–89.

pedal marking setting the stage for the finale, as though to play down its incongruity.

One approach to the finale is to realize what it is not. Schumann described the finale of the Chopin B♭-minor Sonata as more mockery than music:

> And yet, if one admits it to oneself, out of this melody-less and joyless movement a strange, horrible spirit complains to us that holds down with an overpowering fist whatever would resist it, so that we listen as though charmed and without grumbling to the end,—however also without praise: for music it is not. So the Sonata ends, as it began, puzzling, like a Sphinx with a mocking smile.[6]

Schumann considered the Chopin finale incongruous also, the whole sonata "four of his maddest children." Next to the Chopin, Beethoven's sequel to the march is anything but melody-less, joyless, or complaining. Yet in a sense it is puzzling, if not like a Sphinx, like a human face—if not with a mocking smile, at least smiling. Chopin's finale has been prepared by the darkness with which the march ends, Beethoven's by an ending in a pedaled haze of major. Czerny writes of this movement:

> It must create interest through evenness of touch, through subtle nuances of rising or falling movement, without stepping out of character through an all too sensitive performance or through brilliant bravura.
>
> The two eighths  in m. 6, in the left hand, are to be marked with a single stress. And thus everywhere that they occur as a cadence or half cadence. For example, in mm. 12, 20, 28, 30, 32, 34, etc. One often finds in Beethoven's works that he bases the structure of his piece on single, seemingly unimportant notes, and insofar as one brings out these notes (as he himself used to do) one gives the whole proper color and unity.[7]

Except for mm. 30 and 32, accenting the eighth notes may have had the purpose of establishing a downbeat, providing a counterweight to the untrammeled manner of the movement based on a running manner, sequential passages of broken 6/5 chords, and reversability of parts. In fact, it is the kaleidoscopic exchange of parts from one hand to the other that makes possible the expansion of the musical idea.

To speak once more of parallels, the first movement and the march begin in the tonic key, establishing that tonality definitively. The finale, with its opening descent of coloristic broken seventh chords, begins harmonically ambiguous although it cadences on the dominant, like the Scherzo. Beginning in m. 12, one hears C^7–F, $B\flat^7$–E♭: V of VI, V of V, and finally V of I—this, like the ten-measure extension of dominant harmony in mm. 32–41 and the expiring of the movement in pedaled A♭ harmony, is color writing as well. Finally, the middle section, in C minor, is remotely similar to the keyboard style of the trio of the march.

Beginning with a complete, unproblematic idea in the form of a variation theme may have determined that the sonata as a whole would not be unified by a dramatic situation, as in Op. 13, Op. 27 No. 2, and Op. 57. At the same time, a variation movement represents a means for departure from a pattern, which may have established the unexpected as the norm.

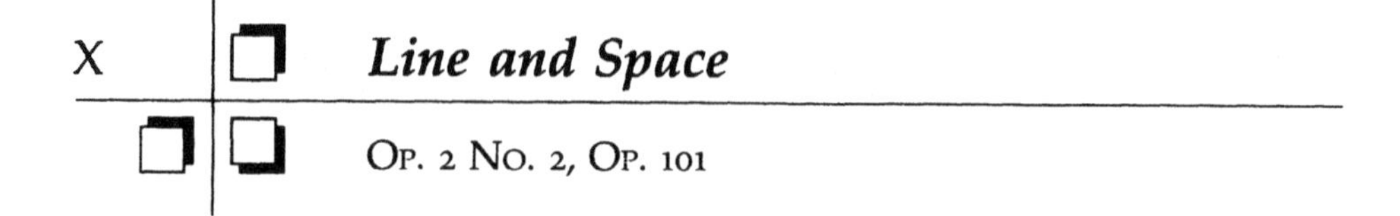

X Line and Space

Op. 2 No. 2, Op. 101

Touch may be the most basic of our senses. Form—repetition, departure, and return—is the means by which the mind recognizes continuity. Continuity, for the pianist's fingers, is the physical feel of musical lines and shapes, perceived as keyboard space and the direction of movement. When we play Op. 2 No. 2 or Op. 101 our hands and our muscles discover the surface, the size, and the contours of the same piece of musical clay that Beethoven shaped with his hands. Thus, the composer speaks to the interpreter not through sound alone but also through the feel of the writing—the arm movement and the physical effort it requires. The grams of weight the finger should feel or the arc the elbow should describe cannot be notated, although the musician/pianist will understand as though reading an unwritten staff between the clefs.

Op. 2 No. 2

The pianist who finds too few notes in Op. 2 No. 1 may occasionally feel that there are too many in Op. 2 No. 2. Both the A-major Sonata and the C-major, Op. 2 No. 3, surpass the F-minor Sonata in technical demands. In its vertical sonority and its clearly defined sections, the treatment of the keyboard in the C-major Sonata sounds orchestral. The A major, by comparison, is linear, suggestive rather than literal, smooth in its flow from section to section, and sophisticated in its invention.

The effectiveness of the first movement of Op. 2 No. 2 lies in Beethoven's ability to adhere to a basic procedure. The first eight measures are unison writing in one direction, downward. In addition, the listener remembers the rhythmic patterns and the resolution on the dominant. With direction of line established as the basic procedure, contrasting ideas begin to emerge in m. 9: a strong resolution on the tonic, part writing, linear direction upward, and rhythmic evenness.

Considering that, except for three instances of the tremolo figure, there are no accompaniment figures in the movement and that the writing is largely unison or imitative, the continuity of the piece consists of the interaction of linear direction. After some sixteen measures, the face of the piece has been sketched, and details such as the *pianissimo* over the sudden zigzag direction in single measures (Ex. 10.1), the opposing lines between the hands (Ex. 10.2), and the extension of the line in eighth notes, *fortissimo,* an octave and a sixth apart (Ex. 10.3) create a personality that is quick-witted and self-assured. The reason for the separate slur and *pianissimo* in mm. 17–18 (Ex. 10.1) may be that the melodic line turns; instead of continuing in one direction, it anticipates the twisting of the E minor second theme.

Ex. 10.1. Op. 2 No. 2, I, mm. 16–19.

Ex. 10.2. Op. 2 No. 2, I, mm. 32–36.

Ex. 10.3. Op. 2 No. 2, I, mm. 39–42.

By isolating "straight" lines as the controlling feature of the writing, Beethoven created a foreground behind which the twisting and turning idea in E minor could be introduced. Although this theme is already easily distinguishable from the broad stripes of the movement as a whole, Beethoven darkens its individuality by:

introducing the theme with a *rallentando*, exposing a half-step neighboring tone figure;
setting the theme in minor;
holding back the tempo by indicating *espressivo;*
underscoring the half step with a *sforzando* over the lower note, then continuing with another half-step descent;
confining the theme within the range of a perfect fourth;
repeating the theme sequentially in G major, B♭ major, and D major over a stepwise ascending bass lasting eighteen measures and covering the interval of a ninth;
quickening the pace by abbreviation (mm. 72–75);
and concluding the section with dramatic posturing on the d♯ diminished seventh chord, the same harmony with which the E minor theme was introduced twenty-one measures earlier.

The E minor theme, searching in tonality and disturbed in character, introduces an opposing element to the unencumbered manner with which the movement began.

The difference between the opening theme and the second theme, the technical difficulty of the writing, and the physical fulfillment itself of playing the music share a common denominator in what the sonata is "about": the meaningful exploiting of keyboard space. The linear and strongly directional writing of the first forty-five measures, unlike the writing of Op. 2 No. 1, consumes keyboard space, as do the broken octaves that Beethoven fingered to be played with the right hand alone (Ex. 10.4). There was nothing to prevent him from assigning the first note of each triplet to the left hand, or even leaving the passage unfingered, yet he deliberately chose an uncomfortable and risky fingering. The slightly narrower octave span on pianos of the time would have been offset by their lighter touch, making accuracy even more unlikely. Since playing the broken octaves with one hand involves stretching, Beethoven chose a fingering to ensure the sensation of space, as does crossing the left hand over the right, over a distance of four and one-half octaves (Ex. 10.5). In the development, imitative entrances at an interval exceeding the span of the average hand likewise produce the sensation of space (Ex. 10.6).

Ex. 10.4. Op. 2 No. 2, I, mm. 84–85, 88.

Ex. 10.5. Op. 2 No. 2, I, mm. 130–37.

Ex. 10.6. Op. 2 No. 2, I, mm. 181–83.

Keyboard space is exploited also by opposite means—instead of consuming, restricting it with melodic lines that are compressed in range. The second theme is just such a melody line, introduced, as noted earlier, by a neighboring-tone figure. The thirty-seconds in the opening theme are crowded into the space of a perfect fifth and rhythmically into the brief duration of an eighth note.

If, in the first movement, Beethoven exploited the polarity of sweeping lines and confined, twisting melodic units, in which lines prevail, the conspicuous presence of the neighboring tone in each melodic unit in the *Largo appassionato* (the changing tone in Ex. 10.7c is an ornamented neighboring tone) makes this movement the emotional opposite of the first movement. As *the* building block of the Largo, a concentration of musical devices invests the neighboring-tone figure with self-conscious solemnity: the slow, measured pace, the widely spaced part writing, the tautness of the repetition of the f♯ in the melody line, and the *tenuto sempre* of the top line set against the *staccato sempre* of the bass line. In this movement the neighboring-tone figure becomes associated with part writing, some of it imitative and much of it utilizing variation, another musical feature setting the Largo apart from the first movement (Ex. 10.7). The linear idea, when it does emerge, provides one of the most earnest and weighty episodes in the movement, its effect so unlike the dash and brilliance of the first movement. Here it lumbers upward, the embodiment of enormous effort, as if to rise above the shock of the entrance of the theme, *subito ff*, in D minor (Ex. 10.8).

Ex. 10.7. Op. 2 No. 2, II, a. mm. 1–2; b. mm. 8–10; c. mm. 19–20; d. mm. 50–51; e. m. 68.

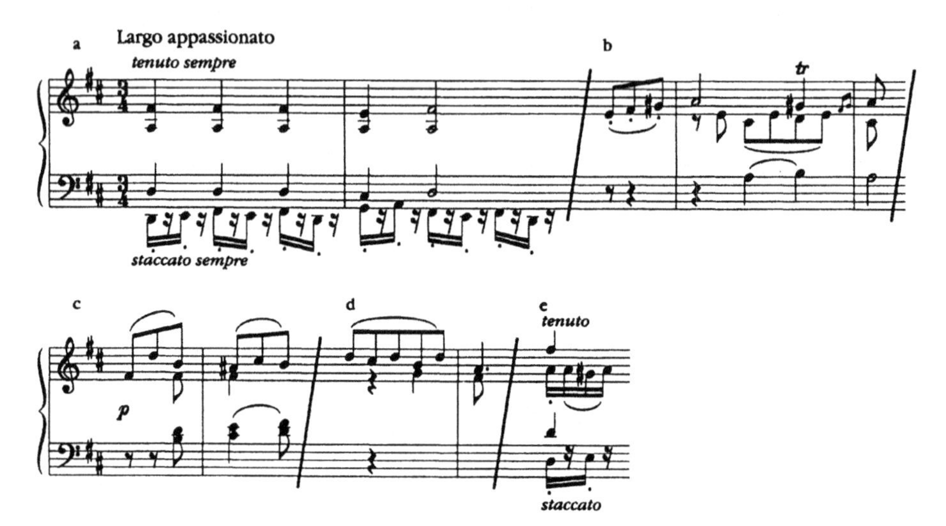

Ex. 10.8. Op. 2 No. 2, II, mm. 60–64.

Not every phrase containing a neighboring tone is equally intense; the character of the alternating sections in A major, B minor, and D major brings release (and therefore a feeling of moving away) from the measured self-awareness of the theme. The distinction between touches throughout the movement and the stepwise descent into the final reprise make the movement particularly gratifying to play. The sensuous, as Thomas Mann wrote, is the way of the artist to the spirit.

Neither the sustained thrust of the first movement nor the *appassionato* of the second characterizes either the scherzo or the finale. Material does return in the scherzo that, if not always in the form of a neighboring tone, moves within a small space (Ex. 10.9). In the Minore, the melodic turns in direction in the two-measure segments are marked with *sforzandos.*

Ex. 10.9. Op. 2 No. 2, III, mm. 16–19, 21–23.

The opening of the Rondo treats line and space in a flamboyant manner with an arpeggio rising three and one-half octaves and a two-note slur falling an octave and a sixth. At the first reprise (m. 41), the arpeggio spans an additional octave, and following the A-minor section it is transformed into four and one-half octaves of A-major scale, a sweeping treatment of the keyboard and a compressing of notes reminiscent of the first movement. With the narrower range and stepwise movement of the second half of the theme, the melodic line presents a balance between consuming and conserving space.

The arpeggio ascent that links the movement to the exploiting of line in the first movement is here not so much a brilliant, bold act as an extravagant sweep, as though reaching the e♮ above the staff had been a miscalculation needing correction. The *sforzando* over the e^2 in m. 4 does not recur in any reprise; instead, the emphasis is achieved by ornamentation and increased rhythmic activity (Ex. 10.10).

Ex. 10.10. Op. 2 No. 2, IV, mm. 43–44, 102–103, 137–38, 175.

The second half of the theme includes also a descending tetrachord, e^2–b^1, which

Beethoven uses as the framework for the imitative section, mm. 8–12, and for the second theme (Ex. 10.11). The Alberti accompaniment to this theme, which extends beyond the octave, is consistent with the feel of spatial expansion in the keyboard treatment of much of the movement (Ex. 10.12). Finally, the sixteenths in the transition, beginning in m. 16, are an incomplete composing-out of the second half of the main theme (Ex. 10.13).

Ex. 10.11. Op. 2 No. 2, IV, mm. 26–28, 32–37.

Ex. 10.12. Op. 2 No. 2, IV, mm. 27–28.

Ex. 10.13. Op. 2 No. 2, IV, mm. 16–21.

The memorable landmark in this *grazioso* movement is the stormy A-minor episode with its staccato, *fortissimo* triplet eighth notes—and the brief passage of legato, *pianissimo* triplet eighths. In this section, one measure (Ex. 10.14) is equivalent, by stretching the imagination, to an expanded neighboring tone, the significance of which Beethoven does not permit us to forget, since each such figure, except for the statements in *pianissimo*, is marked with a *sforzando* on the topmost note.

Ex. 10.14. Op. 2 No. 2, IV, m. 57.

One does not find in every sonata of Beethoven a chain of events leading to a peak of intensity in the final movement. Tension and its resolution in this sonata waxes and wanes, based on the polarity between opposing impulses: long, one-directional lines versus compressed turning patterns. It is noteworthy that the motive containing the neighboring tone first appears in minor in the opening movement and that it achieves an imposing stature in the *appassionato* seriousness of the second movement. Thereafter, the figure occurs in phrases in minor in the Scherzo and, most emphatically, in the eruptive A-minor section in the Rondo. If play with bold, directional lines is equivalent to an uninhibited, aggressive manner, the turning motive, as it continues throughout the sonata, symbolizes a trait of seriousness, providing a core of substance within the piece as a whole.

Op. 101

Did the character of the work determine—or was it molded after—the person to whom it was dedicated? Count Ferdinand von Waldstein, for example, was described by those who knew him as "extremely educated, witty, and a proficient linguist."[1] Archduke Rudolph was honored with the dedication of several of Beethoven's most imposing works—the Fourth and Fifth Concertos, the Sonata Op. 106, the "Archduke" Trio, and the *Missa solemnis*.

Op. 101, finished in November 1816 and published the following year, is dedicated to Dorothea von Ertmann, a student of Beethoven's who was described by Schindler as "one of the foremost pianists in the musical world of Vienna of that day."[2] Judging from what Schindler, Mendelssohn, and Reichardt wrote, her playing could be both sensitive and powerful, insightful, and instinctively "right." In a letter that may have accompanied a copy of the sonata, Beethoven wrote, "Please accept now what was often intended for you and what may be to you a proof of my devotion both to your artistic aspirations and to your person—."[3] Schindler goes on to say that Dorothea refused "to play any piece of music that did not suit her individual style," believing that "not everything is appropriate for everyone." A phrase from Czerny's commentary on Op. 101 might have been applied to the Baroness' playing as well: "this composition that dispenses with all external embellishment . . . ."[4]

The "Eusebius" qualities of the sonata may be obscured by the pianistic and intellectual brilliance of the writing. Nevertheless, it is significant that Beethoven revealed an extramusical association for only the quiet movements, characterizing them as "Impressions and Reveries."[5] Moreover, Op. 101 is a less straightforward piece than the other *Hammerklavier* Sonata, Op. 106.

As is so often the case, the first line reveals the musical character of what is to follow. Listing these points in the order of appearance, there is

an absence of harmonic "directness";
contrary motion between voice parts;
dynamic rising and falling;
a continuous melodic line;
a voice part sustained by syncopated notes tied to strong beats;
a *poco ritard* leading to a fermata.

Harmonic and melodic elements that are ambiguous or unresolved also offer clues to the character of the movement as a whole and its performance:

The expansion and contraction of the line begins and ends with a simple E-major triad that sounds convincing as a tonic, although it is dominant harmony.
The lowered seventh is treated as a passing tone and not as a note requiring resolution.
Although the fleeting cadence in m. 4 is a half cadence in A major, the fact that the chord of resolution is again E major with the fifth in the soprano, as in m. 2, reinforces the ambiguity.
Beginning in m. 7, the tonality *is* E major and remains so throughout the relatively brief exposition of thirty-three measures.
Finally, not until m. 25 is there a perfect authentic cadence.

Silence virtually never interrupts the swells in the writing, the long Wagner-like lines rising and falling and pulling in opposite directions. Marx describes the effect: "nur Verlangen, nicht Vollbringen . . . nur Aufschwung der Phantasie, nicht greifbare Ziele" (only longing, not consummation . . . only soaring of fantasy, not tangible goals).[6]

In addition to the ambiguity of the harmony, the widely separated points of resolution, and the contrary motion between voice lines, there are tangible qualities: tied-over weak beats feeling like syncopations, complicated phrasing with an added *sforzando* on the third eighth [musical notation], other *sforzandos* on weak beats, fermatas, and the indications of *espressivo* and *molto espressivo*—all physical sensations of musical longing. They are notated in Ex. 10.15 with arrows indicating rhythmic holding back produced by stress of various sorts.

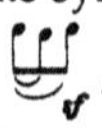

Reading Mendelssohn's description of Dorothea's playing when he visited her in 1831, one can imagine the effect of the first movement of Op. 101 under her fingers.

> She plays the Beethoven things beautifully, although she has not studied for a long time, often exaggerates the expression a little and holds back a great deal and then hurries again; however, she plays single pieces gloriously, and I believe I have learned something from her.[7]

In light of the fluency of his own music, what seemed like exaggerated pacing to Mendelssohn may not have seemed the same to the Schindlers of his generation. Reading his *Beethoven as I Knew Him* leads one to suspect that Schindler was an

Ex. 10.15. Op. 101, I, mm. 14–15, 18–21, 40–42, 49–50, 84–88.

embittered survivor of an earlier era, playing up his contact with Beethoven to conceal his inability to compete with the playing musicians of his day. Nonetheless, there must have been a grain of truth in his complaint that Mendelssohn "saw all music from a virtuoso's point of view," chasing an orchestra "in double quickstep" through a piece.

> Mendelssohn . . . carried his authority as a true aristocrat of music from country to country, from one music festival to another, until it was inevitable that he should be regarded everywhere as the highest model for the performance of every type of music, especially as his productions were supported by eminent qualities of another sort.[8]

In a movement like Op. 101, I, the holding back and moving ahead is already written in the score. The marking *espressivo e semplice* in mm. 25–26 probably applies through the beginning of m. 33 because of the tied third and sixth beats, which encourage holding back. In mm. 48 and 49 the *sforzandos* on the third and sixth beats hold back the tempo, while the two measures that follow seems to move ahead, even if the original tempo is only being resumed. The *molto espressivo* in mm. 52–57 follows an unusually strained passage that ends *subito piano* under a fermata. Holding back (*molto*) here sounds interpretively natural because, in so doing, the return to the reverie of the reprise becomes a gradual psychological recovery.

The Schenker-type schematic in Ex. 10.16 depicts the development section as the most active, suggesting that the E-major chord retains its predominance into the recapitulation, where it finally resolves to A major. This, it is submitted, accounts for the absence of a strong tonic at the beginning of the movement. The relationship between b and g♯ has interpretive implications. The b in m. 12 is a "sense-point," which is reiterated in m. 13. The release felt on returning to the b¹ in m. 15 is a result of the repetition of that pitch in mm. 12 and 13 and the *crescendo* and effortful articulation in m. 14. Like the blocking of stage movements, the pitch b has become an important area of the stage.

Ex. 10.16. Op. 101, I.

The b¹ in m. 15 settles on g♯¹; melodically, it does not just "go" there—a subtle difference that calls for just as subtle relaxing of the tempo. Thereafter, the seesaw movement between g♯ and b continues until m. 24, where the g♯³ is marked with a *sforzando*, although b seems to regain its preeminence on reaching the end of the exposition. Marx says of the first movement, "In no previous composition is the observation of moderation and the most delicate wave-line of rising and falling so necessary and the avoidance of all hasty nuancing and rough contrasts so much the rule as here."[9] The sonata is psychologically complex music: the *nur Verlangen* of the first movement consummated in the *Vollbringen* of the finale.

The march (according to Beethoven, "march-like") is not a piece to accompany the stamping of feet and swinging of arms but, as Marx describes it,

> A strange hybrid . . . this heroic expedition that ventures only into fantasy. Here is nothing to be found of pomp or defiance or of material power and its dimensions inherent in every march, even the funeral march of the Sonata, Op. 26. Not an outward act that is depicted here but rather a fantasy of deeds that could have happened, dreamed heroic traits that, however, high-minded and audacious, reach up to the stars.[10]

In what specific ways is this not a normal march but a heroic expedition into fantasy? One, it is in F major, not an unusual key for a march, but a colorful tonality within the context of A major; it begins as a third relationship to A major, a distant tonal land. It is also contrapuntal, too complex for an ordinary march, just as Haydn's more contrapuntal minuets are no longer courtly dances. Its character is anything but bombastic: twenty-five of the fifty-four measures predominantly *piano* (three of them *pianissimo*), eighteen measures of *crescendo* (ending *forte-piano*, a su-

bito piano, a *forte,* a *diminuendo,* and a *fortissimo*), and no more than eleven measures of *forte* or *fortissimo.* Other peculiarities are the articulation (a scooping gesture stressing the sixteenth upbeat that is unusual for the incisive beat of a march), the four measures of long pedal in the middle of the second half, and the introduction of triplets against the sixteenths. In the second half of the march, *dolce* appears twice.

The trio is more severely contrapuntal—a canon in two voices hardly seems suited to the character of a march. After a time, one becomes accustomed to its strangeness in the way the two voices cling to one another in a strained *dolce.* Can we ever know why Beethoven wrote a canon at this point in the sonata, or whether it has anything to do with the musical plot of the sonata, or, for that matter, what is the musical plot of the sonata?

The first movement and the march proper are marked by an extravagance of the imagination for lines that expand and come together again. Although the second section of the march begins with parallel motion, contrary motion is resumed in mm. 14, 24, and 33 and thereafter virtually to the end of the march (Ex. 10.17). Compared with the march, the canonic writing sounds bare, matter-of-fact, and severely disciplined, and produces lines that generally move in the same direction. Each of the passages of imitative writing between voices moving in parallel direction in the march (those in Ex. 10.18, for example), is marked *piano,* as, in general, are other passages in which the lines move in the same direction (mm. 4–11 and 52–53). Thus, direction of line becomes an issue and the march and trio seemingly the field on which the dominance of contrary versus parallel motion is first contested.

Ex. 10.17. Op. 101, II, mm. 14–16, 24–26, 33–34.

Ex. 10.18. Op. 101, II, mm. 12–14, 19–21, 30–33.

The most telling feature of the Adagio is the *una corda* marking, giving the impression that this is the innermost of the inner, beyond even the *innigsten Empfindung* of the first movement. The marking *sehnsuchtsvoll* is found nowhere else in the Sonatas. How does one play *sehnsuchtsvoll*? The tempo must allow time to hear the melodic pull within as though the triplet needed to be coaxed into moving. Melodic pull may have been Beethoven's reason for not extending the second brace throughout the six notes, the two sixteenths visually receiving greater stress. In keeping with the *sehnsuchtsvoll* marking, it is advisable to think constantly about relationships with earlier events in the sonata: the through-composed melodic line and the expansion and contraction of the lines in mm. 5–8, like the continuous melodic line of the first movement and its lines moving similarly in contrary motion; the two-voice imitation reminiscent of mm. 19–24 (and its parallel passage) in the first movement; and the descending diminished seventh chords in mm. 14–16, resembling the progression in mm. 85–86 of the first movement.

The two-voice imitation that maintains motion in mm. 9–13 of the Adagio is linked in one's memory to the canon and to similar imitative writing and two-voice writing in parallel direction in the march. The reappearance of phrases from the opening of the first movement, positioned immediately preceding the triumphant bursting forth of the finale, reinforces the association of line with *Verlangen-Vollbringen*, to use Marx's phrase. Dramatically, hearing the opening phrase of the sonata again, halting and uncertain, is like one final look back before the determination (*mit Entschlossenheit*) and the symbolic victory of parallel lines in the theme of the finale.

The finale also has roots in what has preceded it. The imitation between the hands in the principal theme is canonic procedure, if not strictly canonic; and, without even taking the fugal development section into account, the movement follows the contrapuntal nature of previous movements. The fugue itself, besides being the most intense form of development, represents the consummation of all the previous imitative writing just by virtue of being a fugue. There are other minor similarities with preceding movements. Eight measures into the finale, the tempo is already interrupted by fermatas, as in mm. 5 and 6 of the first movement. The second theme (Ex. 10.19) reaches upward—a longing gesture like previous melodic material (Ex. 10.20), as well as the figure already quoted from the Adagio. Like the march, the exposition of the finale contains a fleeting blur of held pedal in mm. 87–88, and, like the march also, a short *dolce* phrase (mm. 81–87) appears unexpectedly in the midst of a frenzy of activity.

Ex. 10.19. Op. 101, IV, mm. 66–76.

Ex. 10.20. Op. 101, I, mm. 44–48; II, mm. 1–4, 68–70.

As in the principal theme of the finale, the basic direction of the fugue subject descends, within which the sixteenth-note groups rise—as do the sixteenths in the second theme and in the closing theme. Detached eighths, for the most part, descend throughout the development; the sixteenth groups in the countersubject descend. In order not to lose the argument in a maze of detail, the examples given below are chosen to illustrate the use of direction for dramatic effect. The contrary motion between the sixteenths continues up to the rising sequence beginning in measure 162—a point easily remembered, since the writing feels more chordal to the fingers and moves consistently in the direction of the treble (Ex. 10.21). In mm. 189–93, the tied quarters in the top part, if replayed, suggest the detached eighths in the second half of the subject in augmentation (Ex. 10.22).

Ex. 10.21. Op. 101, IV, mm. 182–84.

Ex. 10.22. Op. 101, IV, mm. 189–93.

Beginning in m. 194, rising parallel thirds and descending sixths form extended lines unlike the preceding brief one-beat segments of contrary motion. Measures 201–204 are a veritable battle of directions (Ex. 10.23). Immediately thereafter, lines four measures long cross, covering a range of almost four and one-half octaves (Ex. 10.24).

Ex. 10.23. Op. 101, IV, mm. 201–202.

Ex. 10.24. Op. 101, IV, mm. 204–208.

The dramatic force of the close of the fugue is *the* climax of the sonata: five measures of detached parallel sixths and thirds, descending, marked *crescendo;* four measures of contrary motion in thirds and sixths, marked with *sforzandos* on each off beat; the subject in augmentation, the right hand voices descending in contrary motion; and the final sweep upward, *fortissimo,* in broken E-major triads, extending six octaves. Direction is likewise important in the final three measures of the movement, in which A-major chords suddenly break out of the *pianissimo* and *ritardando.* Throughout the recapitulation, except for the *poco espressivo* ("a little held back," not "a little expressive"), sixteenth-note passages generally move in parallel motion and ascend. The second theme, beginning in m. 252, immediately reaches higher than the parallel passage in the exposition, and the rising melodic sequence that follows is extended by two measures.

Mendelssohn's Sonata Op. 6 shows evidence of having been modeled after Op. 101. Like Op. 101, the first movement is in 6/8 and the key of the sonata (and of course of the opening theme) is E major. If one may presume to read the composer's mind, Mendelssohn also heard the opening theme of Op. 101 as tonally ambiguous. Not only does the arch design of the melodic line resemble that of Op. 101, but Mendelssohn's theme also begins on g♯ and ends on b and includes a syncopated inner voice. Other general similarities include a second movement in ABA form, albeit *Tempo di Menuetto* and not *Marschmässig,* an improvisatory Adagio that begins with the same harmony (and inversion) and the same pitches in bass and soprano (the ensuing melodic line following closely that of the Adagio of Op. 101), the return of thematic material from the first two movements, and the joining of this movement to the finale. Mendelssohn carries the cyclic element further by reintroducing themes from the first movement, including the opening theme, at the close of the finale.

Like Schumann's Eusebius and Florestan, the *zwei Seelen in einer Brust* of Op. 101 give the sonata a depth of character and a profundity that goes beyond a technical/cerebral *tour de force.* The two souls might be conceived as opposing lines (Eusebius) and parallel lines (Florestan). The canonic trio of the march and passages of the Adagio point ahead to the generally one-directional lines in the finale. As though this were too simple a solution, the development section introduces a fugue to carry the conflict between opposing and parallel lines to a soaring, brilliant conclusion.

XI Movement as Energized Color

Op. 53

Once the technique to articulate non legato sixteenths has been developed, the keyboard patterns of the "Waldstein" lie well under the hands. Although the writing may lend itself to common virtuoso display, the extended *piano* and *pianissimo* writing (the first movement contains roughly twice as many indications of *pp* or *p* as *f* or *ff*) suggests a virtuosity through which notes shimmer instead of blind.

Ironically, the raw material out of which this quality of sound was created was something quite earthbound: exercises in the form of sequential scale passages in tenths, in contrary motion, and in canon. The sketchbook containing these exercises (and, a few pages later, sketches for Op. 53) was used by Beethoven primarily in the year 1803; it also contains sketches for the Third Symphony, *Leonore*, the Fifth Symphony, and the Triple Concerto, as well as the opening measures of the Fourth Piano Concerto.

Ex. 11.1. Beethoven sketches transcribed by Nottebohm.

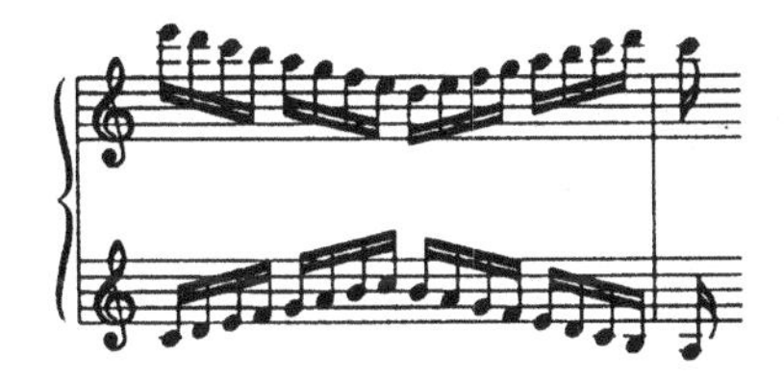

As Nottebohm writes,

> The keyboard exercises . . . have a similar appearance. Certainly Beethoven did not just write them out, but instead he also played them along with others that were not written. One may assume that this cultivation of piano playing and a manner of practicing was not without influence on the brilliance and the running nature of the piano composition that was taken up soon after the notation of the exercises.[1]

He then quotes Beethoven's first sketch for the "Waldstein," material that will form the climax of the development, the descent into the reprise. As Nottebohm remarks, "The predominant character is thereby established."

Ex. 11.2. Op. 53, I, sketch, from Nottebohm.

Why would Beethoven have been attracted to Hanon-like exercise material?

What musical qualities would he have heard in these scale exercises and the perpetual canon that could be lifted to the level of a major work? As the grieving woman in Amy Lowell's Poem "Patterns" protests as she walks the "patterned garden paths" in her "stiff brocaided gown," thinking about her lover's death,

> . . . For my passion
> Wars against the stiff brocade.

Like gymnasts and trapeze performers, keyboardists—when hands and fingers are busy with quick leaps and hand-crossings and fast octaves and passages—have always been engaging to watch, especially if they act out the score with stage-stamping or grimacing. One might imagine the many eyes, now closed, that were riveted for the moment on the display shown in Ex. 11.3. The rhythm and the pattern of sixths last throughout all but two of the succeeding eleven measures. Both the Cramer piece and the "Waldstein" are lengthy works in which technical patterns prevail. Unlike a short character piece using such patterns, such as a Chopin etude or prelude, a sonata-allegro depends on, if not conflict, departure and return within the musical plot. How did Beethoven avoid writing an extended exercise when he was creating the Op. 53 from exercise material?

Ex. 11.3. Cramer, Op. 6 No. 3, I, excerpts.

As Nottebohm remarks, Beethoven's first sketches are often commonplace, but they contain some detail that the composer's mind seized as a new starting point. For example, the sketch for *Andante favori* WoO 57, originally intended as the slow movement for this sonata, illustrates the sort of kernel to which Nottebohm was referring (Ex. 11.4).

Ex. 11.4. WoO 57, SKETCH, FROM NOTTEBOHM.

The exercises and first sketches for the first movement of the sonata indicate that it would be a "motion" piece. What kept it from turning into a frenzied running in circles was a "kernel" of sameness that was made to sound motion*less*

through simplification. Eighths were substituted for the sixteenths in the initial sketch, and, by beginning after the downbeat, the repeated thirds were made to sound as though they had been snatched up in a rhythmic movement already begun—as though the piece had already been playing through all eternity. The player hears this ongoing, seemingly never-ending rhythm and simply gets in step. Beginning with a single note on the downbeat, one may feel like a runner in a relay race, grasping the wand from Beethoven. The surest way to banish the spirit of the music is to resolve to play it comfortably.

Beethoven succeeded, where Cramer (in Ex. 11.3) did not, because he possessed an imagination for musical imagery, or color. Notes were not just notes but sounds; and sounds were the playthings of fantasy; and fantasy is the ability to associate anything with anything else. The repeated thirds are rhythmic repetition, but beyond that they are energy; the repeated thirds are C major, but beyond that they are a color effect. Melodically and harmonically nothing moves until the end of the second measure. Hearing the passage repeated one step lower, in B♭, affirms the intent of a color effect. When the theme returns as a measured tremolo, the rhythmic propulsion within the sameness of extended pitches confirms the lesser importance of the melodic line.

Writing such as this is not a square-cut roll of fabric to be made into a suit but more a remnant, like a remnant of a historical gown or a military uniform from which the imagination reconstructs the experience of living and thinking and feeling it once clothed. Such an imaginary reconstruction provides the living link of the present to the past. Here, the working of fantasy associating movement and color transforms a landmark of the repertoire into an enigma whose components can never be separated. Movement and color are so intertwined that it is impossible to decide whether harmonic color arrests movement, or rhythmic movement isolates harmonic color. The devices by which various degrees of movement and intensities of color are projected include metrical relationships, dynamics, the pace of harmonic change, and the use of the pedal.

Metrical Relationships. Throughout the sonata, levels of activity are established by varying the subdivision of the beat. A triplet figure adorns the second theme: it is later replaced by sixteenths, and these by a trill (Ex. 11.5). The five-note tag in m. 4, to which our ears are alerted by the grace note, returns as the opening five-note phrase of the E-major theme. The rhythmic relationship is augmentation of four to one (Ex. 11.6). The thematic derivation is amply confirmed:

1. In addition to the grace note, a detail not present in the sketch, the five-note tag is separated from the opening theme by rests and the higher range at which it is placed; besides the regularity of its five-note segments, the E-major theme achieves individuality as the only lyrical idea of any length or completeness in the movement.

2. The five-note tag is preceded by a stepwise melodic ascent through a third, the same melodic structure that introduces the E-major theme in mm.

31–34. (Czerny writes, "The transition to E major *staccato* and held back [*ritardiert*].")

3. The tag consists of five descending pitches. Originally, the slur groups did not match in length (Ex. 11.7); in its present form, of course, the five-note pattern is maintained except for mm. 41–42.

4. The slur over the tag creates a feeling of lift; the descending slurred grouping in the second theme has the same effect of exhaling and release. Czerny writes, "peacefully *legato*, hymnlike, but not dragging."[2] The relationship between the "tag" and the E-major theme implies that the slur groups should be clearly articulated.

Ex. 11.5. Op. 53, I, mm. 50–51, 58–59, 71–74.

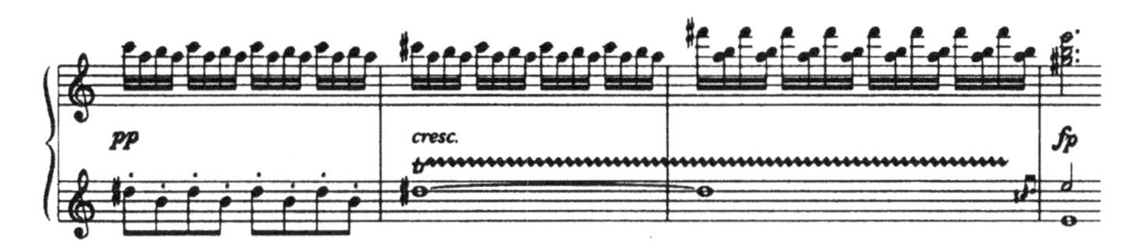

Ex. 11.6. Op. 53, I, mm. 4, 35–36.

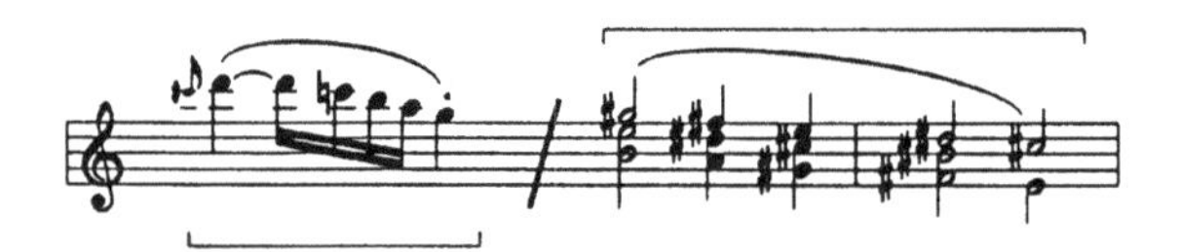

Ex. 11.7. Op. 53, I, sketch, from Nottebohm.

The passage beginning in m. 74 (which is related to similar material beginning in m. 23) outlines a triad; the continuation, although in longer note values, spells out triads more rapidly (Ex. 11.8). The ascent of a third, e–f♯–g, in the opening theme reappears in augmented form in episodic material (Ex. 11.9).

Ex. 11.8. Op. 53, I, mm. 23–24, 74–75, 76–78.

Ex. 11.9. Op. 53, I, mm. 2–3, 31–32, 50–51.

In the Rondo, the alternating sections are principally in a subdivision of triplet sixteenths, while the basic subdivision is duple sixteenths. Czerny's concept of the movement instinctively took this into account: "As peaceful as the beginning must be, the liveliness must be increased with the entrance of the *ff* and the triplet passage that follows; the previous calm returns with the re-entry of the theme."[3] Of the two statements of the theme in the Prestissimo, the first approaches double diminution, the second remains in approximately the same tempo as that of the theme at the opening of the movement (Ex. 11.10).

Ex. 11.10. Op. 53, III, mm. 403–404, 485–88.

Dynamics. Sudden dynamic shifts and strong accents are an effortful and sometimes awkward muscular experience, braking the forward flight of the tempo. Any *crescendo* to a *subito piano* requires a muscular adjustment; Ex. 11.11 is one of many.

An *sf* cannot sound like an accident but must feel deliberate (Ex. 11.12) and may hold back the tempo (Ex. 11.13).

Ex. 11.11. Op. 53, I, mm. 22–23.

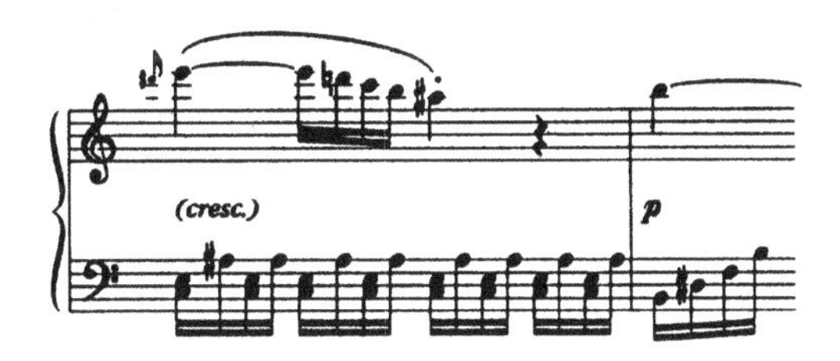

Ex. 11.12. Op. 53, I, m. 11–12.

Ex. 11.13. Op. 53, I, mm. 255–56; II, mm. 9–11; III, mm. 360–62.

In mm. 272–74 of the first movement, a passage that presses ahead, Czerny recommends a fingering that prevents a slick performance, making the ascent instead one of noticeable exertion (Ex. 11.14). The *sforzandos* in mm. 99, 103, and 107 of the Rondo, as well as those in the passage beginning in m. 221, help restore the opening calm, as Czerny suggested. Similarly, the *sf* in the second phrase of the second theme of the first movement invites one to dwell on the g♯ and the closing of the phrase (Ex. 11.15). In the return to C major and the preparation for the entrance of the Rondo, the *sf* in the left hand is placed over a♭, emphasizing the delay in resolving on the dominant (Ex. 11.16).

Ex. 11.14. Op. 53, I, from Czerny.

Ex. 11.15. Op. 53, I, mm. 37–38.

Ex. 11.16. Op. 53, II, mm. 23–24.

Pace of Harmonic Movement. The relationship between outward activity and harmonic content has already been mentioned. For all the many notes, the music remains suspended harmonically for relatively long periods of time. The theme of the first movement fills almost two measures with repetition of the same chord, an indication of things to come. The episode leading into the second theme (mm. 23–29) is suspended over a pedal tone for six measures plus one note, after which the harmony does not change for an additional six measures. Beginning in m. 66, an E-major six-four is retained for four measures, followed by four measures of dominant harmony.

It is unnecessary to point out each such instance, although mention should be made of the harmonic acceleration in the development, beginning in m. 112: 4 (measures) + 4 + 4 + 2 + 2 + 2 + 2 + 2 + 1 + 1—at which point the dominant of C minor is reached. To appreciate the enormous force of the return, the relatively uneventful extension of the dominant seventh in the sketch should be compared with the finished score, in which Beethoven prolonged the pitch f^3 for three measures, then plunged two octaves within one measure to effect the resolution. In mm. 70–78 of the Rondo, the *sf* over the e♮'s keeps that pitch in one's mind for eight measures and, thereafter, the pitch a for another eight measures. The actual progression e–a in mm. 86–88, marked with *ff* and *sf*, occurs within two measures.

Use of the Pedal. Beethoven's pedal indications in the Rondo have been explained as the result of the lesser sonority of his piano, the presence of a split damper pedal, and the composer's deafness. Czerny comments, however, that the Rondo "ist ganz auf den Gebrauch des Pedals berechnet, welches hier wesentlich erscheinet."[4] *Berechnet* may be translated as "calculated on," "intended," or "premeditated"; *wesentlich* as "essential," "fundamental," or "intrinsic"; and *erscheinet* as "to be evident." Thus, "the effect of the Rondo is entirely calculated upon the use of the pedal, which, it is evident, is intrinsic here to the music."

Nottebohm points out that Beethoven's first sketch for the Rondo was discarded, except for the first note and the implied pedal associated with it (Ex. 11.17). With the next sketch, Beethoven begins, as in the first movement, in the middle of the movement. Nottebohm writes, "One will also notice that the use of the pedal is intrinsic [again, *wesentlich*] to the passage."

The sketches for the Rondo theme (Ex. 11.18) also have a bearing on the use of pedal. The final version is appreciably lighter, principally because of changes in the first two measures. As opposed to going to e or c, an upbeat–downbeat on the same note, g, suspends the direction of the line. Furthermore, replacing the syncopation of 𝄾♩♪ with 𝄽 ♩ | ♩. removes all heaviness from the beginning of the theme. Through Beethoven's pedal the whole achieves a floating effect, particularly since one must play as lightly as possible. (Czerny adds the *Verschiebung* throughout the duration of the *pianissimo.*) Most important, the blurring of tonic and dominant stacks the melody notes and harmonies on top of each other, so that the music stands still. In fact, the great advantage of the short, improvisatory Introduzione over the F-major Andante is that the piece thereby moves from a state of tranquillity to one of immobility.

Ex. 11.17. Op. 53, III, sketch, from Nottebohm[5]

Ex. 11.18. Op. 53, III, sketch, from Nottebohm.[6]

Alternate possibilities are either unconvincing or refutable. Along with the lesser sonority, the tone of the typical piano of the time was also much clearer than that of the modern piano, on which the aesthetic ideal is a homogenizing of sound. On instruments such as ours, therefore, the realization of Beethoven's pedals should present, if anything, a lesser problem, for what has been gained in sonority is offset by what has been lost in pungency of sound.

With respect to the split damper pedal, Beethoven made a note in the margin of the first page of the autograph to the effect that, where he had indicated the pedal, the dampers were to be raised in the bass as well as the treble—a clear warning to avoid the use of the split pedal, if available. Finally, in mm. 101, 105, and 113 of the Rondo, where he had indicated a pedal release beneath a quarter-rest in the autograph, Beethoven replaced the quarter rest with eighth rests (in m. 113 using a red crayon) and indicated that the pedal was to be released precisely with the final eighth rest. Such scrupulous attention to detail is hardly the mark of a person unable to hear what he wanted, whether with the actual ear or the mind's ear.

The blurred pedals of the Rondo furnish the clearest examples of the dimension of color. Mention has been made of the duration of harmonies, that such passages encourage the hearing of harmonies as sounds and sound qualities *per se*. The placing of the second theme of the first movement in E major and, later, in A major—each a third relationship to C, as well as the original plan to write a slow movement in E major (Ex. 11.4), is further indication of the importance of color for this work in Beethoven's mind. A deceptive cadence has the same color effect in the passages in Ex. 11.19.

Ex. 11.19. Op. 53, I, mm. 248–49; III, mm. 440–41.

Alternating between major and minor, as in the passage beginning in m. 235 in the first movement (F minor–F major–[C major]–F major–F minor) and in the theme of the Rondo, mm. 13–19 (C minor–C major), is coloristic, as are the glissandos and extended trills. Staccato marks used to delineate a line and the blurring of a C-major scale, *fortissimo,* to produce sonority are also color devices (Ex. 11.20). Staccato marks in Ex. 11.21 do not so much delineate a line as orchestrate the emergence of the overwhelming color of dominant harmony.

Ex. 11.20. Op. 53, III, mm. 51–57.

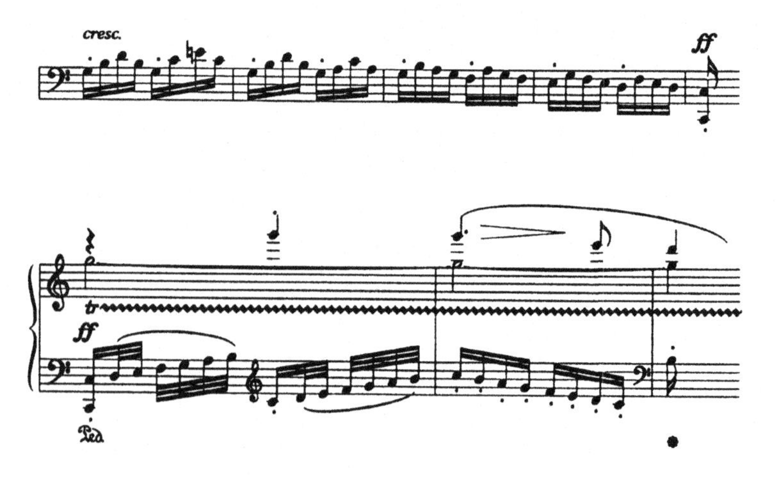

Ex. 11.21. Op. 53, I, mm. 146–55.

In passing, a warning not to play the glissandos as wrist octaves is supported not only by the slur, but also by a remark of Czerny, in which he uses the verb *schleifen*, meaning "to slide," or "draw," or "pull along." For smaller hands, he suggests omitting the lower note of the octaves in the right and the upper in the left, so that each glissando becomes a fingered single-line scale. "In a very fast tempo, the passage played this way does not sound at all empty."[7] For the pianist who does not want to leave out notes but who cannot reach octave glissandos, the fingering given in Ex. 11.22 offers another option.

Ex. 11.22. Op. 53, III, mm. 465–69.

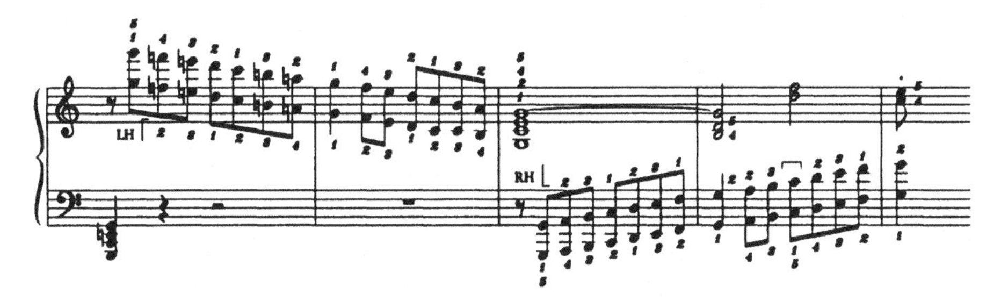

Ex. 11.23, containing examples from Debussy's *Dr. Gradus ad Parnassum,* a piece in which keyboard exercises were also used as a starting point, illustrates coloristic and metrical devices shared with Op. 53 that have been discussed: the use of a pedal tone, as well as the implied use of the pedal to sustain it; the use of staccato to point out melodic movement within passages; the interchanging of major and minor; the suspension of harmonic movement; whole-step modulation; and changes of pace, some of which are indicated in a conventional manner, but the last of which is an *allargando* written in note values.

Ex. 11.23. Debussy, *Dr. Gradus ad Parnassum,* excerpts.

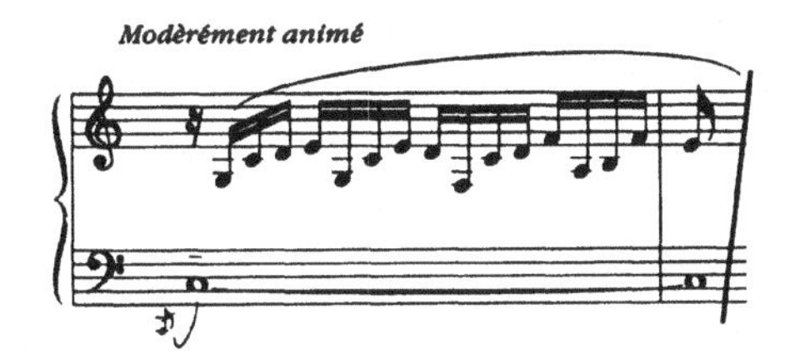

pp
sf
p
I° Tempo
p expressif
piu p
Animez peu à peu
pp
expressif
En animant peu à peu
f
Très animé
f
ff
ff
ff

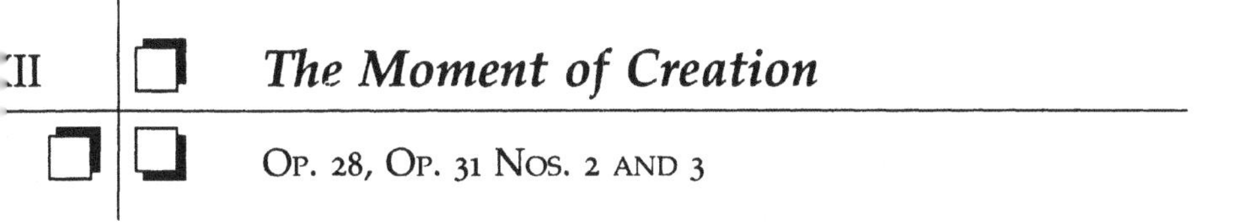

VII The Moment of Creation

Op. 28, Op. 31 Nos. 2 and 3

As musicians, would we choose to have lived in another time? During the 1780s in Vienna to hear Mozart play his own concertos? Or London in the 1790s to hear Haydn conduct from the keyboard? Or Vienna in March 1807 to hear Beethoven premiere the Fourth Concerto? Or conduct the Ninth Symphony? Or hear Chopin play a mazurka or a nocturne? Or attend a Schubertiad?

One could go on and on. Looking at a score is like reading the road signs beside dry creek beds in the American Southwest that warn of swollen streams. Dry ink on a white page is the only trace of the ideas that swept through the composer's mind. Each of the three sonatas in this chapter—Op. 28 and Op. 31 Nos. 2 and 3—begins as though out of nowhere, as though grasped in the act of *preludieren* (to use Czerny's term) and stilled as a specimen of a moment in Beethoven's imagination. Even if one had been alive at the time, it would hardly have been possible to approach any more closely the freshness of the first moment.

Op. 28

Where did this sonata begin in the composer's mind? In what order did Beethoven discover his building materials? Understandably, what follows is speculation.

EX. 12.1. OP. 28, I, MM. 2–10.

Visitors to Beethoven in his later years who wanted to hear him improvise could expect to have their request denied. Instead, one needed only to strike a key and pretend to find something wrong with the sound. Beethoven would then try the key himself, add intervals, sit down, and lose himself in improvisation, unaware of the visitor who had retreated to the back of the room. Here, we may imagine, Beethoven began with the repeated D's in the bass. Like the whirring of the shutters, the sound of these repeated notes must have induced a trancelike state in which the next discovery was the dominant seventh of the subdominant. Especially because these are the opening measures of the sonata, the subdominant sound has the effect of beginning with *otherness* resolving *elsewhere*, delayed by an appoggiatura. The latter, then, was the third discovery: within the context of pedaled repeated D's, *piano*, the expressive pull of the slurred second. The figure is so expressively satisfying that Beethoven repeated it, and repeated it slurred, and repeated it slurred again, stopping on a.

Listening to Beethoven as our mental teacher, the melodic descent of an octave comprises two tetrachords, the D-major triad with a in the soprano being the harmonic answer to the instability of the D^7 five measures earlier, with a^1 in the soprano. He must have heard, as we do, that a is the pitch on which the melodic line is suspended. Descending seconds combine to form each tetrachord. The latter is a formal device, a building block, the former an expressive device, symbolic of whatever sentiments one associates with melodic pull. The last discovery in those early moments of creation, the four measures that conclude the theme, was the contrast of direction and the absence of appoggiaturas, a sensation of being lifted and being released.

Tracing the reappearance of musical elements found in the opening line, the repeated D's continue virtually uninterrupted for thirty-nine measures, the device returning for the first twenty measures of the development, again at the reprise, and twenty measures at the close of the movement. The repeated F♯'s, mm. 219–56, although not as repeated quarter notes, add another thirty-eight measures of pedal. The repeated pedal tone must therefore be regarded as inseparable from the thematic material.

The tetrachord appears throughout the movement, at times more clearly than others. It is explicitly stated in the bass (Ex. 12.2); the reason for the strange *sforzando* on g^1 may have been the integrity of the tetrachord in the soprano. Or, possibly, with the *sforzando* on g in mm. 23 and 31, the aberration V^7–I in G major at the opening of the movement was to be forcibly recalled. The melodic line descends in another tetrachord, $f\sharp^1$–$c\sharp^1$, in the succeeding two measures, and a descending four-note line is repeated in the bass in mm. 40–55 (Ex. 12.3). The abbreviation of the tetrachord to two notes in the bass in mm. 56–59 resembles the intensification in the development shown below in Ex. 12.7. In the second theme, the melodic line unfolds in descending tetrachords (Ex. 12.4), each beginning with a repetition of the two-note appoggiatura figure.

Ex. 12.2. Op. 28, I, mm. 21–23.

Ex. 12.3. Op. 28, I, mm. 40–43.

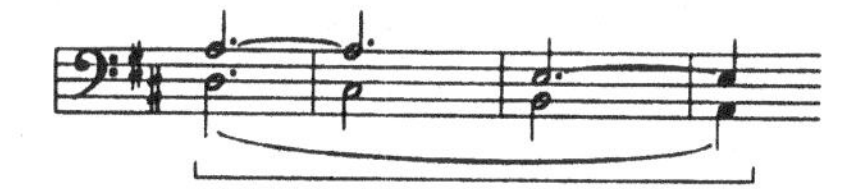

Ex. 12.4. Op. 28, I, mm. 90–98.

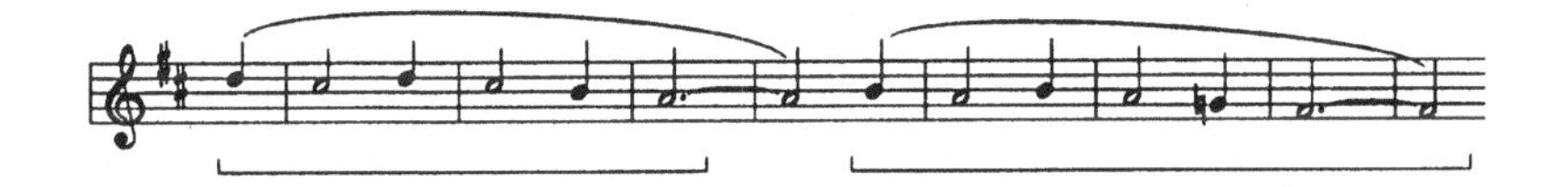

Like the octave compass of the principal theme, the repeated scale passages in mm. 104–108 lie basically within an octave, as do the separate phrases of the closing theme (Ex. 12.5).

Ex. 12.5. Op. 28, I, mm. 135–39.

Compared with the exposition and recapitulation, the development becomes restless, then turbulent in the resolute ascent to f♯ and the peak of importance it reaches. One may well hear the ominous repeated f♯ octaves at the beginning of the development as the harbinger of the double pedal point on f♯ beginning in m. 219, and, for that matter, the V^7–I in G major in mm. 165–67 as a re-emergence of the G-major issue at the beginning of the movement. The contrast in activity between the exposition and the development may be traced back to the differences between the two halves of the principal theme. The first half drifts downward, which is the general melodic direction of the exposition, while that of the development, based on the second half of the theme, generally rises, settling on f♯ in m. 219. The greatly expanded range of the new contrapuntal episode is a factor in the mounting energy, as is the underlying current in stepwise eighth notes, instead of quarters or triad tones (Ex. 12.6). The ascending segment of the principal theme, on which the approach to f♯ beginning in m. 183 is constructed, is intensified by abbreviation. The four-measure phrase becomes a two-measure phrase beginning in m. 199, *subito piano;* then a one-measure phrase in m. 207, marked *crescendo;* finally it is reduced in the right hand to two quarter-note beats (Ex. 12.7).

Ex. 12.6. Op. 28, I, mm. 201–204.

Ex. 12.7. Op. 28, I, mm. 183–86, 199–200, 207, 219.

Beginning in m. 227, F♯-major harmony is prolonged for thirty measures. Why? One may speculate, based on similar events in the movement, that Beethoven was utilizing the unique qualities of the individual members of the major triad in designing his musical architecture: the finality of the tonic, the capacity of the third for subjective response, and the suspended quality of the fifth. The prominence of a during approximately fifty measures of the exposition and d through at least nineteen measures of the development is a reliable indication that the movement is built on the composing out of the D-major triad. The *sforzandos* on chord members in the closing measures of the movement support this observation (Ex. 12.8); and the Schenker-type sketch in Ex. 12.9 represents this composing-out of the triad.

Ex. 12.8. Op. 28, I, mm. 447–55.

Ex. 12.9. Op. 28, I.

In m. 40, after thirty-eight measures of uninterrupted sound, the music seeks a new direction, with movement back and forth between A major and E major. The shortening of these four-measure phrases to two measures, uninterrupted by rests and leading to the single note e in mm. 61–62, establishes the new direction. The character of the fleeting cadence in mm. 2–3 returns in the "elsewhereness" of the long play with a C♯-major triad and an E♯ diminished seventh in mm. 77–90. The *sf* on the A-major sixth chord in m. 103 and on the six-four in m. 131, each with e in the soprano, confirms the primacy of that pitch following its appearance in mm. 61–62. The one-measure scale passages beginning in mm. 104–108, each starting with a triplet and ending with a quintuplet, and the melodic leaps represent the notation of an effortful reaching from a to e.

The f♯, which is heard only in passing in the theme, is brought to the foreground in the development with a third-relationship harmonization. The association of f♯—the third of the triad, its most subjective member, and the determinant of major or minor—with the most agitated and the most striving moments in the movement creates an unforgettable climax to which the interpreter can compare the lesser intensity of the exposition and the recapitulation.

How swiftly should this movement be played? Is the tempo to be felt in three or in one? The answer lies in what the appoggiaturas mean to one's sensibilities. Beyond that, other features encountered on the first page also influence the choice of tempo, including sudden bursts of quicker notes, necessitating uncomfortable shifts of hand position (Ex. 12.10), and *sforzandos* on unstable harmonies occurring on weak beats, often on an appoggiatura or a suspension—a development of the instability in the first three measures of the sonata (Ex. 12.11).

Ex. 12.10. Op. 28, I, mm. 26–29, 104–105.

Ex. 12.11. Op. 28, I, mm. 29–39.

Czerny must have heard Beethoven play the Andante, possibly on several occasions, since he tells us that the composer was fond of playing this movement. He expresses concern for a distinction between legato and staccato and for strict tempo in the D-major section, which he describes as "marchlike." The varied reprise, for all its expressive qualities, should not be permitted to drag, he writes, likening the movement as a whole to "a simple story, a Ballade from past time."[1] The Andante is a reflective piece, always going. In spite of its sameness, details in the writing make the movement feel tense: the contrast of touch between the hands requiring the most careful pedaling; the unnaturalness of a *crescendo* to a sudden *piano* and of a *sforzando* on a weak beat recurring again and again; and the difficulty of playing legato octaves above detached sixteenths. Even in the released quality of the D-major section, intended to sound casual, distinguishing between thirty-seconds and triplet sixteenths keeps the player on guard. Other details contributing to the tension include subtleties of articulation and rests within an inner voice line (Ex. 12.12).

Ex. 12.12. Op. 28, II, mm. 50, 52–53, 71, 73–75.

Czerny makes two points with respect to the Scherzo: Always separate the two eighths from the following quarter , and, in the Trio, accent each f♯ in the right hand. The pitch f♯ makes the beginning of the movement tonally ambiguous, sounding like the dominant of B minor instead of the mediant of D major. This is partly because the four a's beginning in m. 9 are unmistakably the dominant of D major; therefore, the ear wants to hear f♯ as another dominant. The main reason, however, seems to lie in the B-minor tonality of the Trio, in which each phrase begins on the same f♯. The ambiguity is still heard in the *da capo,* even if one *knows* the key is D major. Beethoven's dynamic indications, increasing from *forte* at the repeat in m. 17 to the *fortissimo* that occurs only on the overlapping D-major triads with d in the soprano in m. 57, represent an insistence on correcting any misunderstanding.

Because the rocking tonic pedal of the first sixteen measures of the Rondo is heard alone, outlining a tetrachord with hardly more than a snatch of melodic writing above it, it is more "thematic" than the pedal in the first movement. The many faces of the tetrachord throughout the movement, without its accompanying melodic fragment, establishes its predominance. For the interpreter, the importance of the tetrachord within the rocking figure is its ascending direction, for example, the tetrachord patterns in the development section (this is a sonata rondo) and the Più Allegro. The tetrachord figures in the second movement, by contrast, descend (Ex. 12.13).

Ex. 12.13. Op. 28, II, mm. 2, 18–21.

The movements of this sonata share a quiet momentum; even the Scherzo, the harmonic rhythm of which gives a feeling of one beat per measure, is not a driving Allegro vivace. Pitch relationships also draw the separate movements together. Mention has been made that all movements share the same tonic. As in the first movement, members of the D-major chord become the important structural pitches throughout the sonata. F♯ was the focal point of the development of the first movement. In the Andante, the two important pitches of the A-section are d and a (and secondarily e and c♯); in the B-section, f♯ is again in the foreground, as also in the Scherzo, in which each phrase of the Trio begins on f♯. In the Rondo, both bass and treble entrances begin on a, the second half of the theme in the right hand repeatedly reaching up to an a. Compare the parallel passages from the B-section of the Rondo (Ex. 12.14). Beethoven seems to have leaned toward placing *sforzandos* only on the particular A-major triad with a in the soprano and on those positions of the D-major chord in the parallel passage with d or f♯ in the soprano. Other prominent D-major pitches in the Rondo include the a and the d respectively in the ritornello passages (Ex. 12.15 and m. 160) and the f♯ in the Più Allegro quasi Presto.

Ex. 12.14. Op. 28, IV, mm. 36–41, 152–58.

Ex. 12.15. Op. 28, IV, m. 43.

Pitch relationships are unimportant unless consciousness of these "corners of the building" sharpens one's projection of them, through voicing or pacing or dynamics. To make the academic point that f♯ is the structural pitch of the development of the first movement will move no one. Only when thinking of its subjective connotation in relation to other chord members, and when perceiving that Beethoven chooses that pitch on which to scream in the crisis of the movement, only then does the cerebral observation stir the sense of the listener.

Several other parallels knit the four movements together. Sameness and repetitiveness in the accompaniment figure in the second movement and the finale resemble the repeated quarters in the first movement. Throughout the sonata, thematic material frequently lies within an octave (Ex. 12.16). In the Rondo, all the melodic material in the right hand in the first sixteen measures lies within an octave, as does the rocking figure in the bass, the second theme, the melodic outline of the closing theme, and the first phrases of the second side section (Ex. 12.17). As in the first movement, a musical storm appears in the middle of the Rondo with the long line of octaves in the bass—repetitive, sequential, unstoppable. The bracketed notes in Exx. 12.16 and 12.17 form tetrachords, the building blocks of the first movement and the Rondo. The legato broken chords, mm. 17–27 in the Rondo, are based on two tetrachords: f♯–e–d–c♯ in the right hand and d–c♯–b–a in the left. The rising tetrachord in both hands in mm. 79–94 recalls the same rising figure in the bass in the opening measures of the movement (Ex. 12.18).

Ex. 12.16. Op. 28, I, mm. 411–415; III, mm. 1–2; IV, mm. 2–4.

Ex. 12.17. Op. 28, IV, mm. 1–2, 28–30, 43–45, 68–71.

Ex. 12.18. Op. 28, IV, mm. 79–83.

Following the gravitation to f♯, which is restated over and over in the Più Allegro, it would sound inappropriate were the movement to end with scalesteps 5–1 in the treble. Beethoven's ending on f♯, the third of the triad, restores a subjective fervor to the Rondo that, except for the development section, has been missing in the generally even-tempered character of the movement.

Practice, in the customary sense of the term, is not the only time of growth. After a certain point, when the notes have been learned, improvement is often better achieved away from the piano, when one is occupied with a completely unrelated physical activity. At such a time, the mind is free to mull over pitch or key relationships or tempos or levels of dynamic presence. In Op. 28 it is as though the moment of creation *was* the D-major triad and an impulse to explore the subjective connotation of each of its three members. The fact that all four movements share the same tonic note and that members of the D-major triad figure prominently as structural pitches throughout suggests that the sonata *as a whole* represents the moment of creation. The unity of pitch gives the sonata a monumental or statuesque quality, meaning that the D-major triad can be "viewed" from different angles, and that, while it may seem to move, the piece is more reflective than active. The "big moments" of the sonata are always moments of a strength that is never savage or merely wild.

This, in turn, relates to the question of tempo, especially that of the first movement. A notch must be found on the mental metronome that will not sound hurried on the one hand or sluggish, or even deliberate, on the other. The "statuesque" idea supports the intuitive "quiet momentum." (Perhaps Beethoven himself had this intuitive feeling and therefore felt the need to end the fourth movement with a Più Allegro.) A tempo must be found for the first movement such that the quarter notes, if counted as three beats to the measure, will sound reflective starting with the very first measure. A tempo of one beat to a measure, even within the first measure, would fail to capture the moment of creation, appearing as out of nowhere, and the expansive nature of the sonata as a whole.

Op. 31 No. 2

> This sonata is consummate [*vollkommen*]. The unity of the musical idea and the tragic character, the form that is uninterrupted by any episode, the romantic-picturesque of the complete tone picture never fail to make the greatest effect, if the fantasy of the player stands on the same high level with his dexterity.[2]

The writer, Carl Czerny, studied the sonata with the composer, and therefore one may assume that Beethoven himself used similar imagery when coaching the piece: *ernst* (the Allegro "lively, but serious"), *klagend* (from m. 41 "lively and light, but complaining"), *kräftig, heroisch* (the chords from m. 55 on "very strong and heroic"), *stürmisch* (the Allegro, i.e., the development section, "very stormy"), *aus weiter Ferne klagend* (the recitatives "like a lament from a great distance"), *wie ferner Donner* (the pedaled bass in the final measures of the first movement "like distant thunder"), *beinahe blitzschnell* (the tympani figure in the left hand in the Adagio "almost lightning quick"), *rührend und einfach* (the lyrical melody in the Adagio, mm. 31–38 and 73–80 "touching and simple"), *um gewissermassen den Galopp eines Pferdes auszudrücken* (the Allegretto theme "to express, so to speak, the gallop of a horse").

Czerny's words to the contrary, a pianist mindful of audience appeal will be more inclined to play the "Moonlight" or the "Appassionata." The evenness of the finale of Op. 31 No. 2 and the manner in which the movement expires, *piano*, may make the Allegretto a disappointment in terms of dramatic finality, while the finale of Op. 57 can always be made to sound *bravura*. In the Adagio there is a similar austerity of means in the long note values and the double-dotted rhythm; even during the lyrical passage beginning in m. 18, the clipped tympani figure prevents the listener from forgetting the fragmentary quality of the ideas and the tightness of the rhythm. Czerny could not have meant that Op. 31 No. 2 is a consummate work from the standpoint of being a consummate crowd-pleaser.

The D-minor Sonata may be a work of few words, but it is also a work of unfathomable depths. What is the principal theme of the first movement, the broken-chord motive or the slurred eighths? There is no one "main theme." Instead, the sonata begins with a thematic/dramatic situation consisting of three dissimilar elements—the broken chord, the eighths, and the turn in m. 6—from which the remainder of the movement is fashioned. A simpler idea than the ascending broken chord could hardly be found; the half note is its only complexity, making it, as thematic material, barely more than one step removed from pure sound. Its quality of mystery derives from the impression that we are present at the moment of creation, in the act of what Czerny described as *preludieren:* beginning with broken chords and arpeggios to try out the instrument and discover an idea for an improvisation. Was the first discovery the simple rhythmic articulation of the broken chord? It would seem so, and that the next was the effect of beginning on the third of the A-major triad instead of the root? Whichever idea took precedence in the moment of conception, the broken-chord motive retains its individuality throughout the movement. It always ascends. In a slow tempo, it is always marked *pianissimo,* like an unspoken thought. In a fast tempo, the motive is always *forte* or *fortissimo,* like an answer spoken in defiance.

Mozart's use of a similar figure in his C-minor Sonata illustrates the fundamental difference between the composers' personalities. Mozart's theme is also always in ascending form, and, while it is always marked *forte,* it sounds less decisive than Beethoven's theme principally because it overshoots the downbeat (Exx. 12.19a and b) and, just prior to the reprise, its fragments descend *piano* to *pianissimo* (Ex. 12.19c). In Mozart, the one additional note transforms what might also have been a defiant statement into a dramatic question; in the D-minor Sonata, the similar theme has a will of iron, however desperate the situation.

Ex. 12.19. a. Beethoven, Op. 31 No. 2, I, mm. 21–24. Mozart, K. 457, I: b. mm. 1–2; c. mm. 95–99.

The slurred eighths, which, according to Tovey, Beethoven played as though dusting off the keys, are individual enough that any slurred eighths thereafter sound derived.[3] One can imagine the motive as an attempt to capture the indescribable in sound. Like speaking in tongues, loosed from logic and subject to individual interpretation, Beethoven's slurred eighths are set apart from proper, intelligible two-note slurs, which are poorly suited for the speech of wind and flame. Young pianists are often so intent on playing evenly and clearly that they sometimes try to play mm. 13–18 staccato, instead of slurred like vigorous swipes with a large, wide brush, as the notation in Ex. 12.20 depicts. To achieve a breathless quality like that of mm. 2–5, the fingering given for the slurred eighths in Ex. 12.21 makes it impossible *not* to separate between the pairs of eighths. Not all derivations are as obvious. The slurred quarters in mm. 69–74 are the original slurred eighths in augmentation (Ex. 12.22a), and so are the descending half notes in the closing section (Ex. 12.22b), which follow the same descending tetrachord pattern of mm. 2–4.

Ex. 12.20. Op. 31 No. 2, I, m. 13.

Ex. 12.21. Op. 31 No. 2, I, mm. 41–45.

Ex. 12.22. Op. 31 No. 2, I: a. mm. 69–74; b. mm. 75–76.

In his *Über den richtigen Vortrag . . .*, Czerny writes the turn in m. 6 using an f× instead of an f♯, differing from the reading in present-day editions and, for that matter, from his own edition published by Simrock in Bonn and Berlin. The variants in his quotation of the first six measures (Ex. 12.23), including also the *poco ritard.*, the added fermata over the dissonance of the first chord in m. 6, and the *Adagio* written expressly above the turn, lead one to believe that Czerny may have been writing from memory, which would mean from the memory of his study with Beethoven himself.

Ex. 12.23. Op. 31 No. 2, I, mm. 1–6 (from Über den richtigen Vortrag).

The time signature C, instead of ¢, as in his edition of the Sonata, is a further indication that Czerny was writing from memory, none of which should diminish the value of information from this very gifted student of Beethoven. Neither should the following, from Czerny's "Erinnerungen aus Meinem Leben," be taken as mere boasting: "I possessed such a successful musical memory that, not counting other composers, I was able to play by memory completely exact everything that Beethoven wrote for the fortepiano, a natural gift that has still not left me, even now."[4]

Whatever the individual player decides, the f× sharpens the connection between the turn and related material: the melodic fragment in mm. 22–28 (Ex. 12.24a), in mm. 55–59 (Ex. 12.24b), in the left hand in m. 41 (Ex. 12.24c), more remotely in the general contour of the right-hand line (Ex. 12.24d), and equally so in mm. 121–33 (Ex. 12.24e).

Ex. 12.24. Op. 31 No. 2, I: a. mm. 22–24; b. mm. 55–57; c. m. 41; d. mm. 43–45; e. mm. 122–23.

Characteristics of the opening line that determine the structure of the movement and its interpretation include the segmentation in three clearly differentiated ideas, indecisiveness (there are three indicated tempos, in addition to which the line begins and ends on the dominant), and a highly concentrated manner. Discovering how these interact is to realize what Czerny meant by "consummate."

To begin, the segmentation is a microcosm of the overall structure of clearly defined sections similar to the components of a pre-fabricated house. These sections seem the more blocklike because they are restated virtually intact; for example, the rising sequence of mm. 21–41 is repeated in the development in mm. 99–121. Although the blocklike, repetitious structure is a kind of musical fatalism, the preeminence of either the broken chord or the eighths is never decided during the course of the movement. Is the opening Largo the actual beginning of the movement, or is it the beginning of twenty measures of introduction leading to the real beginning in m. 21? The shift in the character of the broken-chord motive from m. 1 to m. 21 is as momentous as Faust's attempts to translate the first verse of the Gospel According to St. John:[5]

> Geschrieben steht: "im Anfang was das W o r t !"
> Hier stock' ich schon! Wer hilft mir weiter fort?
> Ich kann das W o r t so hoch unmöglich schätzen,
> Ich muß es anders übersetzen,
> Wenn ich vom Geiste recht erleuchtet bin.
> Geschrieben steht: im Anfang war der S i n n .
> Bedenke wohl die erste Zeile,
> Daß deine Feder sich nicht übereile!
> Ist es der S i n n , der alles wirkt und schafft?
> Es sollte stehn: im Anfang war die K r a f t !
> Doch, auch indem ich dieses niederschreibe,
> Schon warnt mich was, daß ich dabei nicht bleibe.
> Mir hilft der Geist! Auf einmal seh' ich Rath
> Und schreibe getrost: im Anfang war die T h a t !
>
> [It is written: "in the beginning was the W o r d !"
> Here I already stop! Who will help me further?

I cannot possibly esteem the W o r d so highly,
I must translate it another way,
If I am truly enlightened by the spirit.
It is written: in the beginning was the M i n d .
Consider well the first line,
That your quill is not too hasty!
Is it the M i n d that produces everything?
It should be: in the beginning was the P o w e r !
Yet, also when I write this,
Already something warns me that I should not stay with it.
May the spirit help me! Suddenly I see what to do
And write, relieved: in the beginning was the D e e d !]

The character of the rising sequence beginning in m. 21 of the D-minor Sonata is also that of the "deed," although the passage culminates with a sustained diminished seventh chord, nowhere harmony, as though it had been only a transition (Ex. 12.25a). In like manner, the extended episode of slurred eighths suspended over the dominant of A minor descends with diminished seventh harmony, the resolution of which is downplayed (Ex. 12.25b). The succeeding two cadences in A minor, in mm. 62–63 (Ex. 12.25c) and 74–75 (Ex. 12.25d), in which the dominant is retained as a pedal point, are similarly weak. (There are grounds for not playing m. 75 *piano,* as in the parallel passage in the recapitulation. Czerny writes, "very *crescendo* to the *forte* [m. 75] which first lets down in mm. 83 to 86."[6]) Curiously, the cadence expires and is then made emphatic with the repeated tonic (Ex. 12.25e).

The rising sequence of mm. 21–41, the "deed," reappears in the development (though not where it would be expected, in the recapitulation) and ends on the dominant harmony, which plays itself out for eighteen measures. The very length of this extension makes indecision the basis for the dramatic plan of the movement, in which will—or purposefulness or action—finds no goal to grasp. During this episode, a figure related to the turn motive is repeated again and again, wearing itself out, tantrum-like, until it can only re-resolve on the dominant (Ex. 12.26).

Thus, the movement is consummate in resembling an ultimate question that will not go away. The recitatives, the only lyrical writing amid the formal blocks of the movement, assume the reality of a solitary speaker who makes a muffled comment, perhaps about the conflict of forces beyond human control. These recitatives, audibly set apart by the long pedals—like a voice within a vault, as Beethoven is supposed to have said[7]—remain for all time a personal narration, symbolizing that "it is *I*" who is imprisoned within this depiction of fatalism. Perhaps, also, because the movement sounds musically undecided, the last movement begins with reiterated resolutions. The D-minor Sonata presents an inexhaustible number of interpretive possibilities, to the point that one is prepared to rank it as the most thought-provoking, if not shattering, of all the sonatas.

A third characteristic of the opening line is its intense concentration. We somehow think more readily of the intensity of color than that of sound. Concentration

Ex. 12.25. Op. 31 No. 2, I: a. mm. 37–41; b. mm. 50–55; c. mm. 62–63; d. mm. 73–75; e. mm. 86–89.

Ex. 12.26. Op. 31 No. 2, I, mm. 134–38.

dimin.

here is the slowness of the arpeggio and the exact spacing of its successive members, the listening-within of the *pianissimo* level, and the dramatically correct length of the fermata. The timing of these elements of concentration must have occurred to Czerny as well, since he advised beginning the counting with the top note of the arpeggio and added a fermata to the chord at the beginning of m. 6. Additional evidence of concentration—of the intensity of color—includes the prevailing minor tonality throughout the movement; the only passages in major are the broken-chord statements in a slow tempo. Concentration also describes the process of immediate development and the abbreviation of sequential sections into increasingly smaller units; mm. 21–41 are subdivided 4 + 4 + 2 + 2 + 2 + 2 + 2 + 1 + 1, a procedure to be found in mm. 110–50 of the last movement as well.

For the player there are no throw-away notes or nuances, since so much is being said with so little. Concentration—not just pitches and rhythms *per se* but the sense they make—is part of the notation of the music; clarity of technique is nothing without intensity of concentration. The triplet figure beginning in m. 21 is not an unmeasured tremolo but a back-and-forth motion within a triplet subdivision that must be marked with accents if its energy is to be released. To that end, the fingerings given in Ex. 12.27 may be helpful; they allow for a shifting of the hand position to avoid accumulation of tension.

Ex. 12.27. Op. 31 No. 2, I, mm. 21–22, 99–118.

The arpeggiated B♭-major chord at the beginning of the second movement appears out of the pedaled D-minor sound—the "distant thunder," as Czerny characterized it—at the close of the first movement. The arpeggiation corresponds to the opening of the first movement, with the difference that the lowest note is the fundamental and not the third of the triad. The effect is thus one of greater repose and stability. Beneath the outward calm, the Adagio moves apprehensively because of rhythmic, melodic, and dynamic details. The double-dotted figure would have sounded more *cantabile* had it been written as a simple dotted eighth and sixteenth. In Beethoven's notation, one becomes aware of waiting, followed by a twitching movement, a rhythmic peculiarity introducing a pervasive strangeness that precludes informality and familiarity. The tympani figure, mm. 17–30, is another such brief rhythmic act of impersonal stiffness in an episode of lyricism and warmth, like the measured movements of a ceremonial guard, whatever human feelings exist within the uniform. Czerny writes that the figure is "to be played with the greatest possible lightness and shortness, almost lightning quick . . ." He also writes that the *cantabile* theme beginning in m. 31 should sound "touching and simple, not stretched."[8] Here, as in other instances of the double-dotted eighth and thirty-second rhythm, the melody is already stretched; Czerny merely cautions one to avoid sentimentality.

Another element creating uneasiness in the Adagio is the interval of a minor second, darkening the prevailing major of the voice lines and accounting for the tightness of movement within these lines (Ex. 12.28). The melodic line in the transitional passage in m. 60 includes additional minor seconds lacking in the parallel passage (Ex. 12.29).

Indications of an abruptly discontinued *crescendo* also make the slow movement sound constrained. In one instance, the modulation to C major within mm. 26–30 is resisted by a tonic pedal; the key reached is still C major, but it is muted by the

Ex. 12.28. Op. 31 No. 2, II, mm. 2–3, 4–5, 6–8, 11–13, 14–16, 18–19, 20–21, 24, 25, 26–27, 30, 34, 35, 38–39, 45–46, 47–48, 84–85, 88–89, 91–92, 93–94, 98.

Ex. 12.29. Op. 31 No. 2, II, mm. 60–63.

subito piano in m. 27. After four measures of harmonic and dynamic straining, the F-major theme sounds the more peaceful and released.

Naturally, the movement will sound neither calm nor uneasy if the tempo is not strictly maintained, as Czerny advises: "It [the *Adagio*] must not drag, and the tempo must be held exactly constant." However, he also suggests, "In m. 55, *crescendo* to *forte*, and *accelerando*, then *piano* and *rallentendo* in m. 58." Czerny did not insert markings of this sort in his edition of the sonata, revealing an adherence to the original that later editors in his century felt less obligated to preserve. If anyone should be granted credibility as an editor of the D-minor Sonata, it is Czerny, who had studied the work with Beethoven. The following comment is indicative of his faithfulness to the original: "The passages in the left hand (from the 51st measure) light and soft, in order that the theme may stand out *legato*."[9] Beethoven himself left these thirty-seconds unslurred, indicating a nonlegato touch; Czerny faithfully reproduces this articulation in his edition of the sonata.

A question arises about pedaling at the beginning of the Allegretto, where Czerny in his commentary adds long pedals through unchanging harmonies, although, again, not in his edition. Moscheles, who had opportunities to hear Beethoven, includes the same pedal marking, as do Bülow and d'Albert. The latter adds a

Debussy-like slur from the sixteenth at the beginning of each measure (Ex. 12.30). Curiously, neither Bülow nor d'Albert was disturbed by the blur produced here, yet they abbreviated Beethoven's original pedals in the first movement, at which point d'Albert added: "According to Beethoven, the same pedal should be held down to the close of the recitative,—an impossibility on our modern piano."[10]

Ex. 12.30. Op. 31 No. 2, III, mm. 1–4.

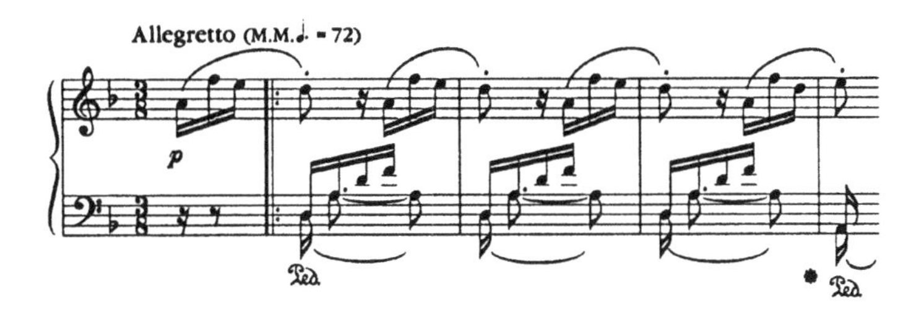

Does one conceive the passage in question harmonically or pedal only sparingly in order not to cover details in the notation? Supporting ample use of the pedal is Schindler's comment that Beethoven was "no miniaturist" and Czerny's oft-repeated description of *harmoniös* passages:

> This movement lasts through the whole piece and is enlivened only through exact attention to *piano, forte, crescendo, diminuendo,* and also through the use of the *pedal* in harmonious [*harmoniös*] places.
>
> The endless, passionate movement gives this *Finale* a fascination and a unity of feeling through which it completes the sonata in a worthy manner.[11]

The Allegretto is a challenge to the pianist's imagination. The movement cannot sound like *Für Elise,* a piece with which it shares musical characteristics in the time signature, minor tonality, subdivision in evenly flowing sixteenths, a less than fast tempo, and a downward melodic tendency. How is one to hear this uninterrupted perpetual motion in two-part writing as a "worthy completion" to the sonata?

As Nottebohm observed, what follows one musical idea in Beethoven is generally a consequence and not something unrelated that has been added on. If conflict between action and indecision distinguishes the first movement and a tense calm characterizes the Adagio, the Allegretto—its sameness, the pendulum-like regularity of its principal rhythmic cell, and the immediate repetition of a section of four, six, or eight measures—sounds predetermined, inevitable, for the constant going prevents any interruption by another, contrasting idea. If the patter of even sixteenths lasting six or seven minutes is to sound not only like an "endless" but also a "passionate rhythmic movement," it is necessary to isolate expressive gestures from the repetitive sameness. To isolate means to make heard, clearly and unmistakably:

the dynamic swells of mm. 9–30, following the uninflected dynamic level of the opening measures;
the breaking out of the D-minor arpeggio in mm. 15–16 following the dynamic swells;
the exact length of the quarter notes in mm. 23–27, followed by the wailing chromatic scale, which does not return again until the final page of the movement;
the outburst of the *forte* episode in mm. 30–43, similar to the sequence beginning in m. 21 of the first movement;
the fury of the *Pralltriller* on each pair of slurred eighths in mm. 43–47;
the lift of the slurred eighths in mm. 59 and 63 against the generally descending lines;
the stamping of the *sforzando* at the beginning of each bar, mm. 87–90;
the dreaminess of the four-note figure at the beginning of the development, which now ascends, outlining a diminished seventh chord;
the *sforzandos* within the *piano* passage, mm. 173–98, which derive their reason for being from sounding contrary to the natural shaping of the four-note motive;
the leap upward to an $f\natural^{3}$ in m. 381 as the widest, highest grasp, after which the piece gradually ceases to continue.

Finally, if the unbending strength of the even sixteenths is not to be lost, the *forte* throughout the sequences in mm. 110–50 must also be unbending.

One may be skeptical of Czerny's statement that Beethoven improvised the theme of the finale after hearing a horseman gallop past his window, since the year to which Czerny assigns the anecdote (1803) is the year following the delivery of the manuscript to the publisher. A date, however, is a trivial matter compared to the substance of the comment. These were people whose imaginations were alive to their surroundings—a horse in gallop, a repetitive figure that never stops throughout the movement, like time—the features above like human gestures. In this spirit, the reader is invited to compare thoughtfully details of imagery in the following poem by Goethe (written after a coach journey from Darmstadt to Frankfurt) with the expressive gestures listed above. While Chronos is depicted in Roman mythology as the god of seedtime and harvest, Goethe identifies him here as the god of time and fate.

An Schwager Kronos

Spude dich, Kronos!
Fort den rasselnden Trott!
Bergab gleitet der Weg;

Ekles Schwindeln zögert
Mir vor die Stirne dein Haudern.
Frisch den holpernden
Stock Wurzeln Steine den Trott
Rasch in's Leben hinein!

Nun schon wieder
Den eratmenden Schritt
Mühsam Berg hinauf.
Auf denn, nicht träge denn!
Strebend und hoffend an.

Weit hoch herrlich der Blick
Rings ins Leben hinein
Vom Gebürg zum Gebürg,
Über der ewige Geist
Ewigen Lebens ahndevoll.

Seitwarts des Überdachs Schatten
Zieht dich an
Und der Frischung verheißende Blick
Auf der Schwelle des Mädchens da.—
Labe dich!—Mir auch Mädchen,
Diesen schäumenden Trunk
Und den freundlichen Gesundheitsblick!

Ab dann, frischer hinab!
Sieh, die Sonne sinkt.
Eh' sie sinkt, eh' mich faßt
Greisen im Moore Nebelduft,
Entzahnte Kiefer schnattern
Und das schlockernde Gebein—
Trunknen vom letzten Strahl
Reiß mich, ein Feuermeer
Mir im schäumenden Aug',
Mich Geblendeten, Taumelnden
In der Hölle nächtliches Tor!

Töne, Schwager, dein Horn,
Raßle den schallenden Trab,
Daß der Orkus vernehme, ein Fürst kommt,
Drunten von ihren Sitzen
Sich die Gewaltigen lüften.

To the Coachman Chronos

Hurry up, Chronos!
Onward, the clattering trot!
Downhill leads the road;
Your dallying makes me nauseously dizzy.
Lively, whether or not it jolts,
Over stump and stones the trot
Quickly into life.

Once more the panting pace
With effort up the mountain!
Upward then, not sluggish
Striving and hoping onward!

Far, high, magnificent the view
Around us into life,
From peak to peak,
The eternal spirit hovers,
Presentiment of eternal life.

Alongside the shelter's shade
You are drawn
And a glimpse of promising refreshment
On the girl's doorway.
Refresh yourself!—For me also, young woman,
This frothy drink,
This fresh glimpse of health!

Down, then downward!
See, the sun is setting!
Before it sets, before the fog in the moor
Lays hold on me, old man,
Toothless jaws chattering
And bones knocking:
Drunk from the last beam of light
Drag me, a sea of fire
In my watering eyes,
Me, dazzled and staggering
Into the dismal gate of hell!

Sound your horn, coachman,
Let the thundering trot clatter,
That Orcus may know, a prince is coming,
Down under, the powerful
Rise up from their seats.

Op. 31 No. 3

Although Op. 31 No. 3 is one of the most accessible of the sonatas, the character of the opening measures is enigmatic. Czerny writes,

> This sonata is more in a style of conversation than of portrayal and differs from the elegiac-romantic character of the preceding sonata through its witty serenity. The beginning is like a question, to which the answer follows in the seventh measure, for which reason it must exhibit a certain indecisiveness in tempo and expression that first after the fermata, and preferably from the sixteenth measure on, yields to a resolute execution; therefore, from here also the metronome can be duly observed.[12]

Although the principal theme of the first movement comprises at least three separate ideas, only the dotted figure, in terms of subsequent development, is treated as though it were the actual theme. Because it is so brief and begins on supertonic harmony, the figure sounds noncommittal, somewhat like a smile upon making an acquaintance. In a different sense, the figure *is* a question, inviting the imagination to hear a natural swell and lift that the piano cannot produce. Played exactly in tempo, without the imagined swell and lift, the figure will have no charm or wistfulness. It must sound as though it began in mid-air, unaware of a tempo.

The figure is also of uncertain tonality. The movement could have continued in A♭ major, as in Ex. 12.31. The A♭ six-five, perhaps more so than the beginning of the other two sonatas, is the stilled moment of creation, the moment preceding even the pen. Even after playing the sonata for years and knowing that the piece is in E♭ major, the *somewhere* effect of the beginning is new with each playing. The sound is that satisfying in itself, one would be happy to have it go *nowhere.*

Ex. 12.31.

Rest-silences are rare in this movement and are always associated with the dotted motive. The immediate repetition of the opening measure is another indication that the sound is to be understood as self-contained aural color. Furthermore, the repeated chords that form a passageway, *crescendo, ritardando,* to the E♭ six-four, *sforzando,* confirm the impression that one has heard, in the opening measure, a "creation sound." The contrast between the purposive chromatic ascent and the brief but busy cadence is the first hint of a less than serious intent, although only once during the movement does the humor become broad: the extended passage of repeated chords that introduce the development and are followed by the mock anger of the cadence in C minor, then by the flippant ritornello.

The opening motive is puzzling because its simplicity is not childlike. We learn more about it from the many ideas throughout the movement that stem from it. Because Beethoven managed to say so little at the beginning, any figure that subsequently falls or repeats must be seriously regarded as a possible derivation of the direction and the stress and lift within that motive. Thus, other than explicit (and varied) restatements of the theme (Ex. 12.32a), melodic material of the movement generally drops, including two-note slurred figures (Ex. 12.32b) and the second theme (Ex. 12.32c).

Ex. 12.32. Op. 31 No. 3, I: a. mm. 18–22, 158–61; b. mm. 35–36, 43–44, 83–84; c. mm. 45–49; d. mm. 193–99; e. mm. 72–77; f. mm. 178–82.

More distantly related to the motive are those lines that include a descending trill and resolution or a series of such short trills. A passage of trills in the recapitulation is extended by repetition, during which 2/4 meter is superimposed upon 3/4

(Ex. 12.32d). If the passages of immediate repetition in the Allegro are tallied, the total amounts to approximately half the number of measures in the movement. Examples of altered meter within a repeated pattern are fairly frequent (Ex. 12.32e). In mm. 178–82, the notation of one beam for a complete measure ensures absolute evenness and avoids stress on any particular beat (Ex. 12.32f). Perhaps the purpose of altered meter, like immediate repetition, was to reproduce the unattached, floating quality of the first two measures of the movement.

Repetition solves the problem of beginning once more in mid-air at the reprise. Beethoven reintroduces the pitch c while moving chromatically into an F-minor triad in first inversion, which is repeatedly broken until it establishes its own tonality. Through repetition the quality of the chord is isolated, stripping it of any trace of harmonic function. It is not surprising to find also in the remaining movements relatively long examples of static harmony, of which Ex. 12.33 represents only a sampling. In addition, the opening theme of the fourth movement is itself a repetitive figure.

Ex. 12.33. Op. 31 No. 3, II, mm. 42–45, 76–79; III, mm. 24–30; IV, mm. 34–42, 54–60, 64–76, 144–51.

The play with subtleties and surprises above the cool, matter-of-fact momentum of sixteenths is a reasonably good indication that *vivace* in the tempo marking of the second movement should not be translated as "fast," but as "full of life." Even in the staccato broken chords in mm. 76–80, where a *crescendo* might have been anticipated, only offbeat *sforzandos* are indicated. There are other eccentricities, such as the *sforzandos* in the theme (Ex. 12.34a)—missing when the theme is in a key other than A♭—and the swell over the cadence in mm. 8–9, like a caricature of the preceding cadence (Ex. 12.34b). Less subtle are the *fortissimo* chords in mm. 34–35 (Ex. 12.34c), the *crescendo* to a *subito piano* in mm. 81–83 (Ex. 12.34e), the rolled "fist" figures in mm. 90–96 (Ex. 12.34f), and the offbeat *sforzandos* at the close of the development (Ex. 12.34g). At too quick a tempo the repetition of the thirds (Ex. 12.34d) is unreliable, and the two-note slurs in the last lines of the movement become entangling. Even if one were to ignore these factors in the music, the position of *vivace* in the tempo marking suggests a modifying adverb and not an actual tempo marking.

Ex. 12.34. Op. 31 No. 3, II: a. mm. 1–3; b. mm. 8–9; c. mm. 32–35; d. mm. 42–44; e. mm. 81–83; f. mm. 90–92; g. mm. 97–100; h. mm. 163–65.

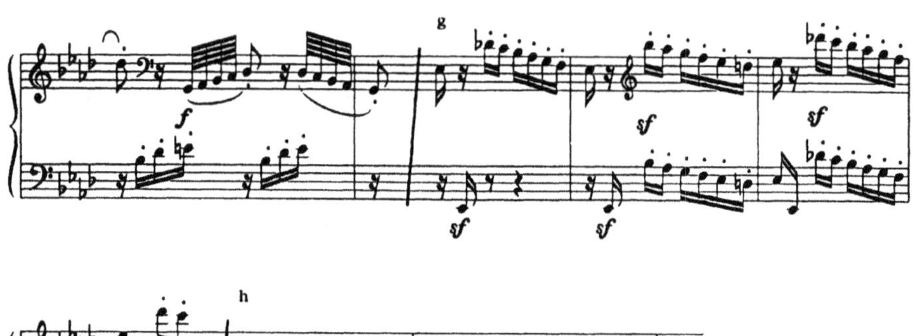

The F-minor section, mm. 9–15, recalling the opening of the first movement in pitches, harmony, and direction of line, is set apart from the rest of the movement by unison writing, a *pianissimo*, many rests, and a *poco ritardando*. A further tinge of minor is diffused throughout the Allegretto, partly the result of long passages of play with a diminished seventh. Also, just as the F-minor section emerges from the opening phrase in A♭ major, other phrases beginning in major have a noticeable tendency to darken: the phrase beginning in F major in m. 34, the statement of the theme beginning in F major in m. 64, and an analogous statement beginning in C major in m. 83. The minor shading creates a capricious, even eccentric mood, and prevents the character from being merely clownish.

Tovey described the Menuetto as a "peaceful dance for gracious souls who deserve their leisure."[13] The Trio and the Menuetto are so familiar, especially through the variations for two pianos by Saint-Saëns, that their differences may pass unnoticed. The Menuetto is almost entirely under legato slurs, the Trio mostly detached. The former is rich in independent lines, while part writing plays almost no role in the more homophonic Trio. Phrase endings in the Menuetto, except for the cadence immediately preceding the coda, are feminine; both halves of the Trio terminate on the downbeat. The flat sixth appears in both the Menuetto and the Trio, and, in the Menuetto, the flat second scale step as well; both pitches appear in the top voice of the Menuetto and are repeated, so that the minor color becomes a strong determinant of character, as in the Allegretto.

Unlike Op. 31 No. 2, this sonata was provided with a brilliant finale to place in perspective the whimsy and grace of its earlier movements. The finale charges forward with few interruptions—fermatas over dominant seventh harmony and others to delay the end of the movement (along with a *ritardando*). The spinning-out of pianistic figures becomes the vehicle for enormous energy. Even the single note d in the accompaniment figure (Ex. 12.35) increases the forward spin. The scooping of the slurred eighths, which ought to be heard as though notated as in Ex. 12.36, has an unstoppable thrust, like the movement of the agitator in a washing machine, abetted by the numerous *sforzandos* associated with repetitive figures and the variation of the theme in the development (Ex. 12.37). Czerny compares the movement to a *Jagdstück*, a useful image to convey the furious haste. Finally, the dominant-tonic figure in the theme (Ex. 12.38) outlines a falling fifth, like the opening of the first movement.

Ex. 12.35. Op. 31 No. 3, IV, m. 1.

Ex. 12.36. Op. 31 No. 3, IV, mm. 12–14.

Ex. 12.37. Op. 31 No. 3, IV, mm. 91–93, 127–29.

Ex. 12.38. Op. 31 No. 3, IV, mm. 2–4.

The absence of a slow movement has much to do with the "witty serenity" of the sonata. If, in the first movement, harmonic color draws one's attention away from metrical continuity, extended passages of color in the finale provide the content for sustained, repetitive rhythmic patterns. Harmonic color in the first movement makes the piece stand still; in the finale, it becomes the lubricant for the rhythmic motor.

Although the first movement of this sonata, like the first movement of Op. 90, achieves continuity through motivic development, the process in the latter communicates an intellectual strength that is concealed in Op. 31 No. 3 by the ingratiating character of the piece. Its words seem less carefully chosen, as though easy banter were appropriate to a large circle of friends, while sharing a very private burden requires specific figures of speech. Perhaps we also imagine seriousness as lying closer to the core of Beethoven's being, where the language for the unspeakable had to be guarded by greater cerebral discipline.

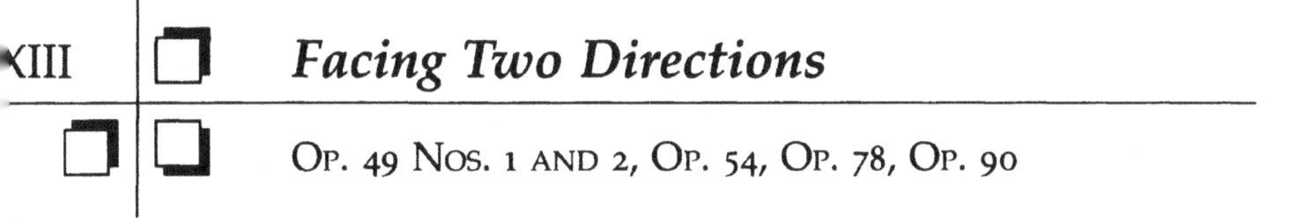

XIII Facing Two Directions

Op. 49 Nos. 1 and 2, Op. 54, Op. 78, Op. 90

The two-movement sonata represents a return, full circle, to the beginnings of the suite in the pairing of contrasting dance movements. Eliminating either an opening Allegro or a traditional Adagio from a typical three-movement sonata rules out an overall departure and return. A two-movement form lends itself to an either/or contrast that is illustrated by Opp. 49 No. 1, 54, 78, and 90. The ultimate, sublime example of such contrast of character is Op. 111, which will be treated separately.

Considered as a group, the opus order of the two-movement sonatas present an ascending dramatic unity and sophistication in the integration of motivic material. Admittedly, the motivic relationship between the two movements of Op. 49 No. 2 is more obvious than that in Op. 90, although in comparison with the latter, the G-major sonata projects little sense of drama.

Op. 49 Nos. 1 and 2

Because of the title, *Leichte Sonaten*, and because of their suitability as repertoire for teaching, the musical substance of these works is likely to be overlooked. The pianist who plays for singers and thinks as a singer will find the angularity of the melodic line in the opening of Op. 49 No. 1 a clue to the substance of the piece. Keyboardists are deprived of the sensation of producing the actual sound and shaping musical ideas *within* the human body. In the melodic line of the G-minor Sonata, the vocal reaching, often for a pitch stressed with an *mfp* or an *fp*, remains meaningless if sixths and fourths represent only the span of notes under the hand. To appreciate melodic distance as a singer, the pianist might practice mm. 5–8 as notated in Ex. 13.1, without pedal, using one hand. For the voice, the appoggiaturas and short slurs in Ex. 13.2 offer an opportunity for communicating warmth and grace.

Ex. 13.1. Op. 49 No. 1, I, mm. 5–8.

Ex. 13.2. Op. 49 No. 1, I, mm. 14–15.

Melodic direction assumes a deciding role from the very beginning of the movement. Reaching upward a fourth to the dominant seventh of G minor and then up a sixth to the subdominant, each time remaining there a full measure, sounds musically strained. In the second theme the melodic reach is downward and freed from effort, permitting the tempo to move ahead, the more so since the line drifts atop an Alberti bass of sustained harmony. While one would not break the melodic line at each barline, the separate slur beginning on c^3 in m. 26, the highest pitch in the exposition, may be interpreted as a vocal stress (Ex. 13.3).

Ex. 13.3. Op. 49 No. 1, I, m. 26.

The musical sense of the development also depends on the direction of the lines. In the sequential material following the E♭ phrase, the line droops; with m. 54 the direction vacillates between rising and falling, the effortful rising line of mm. 58–63 with its pedal point and *sforzandos,* falling back and climbing again, ultimately breaks off short of its goal (Ex. 13.4). Once again, the piano is best treated as a human voice, since, in proportion to what it has to say, the passage is poor in notes, much like a sketch. Here, the reaching—or yearning or desiring—attains its highest point, only to fall short of fulfillment. For a child these measures may be simple or may be difficult; the association of reaching and longing may be beyond the experience of that age. An adult, on the other hand, may find these measures too simple to symbolize anything.

Ex. 13.4. Op. 49 No. 1, I, mm. 58–64.

In m. 92, *sforzandos* are the physical expression of what would be a huge melodic leap for a singer (Ex. 13.5). The most important reason for the repeated *sforzando* on the c in the left hand in mm. 98, 100, and 102 is the one just mentioned—expressive effect through physical exaggeration. The *sforzando* also points out the placement of the closing theme in the bass, and, by sounding ominous, it provides a contrasting background for the G-major ending.

Ex. 13.5. Op. 49 No. 1, I, mm. 92–93.

Although the character of the second movement is new, the musical shapes are not, revealing how Beethoven's fantasy reworked patterns:

the thirds in the left hand (Ex. 13.6);
the lower neighboring tone, followed (though not always) by an ascending leap (Ex. 13.7);
the lower neighboring tone, followed by an accent (Ex. 13.8);
the exchange of theme and accompaniment between the hands (Ex. 13.9).

Ex. 13.6. Op. 49 No. 1, I, mm 1–3; II, mm. 1–4.

Ex. 13.7. Op. 49 No. 1, I, mm. 1–2; II, mm. 20–21, 32–34.

Ex. 13.8. Op. 49 No. 1, I, mm. 3–4; II, mm. 3, 25–26.

Ex. 13.9. Op. 49 No. 1, I, mm. 71–73; II, mm. 137–39.

On the face of it, the G-major Sonata appears to harbor no secrets and therefore may seem less substantial than the G-minor. On the contrary, there are many interpretive opportunities. The principal theme separates into two parts, a flourish and a stepwise line. Although Beethoven left no dynamic markings except for two indications of *pianissimo* in the second movement, the player can throw interpretive light on the two-part structure by means of dynamic contrast and punctuation between the two parts, making a conscious declaration of the significance of each that is typically Beethoven. Played *forte,* the flourish stands out like a front-page headline; the lyrical response, *piano,* like the lines of a calligrapher's art. In the extension of the lyrical phrase a few measures later—with its chromatically ascending line, the eighth rests, and the inactivity in the left hand—one can imagine a written cadenza, an opportunity for lingering before the rhythmic squareness of the ritornellos beginning in m. 15 (Ex. 13.10).

The second theme is fashioned after the second half of the principal theme. The change in subdivision from triplets to eighths has a calming effect on the tempo. The alternating of eighths and triplets continues throughout the movement, eighths always being associated with lyrical writing, similar to the contrast that was introduced at the beginning of the sonata. One might play triplet passages *forte,* those in

Ex. 13.10. Op. 49 No. 2, I, mm. 8–12.

duple subdivision *piano*, although with certain exceptions: A *crescendo* sounds right in the measures leading to the recapitulation, and the triplet scales beginning in m. 75, in the key of the subdominant, might be played *piano* to give the tonal digression a distinctive color (Ex. 13.11). The chord and triplets at the beginning of the development and again in m. 56, being related to the first measure of the movement and introducing a minor tonality in this otherwise exclusively major movement, would be convincing if played *forte*.

Ex. 13.11. Op. 49 No. 2, I, mm. 75–77.

The theme of the familiar second movement is also derived from the lyrical portion of the principal theme of the first movement. There is yet another parallel between the latter and the C-major section of the second movement (Ex. 13.12).

Ex. 13.12. Op. 49 No. 2, II, mm. 67–73.

Op. 54

One phrase may awaken a desire to learn a relatively long piece. It may be the elevated moment in the development of the first movement of the Schubert B♭

Sonata or a particular *maestoso* phrase in the last movement of the Schumann C-major Fantasie. In Op. 54, following the short cadenza with its fermatas and momentary *adagio,* the closing lines of the movement sum up all that has preceded. One would like to still this final musical image, for it is always over too soon.

The components of the coda include the long tonic pedal, the triplet subdivision in the left hand with its rhythmic quality of letting go against the duple subdivision in the right hand, the expiring of the harmonic movement in the four measures of F-major triad and three measures of diminished and dominant seventh harmony, and the melody, which has the freshness of a new idea although it is derived from the b-part (or final cadential segment) of the principal theme, moving predominantly in descending thirds.

On what events earlier in the movement does the coda look back? The principal theme is in bar form, a series of three cadences, two of them unstable harmonically and the third extended and definite. It is a peculiar melodic construction that begins by ending twice, and then ends by extending its beginning. It is a melodic line that stands still and then confirms that it intended to stand still. The tranquillity of the coda summarizes the quality of stillness of the opening phrases of the Tempo d'un Menuetto. One must emphasize, however, that the beginning of the sonata does exhibit movement, however quietly and with a halting, measured, ceremonial step. Because of the triplet pedal point, the coda simply flows.

The tonic pedal below yet another cadence and the repetition in the b-part of the theme beginning in m. 8 continue the calm of the opening of the movement (Ex. 13.13). The combination of these three qualities—the repetition, the pedal, and the cadential progression—in the coda communicates a character of daydreaming and nostalgia. The phrase beginning on the third beat of m. 12, again strongly cadential, is extended a full two measures. Repetition of phrases and melodic cells (the sequential thirds), extension, and harmonic attachment to the tonic do not make for staged conflict but are instead a contemplative manner that becomes more and more absorbed in its thoughts.

Ex. 13.13. Op. 54, I, mm. 8–10.

The triplet octaves are the unexpected interruption, almost thirty measures of disruptive, imitative hammering, *forte.* The music has turned aggressive and is seemingly going somewhere. After a page or more of these triplet octaves, how could the opening section be remembered as anything but peaceful? Melodically, the octave passage utilizes the sequential cell found in the opening section of the movement, except that now the thirds are filled in the passing tones. Like the first section, this episode is repetitive and exists by extension—imitation, sequential treatment, and inversion of parts—as though the music were running on out of control. Perhaps the metrical displacement of the two-beat segments, marked by *sforzandos* and producing 2/4 meter, represents an intent to harness the extension.

The path back to the opening section is marked with a tag derived from the thirds in the melody (Ex. 13.14). What is outwardly new is the same motive in a new role. In the remainder of the movement, the opening section returns twice, each time a varied reprise in which sixteenths in the upbeat become sixteenths throughout, the subdivision of the ornamentation becomes progressively smaller, and syncopated rhythms become even sixteenths. If the beginning of this movement is a face, pianists as painters have little difficulty reproducing its likeness; it is the thought behind the face in its changing expressions that remains elusive to the brush—an etherealizing of the musical material, leading to the cadenza and the memorable coda (Ex. 13.15).

Combining the triplet subdivision of the octaves with the duple subdivision of the melody line may be the most moving aspect of the coda. The triplets are the memory of their former selves, the *forte* triplet octaves, and for these shadows to be integrated with the reference to the principal theme is a musical reconciliation so touching that one is drawn to it over and over.

The musical character of the second movement is derived from the stuff of its opening thematic section: the steady sixteenths, the repetition of thematic segments and sequential patterns, broken sixths and thirds, and tonic and dominant pedals marked with accents. The form of the movement defies a neat analysis: A :||: De-

Ex. 13.14. Op. 54, I, mm. 3–4, 58, 62–65.

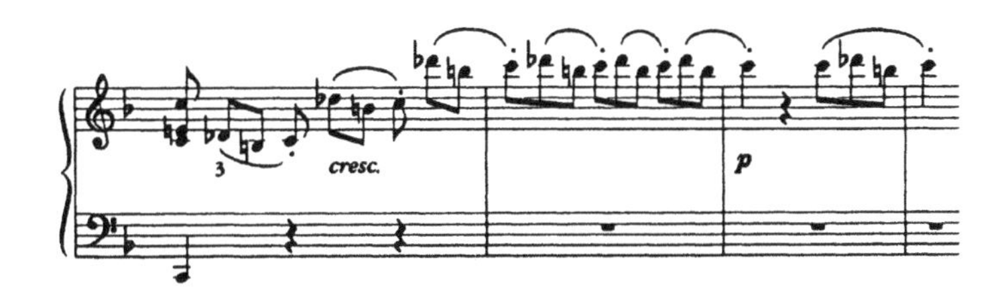

Ex. 13.15. Op. 54, I, mm. 73–74, 109–10, 87–89, 121–23, 123–25, 131–33.

velopment A Development :||: Coda. It is a discursive form that unfolds like a strip of paper the magician has torn in bits. There is no interruption in the sound throughout the movement, which seems to be made up as it goes.

How does a movement as incongruous as this support the unity of the sonata as a whole? Czerny describes the movement as "etude-like" and refers to its "intensifying effect."[1] The latter may be the reason for the long repeat. Postponing the climactic point gives it greater impact. Much depends on keeping the listener's attention from wandering and asking questions about what is going on. It might be difficult to come up with an answer.

Activity is relative, and, within the perpetual motion of the movement, dynamics, the pace of harmonic movement, and character beguile the listener's awareness of the constant patter of sixteenths. The *sfp* on the tonic and dominant in the theme diverts attention from the sixteenths. The rhythmic pattern ♬♬♩♩♩, which occurs only in the opening section and in the A-major statement beginning in m. 23 becomes more insistent in mm. 49–50: ♬♩ ♪♩♪♩ ♪ and mm. 55 and 59: ♫. ♬♩♪ ♩ ♪. In the reprise, m. 115, this tail of the theme on which melodic movement seems to stall is missing, because, as Czerny would say, the composer wants us to be aware of the intensifying effect of the onrushing sixteenths.

The marking *dolce* is found only in the first measure, in which a level of *piano* may be assumed. *Forte* and *sforzandos* set apart the chromatic sequences beginning in mm. 37 and 130, as do the *fortissimos* and *pianos* and the *sforzandos* placed on weaker beats in other sequences, such as those beginning in mm. 65 and 147, turning the even, ongoing sixteenths into a rough ride. The sequential passage just mentioned, which begins *piano* as far back as m. 134, is marked with a *crescendo, sforzandos,* and finally a *fortissimo* as it becomes more chromatic. The *piano* in m. 134 following a passage of harmonic tumult is similar to other instances in the movement in which the writing, following a dynamic intrusion, suddenly stands still, either through a sustained pitch or a repetitive pattern.

Ex. 13.16. Op. 54, II, mm. 45–46, 75–77, 152.

The two movements are related through the three-note figure, bracketed in Ex. 13.16 (a reappearance of the tag in Ex. 13.14), a rising bass in the theme of both the first and the second movements, and the considerable presence of pedal point. The melodic line of the first movement moves in broken thirds descending stepwise, that of the second movement in broken sixths ascending stepwise, the building material for a climactic conclusion to the sonata.

Op. 78

This sonata, written several years later, differs strikingly from the earlier sonatas in spirit and style.

The first movement is tranquil, naive, tender, devout, and to be played neither brilliantly or excitedly, for here also the effect must lie in the beauty of the tone and the evenness of touch. The triplets in the middle section [of the exposition] (from the 24th measure of the *Allegro*) are to be played especially lightly and delicately. . . .

This finale is rather difficult, because it is now and then uncomfortable. The character is humorous, in a joking way, and mischievous. The separated sixteenths are to be played quickly, almost like grace notes. The tempo very lively, and thereby the whole brilliant, on account of which touch and performance must be adapted for this effect. The piece in its entirety, in a secure and clever performance, has an original and interesting effect.[2]

More than the other two-movement sonatas, Op. 78 resembles a torso. The disparity between the two movements borders on the grotesque. One movement, partly because of the repetition, lasts longer in performance time than the first movement of several three-and four-movement sonatas; in fact, in the Schnabel recordings, it is about two minutes shorter than the first movement of Op. 106, while the second movement of Op. 78 takes about the same length of time as the second movement of Op. 106. For the most part, also, the first movement is one of long sung lines. The second movement is brief, a tumble of bits and pieces—as Beethoven was once described in one of his boisterous moods, completely "unbuttoned."

Beneath the velvety exterior of the first movement are two supporting pitches that emerge with a life of their own later in the movement. The Adagio begins on c♯, the melody line then ascending as octave and circling c♯ before coming to rest on that pitch under a fermata. The theme of the Allegro immediately approaches c♯ and, stopping midway on b, ends on c♯ in m. 8. The mind remembers these two pitches and their relationship as an ascending second (Ex. 13.17).

Ex. 13.17. Op. 78, I, mm. 4–8.

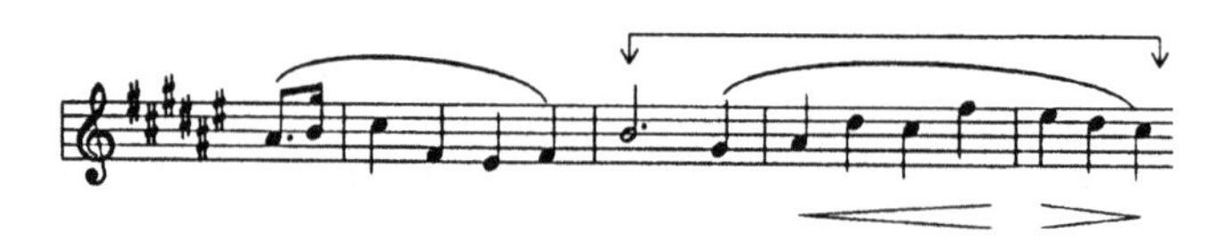

The open-ended principal theme is followed by a variation in which the ascending second gains prominence. The variation is set apart from the theme by the marking *leggiermente,* which can mean non legato, and, for that matter, the sixteenths *are* unslurred (Ex. 13.18). A *subito piano* marks the entrance of the second variation, which adopts the ascending three notes of the beginning of the theme and also ascending seconds (Ex. 13.19). The latter are implicit in the hesitating gesture preceding the fluent continuation in sixteenths (mm. 16–17). The point just described is a line of division in the exposition, the melodic direction previously having been generally ascending (due to the ascending second) and thereafter generally descending.

Ex. 13.18. Op. 78, I, mm. 8–12.

Ex. 13.19. Op. 78, I, mm. 13–18.

The motive that jarringly interrupts the graceful triplet line (Ex. 13.20) is the ascending second with a falling third appended. Although the articulation slur should be clear enough that one would not connect the d♯ to the b♯, knowledge of the ascending second building block provides the reason for articulating the figure clearly and, with the *sforzando*, with conviction. Possibly, also, these three notes have something to declare regarding direction, in that the up-down movement summarizes the general melodic directions of the exposition. Ascending movement is resumed unobtrusively in the chords at the close of the exposition, in which the fourth scalestep rises to the dominant (Ex. 13.21).

Ex. 13.20. Op. 78, I, mm. 31–32.

Ex. 13.21. Op. 78, I, mm. 36–38.

One is led to reflect about the balance of melodic direction in the theme

(Ex. 13.22). The grace of the movement is partly this quality of poise, enabling the player to think in terms of long lines extending over large sections. For example, the general direction of the melodic line throughout the development follows a descending harmonic sequence: D♯ minor–C♯ minor–B major. It is as though, with the descending scales, an accumulation of weight is dropped on the c♯ and e♯ unisons in m. 55, *ff*, all of which is frustrating to the muscles, which instinctively want more notes to support the dynamic level. Through the playing out of the formal plan, the recapitulation ends melodically on f♯ (m. 95), which is them "corrected" by dwelling on c♯ (Ex. 13.23).

Ex. 13.22. Op. 78, I, mm. 4–8.

Ex. 13.23. Op. 78, I, mm. 95–103.

Although we are not yet aware of it, the sharply articulated motive in mm. 31–32 (Ex. 13.20) is the thematic link between the two movements. The purpose of understanding what is happening in the music is not to lecture the listener or to demonstrate an interpretation. Knowing how Beethoven's mind worked in the moment of creation is to establish contact with the original source of comprehension. If only a half dozen persons in an audience understand the piece as well as the player, one must believe that a majority of the rest will sense the player's conviction and, regardless of whether they know why, may be moved by the experience and remember it. The working of Beethoven's intellect—that from a simple Ur-plan of two notes the composer was able to conceive two such dissimilar and complex musical characters—commands the most profound respect.

Many may find the clipped sixteenths, as recommended by Czerny, objectionable. However, not only should Czerny's proximity to Beethoven from his youth lend credence to his words, but the projection of character alone should convince one of the rightness of such a realization. To do otherwise is to rob the sonata of its originality and this movement of its wildness. The slurred sixteenths are only part of the untamed nature. Other features contribute to the peremptoriness: the short 2/4 measures, Allegro vivace; the very short motives that burst upon us, *forte;* the augmented sixth and diminished seventh harmony upon which the motive leaps out before our ears (Ex. 13.24); the diminution of the ascending second to sixteenths, alternating between the hands (Ex. 13.25); the movement back and forth between major and minor; the ungainly feel of mm. 65–69, with sudden shifts of compass and dynamic level (Ex. 13.26); the resolution of such passages on an augmented sixth chord, *fortissimo,* which is then extended for seventeen measures, preceding the final statement of the theme; the *sforzando* on c♯ beginning in m. 168 for the duration of five measures (Ex. 13.27); and the abrupt ending of the movement.

Ex. 13.24. Op. 78, II, mm. 1–6.

Ex. 13.25. Op. 78, II, mm. 22–23.

Ex. 13.26. Op. 78, II, mm. 67–69.

Ex. 13.27. Op. 78, II, mm. 168–73.

Op. 78 is a challenge to the elasticity of one's mind. It is music of the will—a song of the intellect that has its own peculiar expressiveness. In a sonata of such disparate qualities, a playing manner of unreserved exaggeration would seem to be appropriate.

Op. 90

Of the nine sonatas in a minor key, only Op. 10 No. 1, Op. 13, and Op. 111 begin in so impetuous a manner as Op. 90. The impact is immediate, leaving no time to consider consequences; from the first sounds, the situation is heatedly active. The first movement of Op. 90 is so plain-spoken that even a passage such as Ex. 13.28 sounds completely intelligible.

Ex. 13.28. Op. 90, I, mm. 104–108.

Yet, beneath the contest between brawn and tenderness is a piece that is meticulously thought out, to the point of explaining its own interpretation. If musical ideas that are derived from the opening theme are to be clear and compelling, the theme itself, from which these receive their significance, must be played with uncompromising clarity. The derived material indicates that Beethoven heard his opening theme as composed of individual segments, each capable of being developed into an individual character (Ex. 13.29). The upbeat segment "a" recurs as a full quarter (Ex. 13.30a) and as a tied note (Exx. 13.30b–e). Segment "b" is given a lyrical shape in Exx. 13.30d and 13.31a. The full theme occurs in extended form in the upbeat and descending scale in mm. 29–32 (Ex. 13.31b). In mm. 61–64 the upbeat is shortened to an eighth and slurred to the following note (Ex. 13.31c); the figure is rhythmically displaced and clearly broken off by a rest at the same point where the opening theme is articulated by a slur—another good reason for hearing the separation clearly when playing that theme.

Ex. 13.29. Op. 90, I, mm. 1–2.

Ex. 13.30. Op. 90, I: a. mm. 24–26; b. mm. 8–10; c. mm. 16–17; d. mm. 75–76; e. mm. 58–59.

Ex. 13.31. Op. 90, I: a. mm. 10–14; b. mm. 28–32; c. m. 61.

Following the measure-long preparation (m. 54) with repeated g's and the *ritard./dimin.* from *ff* to *p*, the descending line in mm. 55–67 (Ex. 13.32) sounds derived from segment "c." Beginning in m. 91, the one-measure segment "d" is repeated twelve times, counting the alteration in mm. 100–102. In the measures leading to the recapitulation, the segment extends over two measures, then one measure, then two quarter-note beats, and finally three eighth notes (Ex. 13.33). The use of stretto in addition to this rhythmic abbreviation further illustrates the intellectual intensity of the movement. The two-note segment "e" appears in mm. 45–50 (Ex. 13.34) as a rhythmic pattern ascending through four measures; the displacement of the beat adds to the forcefulness of the passage. Despite four measures of repetition, it continues to sound rhythmically awry, as though something we do not want to accept is being forced upon us. With the repeated eighth notes beginning in m. 51, one may hear the e–e♯ and the f♯–g as the same two-note segment "e" in diminution joined to the rhythm of the left hand.

Ex. 13.32. Op. 90, I, mm. 55–56.

Ex. 13.33. Op. 90, I, mm. 136–43.

Ex. 13.34. Op. 90, I, mm. 45–50.

By means of the many derivations, Beethoven placed the opening theme under magnification for the player, who is then obliged to hold the tempo in check to make details intelligible. To play this movement like a gigue, one beat per measure, is to deny life to the opposing qualities in the first eight bars: Although all four phrases are alike rhythmically, the second and fourth are not fragmented by rests and articulation. The latter end stepwise, the others with leaps. The first and third phrases are marked *f* and modulate; the answering phrases, *p*, confirm the new key.

The duality is maintained with few exceptions throughout the movement, *forte* writing being detached or fragmented and *piano* smooth and connected. Although this is not true in every instance, there are many supporting examples. The octaves beginning in m. 24 are marked *pp;* although the line is unslurred, it is not interrupted by rests. The two varied statements of the theme, beginning in mm. 28 and 32, respectively, and marked *f*, are unslurred; the third statement, marked *p* and beginning in m. 36, is slurred. The second theme beginning in m. 45 is distinguished by a *f* and rests, while the descending line in notes of full value is marked *p* and slurred. In the succeeding closing phrase, mm. 67–71, staccato eighths are marked *forte,* while the remaining three measures plus one beat are slurred and *piano.* At the peak of the development, marked *più forte* and *ff,* the sixteenths are unslurred (m. 132); when the idea is continued, *p,* the two voice lines are slurred.

Beethoven establishes at the very outset what the movement is about. Once established, the line between the impulsive and the restrained is kept absolutely clear, however complex the thematic development. Because he has defined the two characters so clearly through touch and dynamics, it was possible for him, in mm. 16–24, to indicate legato slurs *and* dynamic straining simultaneously to create a kind of resigned refrain. Although a *poco riten.* appears in the sketch for the end of the movement (Ex. 13.35), the player will notice that the marking does not appear in the finished score.

Ex. 13.35. Op. 90, I, sketch, from Nottebohm.[3]

From the standpoint of completeness, one may question how the listener can hear the work as cohesive if the action takes place at the beginning and is followed by a long period of relative peace. The best answer may be that the composure of the second movement is the resolution of the turmoil of the first. It is easy to hear that the two movements of Op. 90 are unlike, but it is more difficult to hear specific differences as part of a perspective lasting from the first measure of the sonata to the last. The two movements differ through

the intense minor of the opening chords, *forte* and detached, with g in the soprano versus the E-major opening, *piano* and legato, of the second movement, which clings to g♯;

immediate modulation to the relative major and dominant minor, compared with the closed, lyrical theme of the second movement;

a concise sonata-allegro versus an expansive rondo;

a quick tempo versus a marking of "not too fast";

the spasmodic continuity of the first movement, as opposed to the long lines* of the second;

variety in the piano writing of the first movement in contrast with a generally unchanging style in the flowing subdivision of sixteenths and triplets in the second.

*A propos these unbroken lines, a sketch for the theme included a rest that was later replaced by a note (Ex. 13.36). Since this strain occurs fifteen times throughout the course of the movement, the melodic gap might have become difficult to tolerate.

Ex. 13.36. Op. 90, II, sketch, from Nottebohm.[4]

Because of the uniformity of the writing, the tranquil character, the full and unvaried repetitions of the theme (except for the varied return beginning in m. 230 and the partial statement at the close of the movement), the second movement *sounds* its length. The balanced, suspended quality is a result also of mirroring of the voice lines (Ex. 13.37). In Exx. 13.37d and e and Ex. 13.38, repetitive and sequential imitation further stills harmonic motion, as does the pedal point (and the written trills on the dominant in Ex. 13.37b).

Ex. 13.37. Op. 90, II: a. mm. 8–16; b. mm. 41–48; c. mm. 60–64; d. mm. 221–24; e. mm. 271–76.

Ex. 13.38. Op. 90, II, mm. 265–71.

An important point of contrast between the movements is the shorter first movement with its wide emotional range versus the much longer second movement with its narrower affective field. The first movement generally is "imbalance" and the second "balance"—Schumann's Florestan, Eusebius, and Raro before the fact. The resigned balance that is so touching at the end of the first movement would seem to be the emotional link between the movements: a brief outward quiet turns into sustained inward peace. Moreover, the tempo direction, *Nicht zu geschwind,* supports the character difference between the g♯–f♯ melodic substance and its parallel, g–f♯, in the first movement (Ex. 13.39).

Ex. 13.39. Op. 90, I, m. 1; II, mm. 1–2.

There are more easily recognized links between the first movement and the rondo: The transition beginning in m. 32 of the rondo (Ex. 13.41) recalls the principal theme of the first movement, and, after the development, the return to the principal section of the rondo has an unyielding manner similar to the writing of mm. 104–107 in the development of the first movement (Ex. 13.41).

Ex. 13.40. Op. 90, II, mm. 32–36.

Ex. 13.41. Op. 90, II, mm. 136–37; I, m. 104.

Op. 90 has a spiritual affinity with Op. 111 that the other two-movement sonatas do not. Nevertheless, in its impulsiveness Op. 90 seems a more youthful piece, beginning, as it does, with an unmistakably clear statement. In the first movement of Op. 111 we only slowly learn where the piece is going and what it is going to say; in the later sonata it is as though the principal theme (which had appeared in a sketchbook some twenty years earlier) is being chiseled out of the melodic material of the Maestoso and finally laid bare at the opening of the Allegro.

The rondo of Op. 90, in spite of occasional thrusts outward, does not go significantly further afield than the innocence of its closed theme, whereas the Arietta of Op. 111 travels a long spiritual journey. One is a not unusual rondo, while the other is an unusual set of variations. The character of each individual movement has much to do with its meter. The quick 3/4 of Op. 90 (because the measures are shorter and events occur with greater insistence) sounds more impetuous than the fast 4/4 of Op. 111, and even sixteenths in duple meter pull forward more strongly than a slow triple meter with triple subdivision. While the rondo of Op. 90 always sounds very personal, much of the Arietta seems more "above it all" and impersonal in its sustained rocking and drifting.

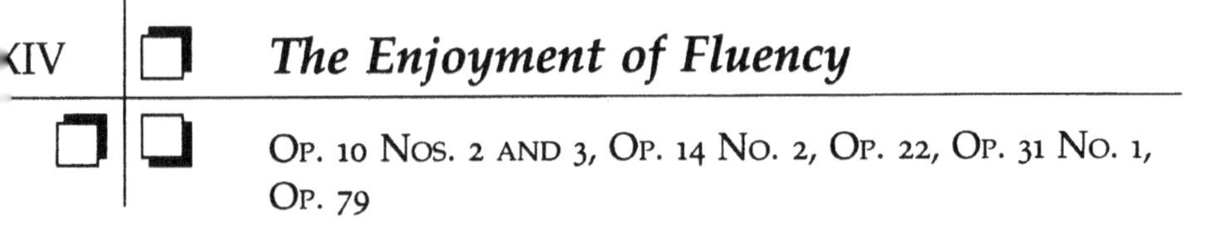

XIV The Enjoyment of Fluency

Op. 10 Nos. 2 and 3, Op. 14 No. 2, Op. 22, Op. 31 No. 1, Op. 79

Not every work from the pen of a Beethoven can be as profoundly moving as Op. 111 or as totally integrated as Op. 13. The appeal of the opening movement of each of the sonatas included in this grouping is not so much soul searching as the enjoyment of wit, brilliance, and imagination. The first movements of Op. 10 No. 3, Op. 22, and Op. 31 No. 1 are sleek, unhindered in their forward momentum; those of Op. 10 No. 2, Op. 14 No. 2, and Op. 79 are only of a somewhat less untroubled character. Yet, with the exception of Op. 14 No. 2, each has a second or middle movement of emotional depth, the *Largo e mesto* of Op. 10 No. 3 being one of the darkest soul-probing pieces of music Beethoven ever contributed to the pianists's repertoire.

Op. 10 No. 2

The first movement of Op. 10 No. 2 resembles a patchwork quilt. The opening theme itself joins two contrasting ideas, the first of which, a four-measure segment of melodic bits and pieces, is relatively insignificant as a theme. Its immediate purpose seems to be providing a beginning for the piece. The eight measures that follow introduce an extended arched melodic line that picks up the opening melodic third and adds a dynamic swell, syncopation, and appoggiaturas. Everything prior to the C-major theme beginning in m. 18 sounds exploratory.

Key relationships, some introduced by sudden modulations, also fit into a patchwork pattern. The half cadence on the mediant is followed immediately by the theme in C major, which progresses still further to G major, where it is confirmed by six measures of movement back and forth between dominant and tonic. By this time, the mind no longer hears G major as the dominant of the dominant of F, because the activity, length, and span of the C-major section, mm. 18–30, have convinced our ears that the opening bars of the sonata were introductory.

More abrupt is the change of mode from C major to C minor, *fortissimo,* in m. 41. The development, which begins with the cadential tag in A minor, then in D minor, followed by further working out in an array of keys, ends where it began, in D minor. Beginning the recapitulation in yet another key, D major, reestablishes the exploratory quality of the beginning of the movement. "Patchwork" also describes the seemingly capricious introduction of new keyboard figures that are just as capriciously dropped. The movement does not have a central dramatic point; instead it jumps from one idea to another with the agility of a comedian's mind, as well as a comedian's sense for timing and effect, caricature, and continuity.

As for the *sforzandos* in mm. 31–35 (Ex. 14.1), where the modulatory urge has gone beyond the dominant of the original key, the purpose of the accents on c, the expected tonic, may have been to weaken the impression of G major. Or, the purpose may simply have been bizarre willfulness. If the four-measure opening was not important as a theme *per se,* it does supply the rising third that appears in the lyrical portion of the theme (Ex. 14.2a), the third within the half cadence on the mediant (Ex. 14.2b), as well as the thirds in the C-major episode (Ex. 14.2c—kin to the lyrical portion of the principal theme, the accompaniment figure of which is also constructed of thirds), in the second C-major theme (Exx. 14.2d and e), and in the closing theme (Ex. 14.2f). The thread of continuity in the development lies in the three-note fragment and the etude-like laughter (Exx. 14.2g and h), with its recurring suspensions relating back to the appoggiaturas in the lyrical phrase in the principal theme.

As befits a sonata of this character, there is no slow movement, although the Allegretto is of a subdued nature. A long slur covers the wandering, circular movement of a melodic line that seems unable to find a stopping point. In contrast to the two-octave plus a third range of this line, the second phrase moves stepwise upward, as though hobbled with offbeat accents and clipped articulation. In response, the return of the first eight measures (mm. 16–38) is interrupted by a repeated two-

Ex. 14.1. Op. 10 No. 2, I, mm. 31–36.

Ex. 14.2. Op. 10 No. 2, I: a. mm. 4–12; b. mm. 16–17; c. mm. 18–20; d. mm. 38–41; e. m. 47; f. mm. 55–57; g. mm. 69–70; h. mm. 77–79.

note slur, marked *rinf.* Beethoven's indication of this dynamic with each of the two-note slurs suggests a relationship between this two-note slur and that in the middle section (Ex. 14.3). Compared with the short, one-measure slurs just mentioned, the repeated chords, lengthened slurred second, slower harmonic rhythm, and the *sforzandos* on offbeats in the left hand further slow the pace of the piece.

Ex. 14.3. Op. 10 No. 2, II, mm. 28, 38–42, 46–54, 70–74.

What effect does the subdivision in eighths introduced in the repetition of the A-section have on the movement as a whole? There are, in the Allegretto, two opposing intentions, long smooth lines and a crazed surface of short articulated groups and offbeat *sforzandos.* With the subdivision in eighths, Beethoven harnesses the uniqueness of both intentions, smoothing their dissimilarities without discarding the strangeness of the abnormal accents.

Czerny writes, concerning the Presto:

> In a fast tempo, this movement makes a brilliant effect if one brings out the theme clearly each time it appears. The *crescendo* must increase strongly up to the 14th measure, after which the following 8 measures are to be played very powerfully, and the remaining 10 measures again softly, throughout which the eighths in the left hand, however, must stand out expressive in their staccato. . . . [1]

The *crescendo* to which Czerny refers is not present in Urtext editions, nor, for that matter, did Beethoven indicate any dynamic level at the beginning of the movement. Of greater interest are the means of continuity by which the composer constructed a movement of this length from so little thematic material, an F-major triad broken into staccato eighths and concluding with a sixteenth-note tail.

The movement begins in a manner of a fugue, continuing by repetition of the subject, a vague suggestion of inversion (Ex. 14.4a), stretto (Ex. 14.4b), imitative writing (Ex. 14.4c), sequential writing (mm. 51–59, 77–80, 119–22), and double counterpoint in the first twenty measures of the recapitulation. In this nearly monothematic movement, newness is found in the tonal color of third relationships and change of mode modulation. The key of D major beginning in m. 69 is positioned just preceding the reprise, comparable to the reintroduction of the principal theme in D major at the reprise of the first movement.

Ex. 14.4. Op. 10 No. 2, III, mm. 23–24, 41–43, 51–53.

The patchwork organization, the spinning out of simple ideas, subtleties of timing, and the continuity of the incongruous make this sonata a piece of entertaining diversion, deepened by an interlude of yearning and inwardness.

Op. 10 No. 3

The Presto of the D-major Sonata resembles Op. 2 No. 2 in exploiting line and direction, but, unlike the latter, it moves forward almost exclusively in quarters and eighths. A dotted rhythm occurs only infrequently and then only as a dotted half note and quarter. The music is like a streamlined body whose movements are so efficient that it is able to move without effort, continuing, it seems, even through the measure of silence at the very end. The articulation slur within the theme (Ex. 14.5a) and the slur over the four-note figure (Ex. 14.5b) lighten the downbeat and promote acceleration.

Ex. 14.5. Op. 10 No. 3, I: a. m. 1; b. mm. 74–75; c. mm. 53–54; d. mm. 3–4; e. mm. 21–22; f. mm. 181–83.

Forward-moving energy occurs simultaneously with a suspended voice part in Ex. 14.5b. The appoggiatura in m. 53 (Ex. 14.5c and all similar instances) is to be played as an even eighth and not as a grace note, according to Czerny.[2] As for the reason the composer did not write even eighths—possibly the appoggiatura indicates a leaning on the first note similar to the first note of the theme, which, in effect, also begins with an appoggiatura.

The movement alternates between forward-pressing energy and standing still, both of which are present in the opening statement. Because of the quick tempo and the evenness of the subdivision, each of the five fermatas stands out as a question mark, heightening the expectation of something new in the offing. The first fermata, in m. 4, is followed by a winding descent using the opening four-note figure. The fermata in m. 22 (Ex. 14.5e)—preceded by an extended *crescendo,* a long ascending line, and *fortissimo* octaves broadened by quarter rests—establishes the dominant of a new tonal center and a new theme. If one regards the point weakened by the absence of the $f\sharp^3$, the single note should be added without hesitation.

The statement of the theme at the end of the exposition, unlike its other appearances, includes a *crescendo.* This, the third fermata in the movement, is followed by a new theme beginning a new section (the development) in a new key, without preparation. The fourth fermata in the movement stands over the dominant seventh at the end of the development, following six measures of the pitch g and four of dominant harmony, an accumulation of concentration that will be released into the appoggiatura in the principal theme.

One encounters numerous derivations throughout the movement. Ex. 14.6a is the four-note opening motive in augmentation. Ex. 14.6b is related by note value and the generally descending line; additional notes have been inserted, creating a criss-cross direction. This same passage would appear to lead to a new generation of descending figure, the closing theme (Ex. 14.6c), which in turn outlines a four-note pattern of three scale steps plus a leap, similar to a quarter-note figure two measures later (Ex. 14.6d). The filling in of a third reappears in the three-note segments in Ex. 14.6e and the ascending broken chords in Ex. 14.6f. The angularity of the new theme in B♭ at the beginning of the development (Ex. 14.6g) may have been derived from the closing theme.

Ex. 14.6. Op. 10 No. 3, I: a. mm. 40–45; b. mm. 87–93; c. mm. 105–109; d. mm. 114–17; e. mm. 31–34; f. mm. 333–35; g. mm. 133–37.

It would be difficult to conceive greater contrast than that between the confidence of the first movement and the dejected mien of the Largo. Schindler, if we may rely on his memory, in commenting on extramusical stimulus in Beethoven's thinking, claimed that for the composer, the Largo suggested through nuances of dynamic shading the mental state of a person in a deeply depressed mood.[3] Dynamics, whether sharply contrasted or nuances, establish immediate contact with the listener's attention and determine how one perceives harmony, melody, rhythm, and the piano writing itself. Here, the dynamic level suspends time, giving the listener an opportunity to react. One example is the measure of *portato* eighths following the turn to the subdominant in mm. 4 and 5 (Ex. 14.7a), another the rests and staccato chords, *piano,* in mm. 20–21, following the *forte* chords (Ex. 14.7b). A measure-long held note, *fp,* in m. 36 likewise allows time for the right hand to react to the dynamic and comment with filigree nothings (Ex. 14.7c).

The short swells in m. 6 (Ex. 14.7d) interact with the neighboring tone and appoggiatura, d♯; the repetition of the diminished seventh chord in this measure receives no stress. In the next measure, the muscular effort that the dynamics summon means that one not only hears but also feels anxiety in the ascent to the rolled diminished seventh. Through devices such as the *crescendo* to a *subito pianissimo* we enter, at the piano, into Beethoven's actual physical world of touch—in this case, the physical sensation of straining—and thus into his mind. "Playing with feeling," as we commonly use the term, is synonymous with being sensitive to physical feeling. This may be the ultimate "piano lesson," that the material instrument—wood, steel, felt, plastic—becomes the flesh-and-blood extension of the human body; on some miraculous meeting ground, one touches Beethoven's touch, as though clasping hands with the composer in life. Another analogy—though incom-

Ex. 14.7. Op. 10 No. 3, II: a. mm. 4–5; b. mm. 19–21; c. m. 36; d. mm. 6–9; e. mm. 9 (also 11, 12) 16–17; f. mm. 23–25; g. mm. 35–36; h. m. 43; i. mm. 68–70.

plete because the human factor is left out—would be comparing the score to a piano roll that, prefashioned, plays the piano, reproducing the same nuances of time that the manufacturer programed into it.

With the Alberti accompaniment in m. 9, the pace of the movement seems to increase; the *rinf.* (Ex. 14.7e) occurring three times in these eight measures underlines the modulation to C major. If the C-major cadence had concluded *forte,* the movement would have sounded at this point more predictable, in contrast to the thoughts of one trapped in a deeply depressed mood, which are unlikely to be predictable. Diminished seventh chords, those nowhere words in musical language, seem predictably to be underscored by a *sf, f, ffp,* or *ff,* as in mm. 7, 19, 23–24, 35, 37, 43, and 68–70 (Exx. 14.7f–i). In this sonata, only the slow movement begins on the downbeat; the thick darkness of its mood required a more weighty beginning.

The parallels between the outer movements are numerous enough to prove an intent to unify the sonata, perhaps because, with the presence of a slow movement of such great passion, it is difficult to conceive of the four movements as one dramatic unit. Like Op. 2 No. 2 and Op. 7, each of which also includes a slow movement of great passion, the emotional depth of the Largo overwhelms, if not the first movement, both movements that follow it. Our notion of "a Beethoven sonata" may be disturbed by what seems to be an absence of profundity in the final two movements. If so, we are in good company, considering Tomaschek's reaction, "It is not seldom that the unbiased listener is rudely awakened from his transport."[4]

Both the first movement and the Rondo begin with an upbeat that is slurred over the bar. (In the Menuetto, the upbeat is tied over the bar.) The ascending fragment (also spanning a fourth) with which the Rondo begins is similar to the descending tetrachord in the first movement, and the principal theme in each movement concludes with a fermata over the dominant. Important-sounding fermatas, all but one on or associated with the dominant, occur throughout the Rondo, much like the pauses interrupting the continuity of the first movement. The B♭ section beginning in m. 33, *fortissimo*, enters just as suddenly as the B♭ section in the development of the first movement.

The traditionalist of Beethoven's day might have observed that the sonata as a whole revealed an imagination that was too profligate, darting in new directions and leaving too suddenly what has only begun. The traditionalist in us becomes so occupied with playing the instrument that we are likely to miss even that point, preferring to honor a "masterpiece" with an outward perfection that is respectable, if also stale.

Op. 14 No. 2

In his *Über den richtigen Vortrag der sämtlichen Beethoven'schen Klavierwerke*, Czerny has relatively little to say about both the Op. 14 Sonatas, although these are works that he either heard Beethoven play or studied with the composer. The first movement of the G-major Sonata he describes as "charming and cheerful," and says that it should be played with delicacy and sensitivity, although in a lively tempo. He also points to the legato and *cantabile* quality of the closing theme, in which the bass and the middle voice deserve special attention, and to the powerful section in the development (mm. 81–98): "mit Feuer und Leben." Czerny calls attention to the *alla breve* of the second movement, suggesting it be played in a "rather lively Allegretto"; and he recommends that the staccato be very short, in order to set up the contrast with held notes. He says of the last movement only: "Very humorous and mischievous. Therefore to be played lively and with facility."[5]

Like many other Beethoven themes, the principal themes of Op. 14 No. 2 and of Op. 22 are fashioned from a triad, although here the likeness ceases. The opening movement of the B♭ Sonata is catapulted on energy created by a flick of the wrist. That of Op. 14 No. 2 is a curious, metrically ambiguous spreading out of a G-major triad. Only by dynamic shading toward and away from b can the listener be convinced that the last note of the broken chord in the right hand (and the first in the left hand) do *not* fall on a downbeat.

The steady sixteenth subdivision prevails throughout much of the movement. In only about two dozen measures is this replaced by thirty-seconds, eighths, or a cadence, not counting the passage in the development where triplets are combined with sixteenths. The beginning motive seems intended only to establish a procedure. The fluidity of the rhythm and the absence of rests and dramatic pauses produce a movement of a largely even-tempered character. As the sonata begins, the theme is ambiguous formally as well, sounding, if not like an actual introduction, at least introductory to the melodic line and even accompaniment figure beginning in m. 8. However convincing its reworking in the development, the theme includes incompatible elements that coexist in an eight-measure period: the intellectual beat versus the heard beat, and harmonic and rhythmic evenness followed by the syncopated, leap-prone line with which the period ends.

Beyond the rhythmic flow, other features establish procedure. The motive being a broken triad, thirds are a primary building block not only in the principal theme, but in the other important themes as well (Ex. 14.8). Another is the presence of passing appoggiaturas that approach triad tones from the half-step beneath. These appear in Ex. 14.8 as well as in the closing theme (Ex. 14.9), the bracket indicating the recurrence of the original motive. The thirds, chromatic passing tones, and appoggiaturas are factors in the suavity of the movement. In Ex. 14.9, the bracketed motive ends on the downbeat. In the development, this melodic tag ends similarly on the beat (Ex. 14.10). In the coda, which is virtually an abbreviation of the first eight measures of the movement, the same motive appears in the same metrical form, the way the ear wanted to hear it at the beginning (Ex. 14.11).

Ex. 14.8. Op. 14 No. 2, I, mm. 26–29, 36–41, 47–52.

Ex. 14.9. Op. 14 No. 2, I, mm. 52–57, 60–63.

Ex. 14.10. Op. 14 No. 2, I, mm. 67–68, 115–22.

Ex. 14.11. Op. 14 No. 2, I, mm. 187–90.

If rests (simultaneously, throughout the parts) were difficult to find in the first movement, the effect of the second movement depends on a background of silence. The contrast within the theme to be varied is not just between staccato and held notes, but also between staccato pitches that generally ascend and legato lines that generally descend. The dominant characteristic of each variation is related to a previous detail: the legato writing of the first variation to the four-part legato strain in the theme (Exx. 14.12a and b), the offbeat portato eighths in the second variation to the syncopated counterpoint in the first variation (Exx. 14.12b and c), and the broken-chord pattern in the third variation to the offbeat chords in the second (Exx. 14.12c and d).

Ex. 14.12. Op. 14 No. 2, II: a. mm. 8–12; b. mm. 20–22; c. mm. 40–42; d. mm. 65–66.

Did Beethoven intend the melodic line in the left hand (Ex. 14.12d) to remind one of the opening motive of the first movement? Did he intend that we hear the melodic twist in the Scherzo (Ex. 14.13) as another derivation of the same motive? If so, there are numerous occurrences to confirm the musical bond (Ex. 14.14). The measures within brackets (mm. 33–34, 37–38) do not conform completely to the pattern in the other examples but do include a chromatic lower appoggiatura. Finally, the themes of the outer movements are similar in being metrically ambiguous.

Ex. 14.13. Op. 14 No. 2, III, mm. 3–4.

Ex. 14.14. Op. 14 No. 2, III, mm. 21–22, 29–30, 33–34, 37–38, 70–73, 76–80, 89, 121–24, 131–38, 181–84, 252–54.

Op. 14 No. 2 is the only sonata of the thirty-two to conclude with a movement expressly titled Scherzo. This is not to say that, in other instances, the finale may not be a scherzo in spirit, as, for example, Op. 10 No. 1, Op. 31 No. 3, Op. 78, and Op. 79.

Op. 22

Consider how a movement with the stature of a sonata-allegro could be constructed out of an idea so brief it occupies less than two seconds of our attention.

The descending melody in mm. 4–7 of the first movement provides no thematic support; although it may sound like the actual theme, it is of no consequence in the movement, recurring only once in the parallel passage in the recapitulation. The opening figure is *manner*—the repetition of a broken B♭ triad releasing its energy like a coiled spring—of greater significance for continuity than the actual pitches. What the mind perceives is bursts of energy: out of something stationary, suddenly action, or, out of the infinitesimal, the creation of energy—the central point of Beethoven the developer.

In his *Death of the Soul,* William Barrett speaks of the difficulty of understanding the idea of energy separate from matter.

> But energy as we know it directly, in the flow of psychic energy in ourselves . . . waxes and wanes as this or that idea or event in our life charges us with energy or makes us droop in despondency.
> . . . Let us imagine a universe that would be the antithesis of the materialist picture of the world . . . . Instead of matter, we posit spirit as the ultimate stuff of the world, and instead of *atoms* we now have Leibnitzian *monads.* These monads are centers of energy in an energic universe.[6]

Thus this music seems always to begin once more in bursts of energy, one following the other: mm. 8–11, 11–13, 16–21†, 22–30*, 30–38*, 38–44*, 44–52*, 52–56*, 56–62, 62–66†. One could go on. In the development, these bursts occur in series of four-measure (mm. 81–89) and two-measure segments (mm. 89–104), followed by a calming of the excitement, leading to the reprise. The sequential repetitiveness of the development and especially the figure in Ex. 14.15 can be rationalized as "good music" only in the sense that harmonic progress is clear. It is the energy that this "music by the yard" generates that commands our attention.

Ex. 14.15. Op. 22, I, mm. 91–92.

Most of these episodic bursts ascend and descend. In those marked above with an asterisk, ascent exceeds descent in length. Comparison of these segments with others in which ascent and descent are of equal length (marked with a dagger) suggests that, in the former, thought and action are swept farther afield, while a more-balanced ascent and descent is associated with stability prior to another burst of energy. However, this does not always hold true; the sequence of two-measure segments in the development is engaged in a search for harmonic stability. By comparison, the four measures of octaves near the close of the exposition (mm. 62–66)—

two measures up, two measures down—are the epitome of the stability of the movement. It is not surprising that there should be no coda. When the movement has finished, it is finished.

Overall, the movement is as unproblematic as its opening material, calling to mind Beethoven's description of the sonata to his publisher, "Diese Sonate hat sich gewaschen."[7] The secondary themes of the movement, like the principal theme, are based on triads (Ex. 14.16). In Ex. 14.16b, the thirds are of course doubled in the left hand. Beginning in the middle of the measure and marked with *sforzandos*, the slur groups sound interruptive and impatient. The uniformity of the building material directs notice away from whatever individuality secondary themes may have and toward the common denominator of energy.

Ex. 14.16. Op. 22, I: a. mm. 22–23; b. mm. 30–36; c. mm. 56–58; d. mm. 62–66.

Doubt may be a valuable teacher. Who has not thought, playing the slow movement, that the beginning phrases of the second section (mm. 12–15) are harmonically redundant? The E♭ major triad has been repeated for nine beats of Adagio—*con molto espressione* ("very held back")—in the first measure of the piece, with the chords marked portato. Moreover, the second section has been preceded by an extended cadence in E♭. The question leads deeper into the nature of the opening idea. In discussing the repeated chords, Eric Blom first quotes Paul Bekker to the effect that the Adagio points toward the Romantic nocturne, adding that Chopin would have written a more "fluid" figure.

> As for Beethoven, the left-hand chords with which this movement opens are merely music that happened to be set down for the piano; they are not music necessarily imagined in pianistic terms. Beethoven did not say: "Here is a piano, let's write something for it," he said: "I must write this music: the piano will do very well for it."[8]

A comparison with opening measures of nocturnes by Field and Chopin illustrates the point (Ex. 14.17). The sounds in these examples have a magical, hypnotic quality, as though to draw us to a world of dreams and fantasy, a deception we accept. While the touch indication in the Beethoven adds a sensuousness and tenderness to the character of the Adagio, the repeated-chord accompaniment becomes a thematic partner, providing harmonic "columns" against which the weight of the appoggiaturas leans. The working out of this thematic partnership in the first half of the development is wrenching. The movement is no longer merely "beautiful"; miles of psychological distance separate the beginning and the development. The E♭ harmony in the beginning measures of the second section confirms the resolution that has taken place in mm. 11 and 12, a resolution in which the dominant seventh chords were marked with *sforzandos*. As in the first movement, there is no coda.

Ex. 14.17. Field, Nocturne in B♭ major; Chopin, Nocturne, Op. 27 No. 1.

The Menuetto and Minore combine the fluidity of the first movement with the passion of the Adagio. It is strange that the left-hand line in the first phrase should repeat the pattern of the principal theme of the first movement—if Beethoven consciously intended that (Ex. 14.18). Did he intend as well that the sixteenths in the melody line should be the figure found in the opening of the Adagio (Ex. 14.19)? Did he intend the melodic cell in the counterpoint in the Minore to be an inversion of the figure in Ex. 14.19 (Ex. 14.20)? Are we correct in being reminded of the first movement by patterns in Ex. 14.21?

Ex. 14.18. Op. 22, III, mm. 1–4.

Ex. 14.19. Op. 22, III, mm. 1–2.

Ex. 14.20. Op. 22, III, mm. 30–31.

Ex. 14.21. Op. 22, III, m. 7; III, mm. 8–10; I, m. 10; I, m. 21.

The Rondo is expansive, its "clinging" quality shown by Exx. 14.22–30.

1. The melodic line is, by and large, stepwise and often chromatic. Its chromaticism is associated with appoggiaturas, its shape often mirrors the contrapuntal line in the left hand, and its compass tends to shrink or to be drawn to a single note, f^2.

2. In a kinesthetic sense, inserting the afterbeat of the trill before the thirty-seconds is rhythmically difficult (Ex. 14.22). It has a slippery feel, regardless of how intently one tries to place it exactly where it belongs. Furthermore, the effect of the *sforzando* over the B♭ triad in mm. 18 and 20 is much like snatching an object that is about to slip away.

3. The written *tenuto* of the broken chords is muscular clinging (Ex. 14.23).

4. The melodic material in Ex. 14.24 is again stepwise, sometimes chromatic, and, most important for our argument, a series of suspensions.

5. The obsession with the opening motive in the imitative return to the principal section, mm. 40–49, involving stretto, rhythmic displacement, and written acceleration, seems appropriately described as "clinging."

6. The ritornello passage in the middle section of the movement, mm. 72–79 and 95–102, expands and contracts, in the manner of a rubber band (Ex. 14.25).

7. Phrasing precisely and giving equal importance to each voice keeps the player's fingers gripping the keys (Ex. 14.26).

8. The melodic line in the second return to the principal section, mm. 103–11, consists for five measures of three pitches (Ex. 14.27).

9. Playing legato sixths with the left hand gives the passage a clinging sensation, as does the passage of two legato voice parts in the same hand (Ex. 14.28).

10. The repetition of pitches in the triplet figure in Ex. 14.29 again produces the muscular sensation of clinging to the keys, as does a circling melodic line compressed within the range of a diminished fifth for the duration of two and one-half measures.

11. The *sforzandos,* the holding of common tones, and part writing in the final example require that notes be held full value. Harmonically, the passage also sounds constrained.

Ex. 14.22. Op. 22, IV, m. 19.

Ex. 14.23. Op. 22, IV, mm. 22–23, 32–33.

Ex. 14.24. Op. 22, IV, mm. 24–25, 30–32.

Ex. 14.25. Op. 22, IV, mm. 72–73.

Ex. 14.26. Op. 22, IV, mm. 88–89.

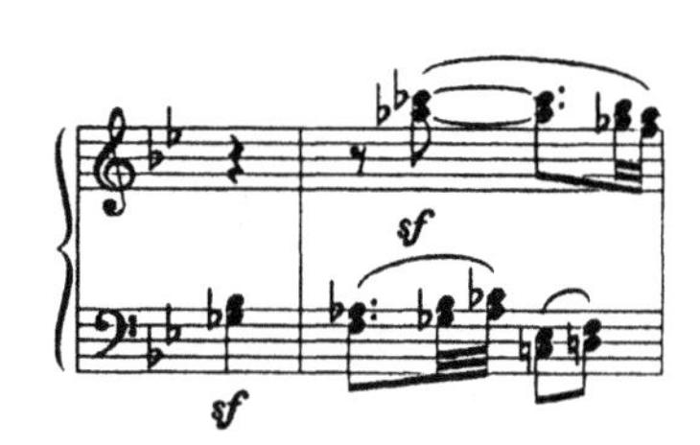

Ex. 14.27. Op. 22, IV, mm. 107–11.

Ex. 14.28. Op. 22, IV, mm. 112–18.

Ex. 14.29. Op. 22, IV, mm. 165–66, 168–71.

Ex. 14.30. Op. 22, IV, mm. 182–85.

Once more, the spirit within the score reaches the mind through physical sensation.

Op. 31 No. 1

Why should a sonata as exuberant and gratifying to the fingers as Op. 31 No. 1 not be played as often as the *Waldstein*? There are conspicuous harmonic and formal similarities between the two sonatas: The opening theme is immediately repeated a whole step lower, there is a pause on the dominant under a fermata, the second subject is placed in the mediant major key, and sequence is the process of continuity in the development. In the recapitulation, the second theme appears in the submediant major, then the submediant minor, before being stated in the tonic key, a procedure followed in the first movement of Op. 53 also. Op. 53 may sound more mysterious to the imagination, but also more distant in its grandeur. Quite the opposite, in Op. 31 No. 1 one is immediately aware of a vital presence in its short measures, short ideas, and the humor of the tied upbeat.

Each movement is unlike the other two, the first of a rhythmic and fluent nature, the second ornate (Czerny calls it a nocturne[9]), and the third lyrical and expansive, resembling Schubert. No movement seems to be motivically related to the others. The distinguishing mark of the principal theme of the first movement is its rhythmic snap, a musical quirk present in approximately one-third of the total measures in the movement. There is no "accompaniment" other than the single tonic triad, and the sixteenths outline a G-major chord. In the single-line writing the rhythmic snap stands out as the identifying mark of the movement. Even the second theme, its syncopation related to the principal theme, is primarily a rhythmic idea, not a sung line. If the rhythmic snap is a kind of joke, the running passages are the laughter.

As might be expected, the writing is generally uncomplicated: unison passages at the octave, with repeated chords, an octave, or a chord to define the main beats. The single complexity is one short imitative passage, mm. 93–95, which is repeated in the reprise. Anything beyond this would have stolen attention from the rhythmic character of the movement. Harmonically also, the music frequently continues in long extensions of single chords—six and seven measures of one harmony, uninterrupted, not being unusual. The second statement of the principal theme begins in F major and prolongs F-major harmony for seven measures. At the close of the exposition, fourteen measures are consumed in repeating the same harmonic/melodic pattern in B minor/major. Just prior to the reprise, play with dominant harmony is extended over thirty-one measures.

Concerning the principal theme, Czerny writes, "The chord in the bass must follow the held sixteenth very quickly and decisively." In his quotation of the theme, he places a staccato dot over the chord, at variance with the Henle edition but in agreement with the original edition, the Vienna Urtext, Bülow, Tovey, d'Albert, and Schnabel. The absence of the dot in Henle is corroborated in the Kinsky *Verzeichnis*,[10] so that the chord or single note is held its full value in each instance that the theme recurs. In the original edition, as in Henle, the quarter-note minor ninth in Ex. 14.31 lacks a staccato dot. The question is beneficially bothersome for the pianist, since merely having to make a decision is healthy. Hold the quarter its full value, and its release must be just as decisive as its attack. Playing the chord staccato isolates the held g♮ and the single line. The important factor is silence, or listening to silence. In any event, if the staccato quarter is not to sound musically unnatural, it can hardly be shorter than the duration of an eighth.

Ex. 14.31. Op. 31 No. 1, I, mm. 182–92.

Unlike the first movement, the 9/8 meter of the Adagio results in relatively long measures. This is only one factor in the spacious, unhurried nature of the piece. The "pizzicato" eighths provide a relaxed background. The trill is literally a spinning-out of the initial dotted half note. The dotted rhythm [rhythm figure] promotes lingering, for the thirty-second note needs time to sing. Appoggiaturas, fioraturas, and cadenzas require a stretchiness in the tempo, in order not to sound stiff or crowded. Because of its length, however, the spacious and unhurried tempo may become wearisome if the interpreter does not recognize differences that need subtle changes of pace.

The melodic line of the B-section, beginning in m. 16 (the movement being a rondo), is plain, compared with what has preceded, and the pizzicato accompaniment is replaced by a neighboring-tone figure (Ex. 14.32). Is this figure related to the trill in the theme? Should one let the tempo move ahead? In any event, the eighths do have the same function as the trill, namely, to sustain and control the shading of sound that would otherwise die away, much as the repeated g♮'s in the left hand in mm. 23–24.

Ex. 14.32. Op. 31 No. 1, II, mm. 16–17.

Although the C-section begins (m. 35) with what sounds like new material, the triadic descent of the melodic line and its accompaniment figure in contrary motion (Ex. 14.33) could well have been derived from the first measure of the theme. For a variety of reasons, the passage of repeated chords beginning in m. 41 passes for a variation of the principal theme: The repeated chords are marked staccato, like the staccato eighths of the broken chords in "A." The harmony alternates between tonic and dominant, and the descending sixteenths follow the melodic direction of the principal theme (Ex. 14.34).

Ex. 14.33. Op. 31 No. 1, II, mm. 36–37, 1–2.

Ex. 14.34. Op. 31 No. 1, II, mm. 42–43.

Although nuances of pacing are not indicated with tempo markings, one may assume that, whatever the pace of the B-section, the original tempo would be resumed in the first repetition of the theme in m. 27. Thereafter, would one move ahead with the onset of the sixteenth subdivision in m. 35? If so, there would be an opportunity for a spacious broadening in mm. 53–57, with the suspensions and dissonances.

Following the sixteenth-note subdivision of the C-section, the eighth note pizzicato is replaced by sixteenths in the next statement of the A-section. Even in the "B" that follows (m. 80), the sixteenth subdivision is continued (Ex. 14.35), and that subdivision is retained in much of the coda. The peace at the close of the movement has much to do with placing the theme in the left hand an octave lower than it has been heard previously (m. 108).

Ex. 14.35. Op. 31 No. 1, II, mm. 80–81, 86.

A sentence from Czerny's description of the finale reads, "The beautiful, very deeply felt melodic theme is to be played as *cantabile* as possible and the four-part harmony reproduced with a firmly held touch." The four-part writing is a factor in the rich sonority of the movement, at times filled in with additional chord tones (Ex. 14.36). The finale of Op. 31 No. 1 sounds suspended as a result of the extended use of pedal (tones) and the manner in which the opening phrase is draped between the dominant of the scale; in Op. 53 this effect is due to long (damper) pedals. Because of the latter, perhaps, and the *pianissimo* beginning, Op. 53 sounds the more peaceful and distant, Op. 31 the more contrapuntal and present. Fullness is effected also by frequent inversion of voice parts and by figures that reach outside an octave (Ex. 14.37). The sound of contrary motion between voice parts, as well as the contrapuntal writing in the middle section, also translates into greater sonority.

Ex. 14.36. Op. 31 No. 1, III, mm. 24–26.

Ex. 14.37. Op. 31 No. 1, III, mm. 31–33, 132–36.

The movement sounds filled out not only in this vertical sense, but also in the expansiveness of its form; there is little inclination to curb its branching out and flowering. As though a prediction of things to come, the opening theme is suspended on a double pedal point and begins with a half-measure upbeat. A pedal point of some sort is present in virtually two-thirds of the movement. The triplet subdivision that appears in the right hand of m. 17 is continuously present except for brief passages throughout the remainder of the movement, adding to the spun-out quality. In a way, the movement plays itself out, as though the musical surfeit led to a kind of exhaustion of possibilities. The final reprise, an improvisatory digression that arrests the flow of the movement with rests and with phrases marked *adagio*, followed by a *presto*, may have seemed in Beethoven's mind the only effective solution for bringing the movement to a conclusive, if also incongruous, close—after digression, a shocking digression.

Op. 79

For most, this sonatina's claim to immortality is probably its place among the "Thirty-Two," and a sonata cycle that omitted it would be incomplete. Tovey says, however, that its idioms resemble the style of Beethoven's third period;[11] this comment is interesting, since it is possible to hear in the theme of the first movement an inverted resemblance to the opening of the Eighth Symphony (Ex. 14.38). Both themes are twelve measures in length, an eight-measure phrase with a four-measure suffix. Both begin by clearly outlining the triad, and, although the respective melodic lines in the first two measures move in opposite directions, the fifth of the triad is the prominent pitch. In each, the fourth scale step is also important, although somewhat more so in the symphony theme. Neither theme contains a dotted rhythm.

Ex. 14.38. Op. 79, I, mm. 1–12; Eighth Symphony, I, mm. 1–12.

There is not one dotted rhythm in the whole first movement of the sonata, nor are there outward symptoms of inner conflict. Of the 201 measures in the first movement, almost exactly half consist of broken-chord figures, not counting those in the statements of the principal theme or tags derived from it, such as that shown in Ex. 14.39. Scale passages of any duration occur only within the second theme and its parallel passage. One of the main objectives of the movement, besides rhythmic fluency, is the exploiting of triadic color, resulting in moments of "musical daydreaming" (such as one hears in the Scherzo of Op. 106, the Arietta of Op. 111, and the first movement of the violin and piano Sonata, Op. 96) that are quite moving next to the vigorous thrust of the first measures of the principal theme. These passages are easily recognized: the twelve measures of broken chord beginning in m. 12 and the pedaled measures of tonic and dominant harmonies in the development, each marked *piano* and *dolce*. The clear contrast between these measures and those marked *forte* and containing *sforzandos* (either unpedaled or with change of pedal) is straightforwardly coloristic. The tonalities represented—E major, C major, C minor, E♭ major—include a third relationship and a change of mode, which are also devices of color. With respect to the predominance of color, the use of pedal point throughout the principal theme should be included, as well as the half-step appoggiaturas beginning in m. 184 (Ex. 14.40). A student's characterization of a Debussy etude as "a pallette and not a painting" would not be inappropriate for this movement.

The tonality of the second theme, beginning in m. 24, is ambiguous. Does it sound like A major or D major? In spite of the presence of the dominant seventh of D in mm. 26 and 30, the dominant seventh of A major appearing as a broken chord

Ex. 14.39. Op. 79, I, mm. 46–49.

Ex. 14.40. Op. 79, I, mm. 184–85, 188–89.

in mm. 20–23 establishes A major, as do the tonic-dominant statements of mm. 32–35. It is not until mm. 36–39, the closing or cadential section, that we feel ourselves securely in D major.

Although melodic lines are of lesser importance in the first movement, the duet in thirds and sixths, the dynamic swells, and the long phrases of the middle section of the second movement combine to give it the character of a song without words. The piano writing follows an ABA form, with the right hand duet in the outside sections and the single line melody in the middle section. In this respect, the movement resembles the Bagatelle Op. 126 No. 5, in which the left hand moves in thirds in the outside sections, in thirds in the right hand in the middle section. One is left unsure, in the left-hand broken chords (Ex. 14.41), which pitch is more important, the tonic or the dominant. Does the section begin with a pedal on b♭? Is the bass note in m. 17 g or e♭ (Ex. 14.41)? For a reason difficult to support, the particular pattern and spacing of the broken chord that produces this aural uncertainty has a "late" sound.

Ex. 14.41. Op. 79, II, mm. 10–12, 17–19.

It is an interesting coincidence, referring again to Tovey's comment, that the melodic line at the beginning of the last movement should outline the melodic line of the first phrase of Op. 109 (Ex. 14.42a). The movement can be heard as a bagatelle, as the haste of brevity. The first B-section is given no more than glance to the side; its effect is that of related ideas strung together: a single phrase ending with a half cadence, followed by a return to the A-section using the rhythmic/neighboring-tone cell of the principal theme, found also at the beginning of the B-section. The fact that this brief pattern is repeated on virtually each beat of the principal theme, that it is used as the melodic substance of transitions that return to the A-section and of the coda, and that it gains significance by being placed against a triplet accompaniment convinces the listener that this is a monothematic piece, another attribute suggestive of a bagatelle.

Ex. 14.42. Op. 79, III, mm. 1–4; Op. 109, I, mm. 1–4.

The "late" quality may be heard in widely spaced writing (Ex. 14.42b) and also in the sketchlike transparency of the writing, in which rhythmic combinations and quick register changes that are otherwise not difficult sound complex.

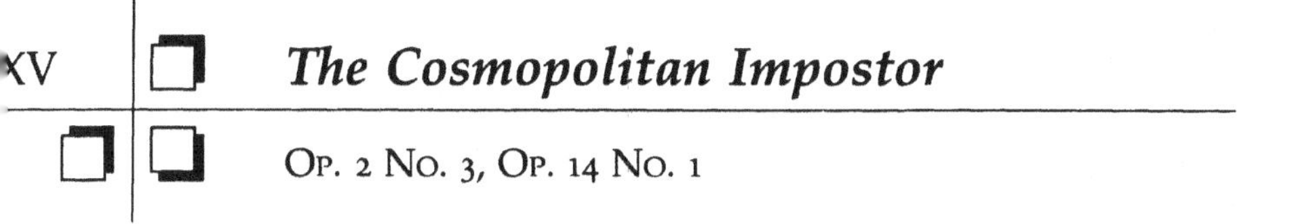

XV *The Cosmopolitan Impostor*

Op. 2 No. 3, Op. 14 No. 1

Throughout its existence, the keyboard has been the central meeting place for every genre of composition. It is the instrument of accompaniment, a chamber music partner, a concerto soloist, and the instrument for orchestral reductions. In a letter to Breitkopf & Härtel, dated July 13, 1802, Beethoven referred to the popularity of transcriptions as an "unnatural mania," saying that the piano and string instruments were so different from one another that the practice should be checked.[1] One wonders what he might have said about Liszt's transcriptions of his symphonies, in which form the piano became a cultural missionary, making the music accessible in places where there were no orchestras.

Thinking in choirs of instrumental sound and independent voice parts is central to Beethoven's keyboard style, just as an operatic vocal style emerges from the Mozart sonatas and the Chopin concertos. Op. 2 No. 3 has been chosen to group with Op. 14 No. 1, the only sonata Beethoven transcribed for strings, because its orchestral manner—in addition to a concerto-like cadenza in the first movement—is its most prominent characteristic.

Op. 2 No. 3

Four bars announce the method of construction of the first movement: Two bars, tonic to dominant, followed by two bars, dominant to tonic; the phrase closed and complete, symmetrical in form. There are four voice parts. The repeated lower-second neighboring tone produces the rhythmic energy of the theme.

The virtuoso in one's nature finds in the piece a brilliant, professional sonata, a brawny piece in which to pretend that the piano, played by ten fingers, is equal to an orchestra of sixty or seventy players. The piano has achieved its position by being an instrument of illusion. It cannot actually sing, yet we pretend to do just that in a Chopin nocturne. Every shade of dynamic produced by the hammer striking the strings is controlled solely by the speed of a key descent of 3/8 inch that may be effected by a pencil eraser as well as the tip of a finger. Yet with these simple movements we become each of the characters in *Carnaval,* suggest the sentiments of a sonnet by Petrarch, sense Brahms's brooding presence, see rockets burst in *Feu d'artifice,* or become an organist playing a Bach toccata in transcription. The C-major Sonata is a *bona fide* original composition for the piano, but a transcription nonetheless of a sound ideal that must be retranscribed by one's imagination when playing.

The principal factor in this orchestral transformation in the first movement is the blocklike construction, individual sections separated by dynamic plateaus (Ex. 15.1). Dynamic nuance is restricted to the second theme, the *calando* in mm. 107–108, and the *crescendo* in the bars preceding the six-four chord in m. 232. The *crescendo* in m. 228 is the sole instance in the entire sonata of either *crescendo* or *decrescendo,* although there are two such "signs" in the slow movement, plus another *calando* in the finale. The orchestral sound ideal reveals itself also in the consistency of voice parts within individual sections, the cadenza, the separation of lines through differing articulation, and the placing of *sforzandos* on inner notes (Ex. 15.2).

In its episodic organization, in which each section—like the principal theme itself—is closed, and in its assertiveness the music has an authoritative character. Through its size, the movement aspires to be equal in stature to a symphony or concerto without necessarily having big thematic ideas. By comparison, the first movement of Op. 31 No. 2, which sounds bare in notes, communicates ideas that are huge in an interpretive sense; and the first movement of Op. 110, which is just the opposite of Op. 2 No. 3 in outward activity, extends across inner distances for which no measurement exists. The sonata is not totally lacking in sophistication, for the four movements are linked motivically (Ex. 15.3), although the similarity is one of pattern rather than of interpretive content, as in Op. 110. In the first movement, new ideas, each well crafted and similar to its fellows, are introduced, one after another, like athletes at a sports banquet who have in common their physically fit bodies and untroubled personalities.

For the pianist, the realization of the orchestral style raises a question regarding dynamics. Because gradualism in the handling of sonority is natural to the instrument, one cannot fault the player who prefers to believe that *crescendo* or *decrescendo* is implied in going from one indicated dynamic level to another. Nevertheless, a *fortissimo* meant to sound like an orchestral *tutti* on the piano ought to be unreservedly purposeful, so that the *effect* will sound greater than the actual difference in

Ex. 15.1. Op. 2 No. 3, I, mm. 25–27, 44–45, 76–79, 112–13, 138–39.

Ex. 15.2. Op. 2 No. 3, I, mm. 69–70, 129.

sonority possible on the piano. For this reason, the episodic and orchestral nature of the piece seems best realized by observing *subito* dynamics, as Beethoven's markings in this sonata indicate.

The choice of E major as the key of the Adagio (like the deceptive resolution on an A♭ chord in m. 218 of the first movement, a third relationship to C major) takes the listener in an instant to a large area of new key color with the suddenness of orchestrating winds after strings. In mm. 53–54 the third relationship and the manner of an orchestral *tutti* are coordinated to produce just such an instantaneous newness. The theme of the Adagio, like the principal theme of the first movement, is in four voice parts, as though written for string quartet. In spite of this "extrapi-

Ex. 15.3. Op. 2 No. 3, I, mm. 1–2, 47–48, 77–79; II, mm. 1, 11, 19; III, m. 1; IV, mm. 1, 119–21, 175.

anistic" connotation, the movement offers considerable opportunity to paint with the sound of the instrument. One reason almost too obvious to mention is that this is a *slow* movement. The most inviting opportunity is offered by the E-minor section, with its hazy atmosphere created by the broken-chord accompaniment and the neighboring tone. The half-step appoggiaturas in the left hand beginning in m. 19 are as coloristic as the accompaniment figure. Neither the dreaminess of the prolongation of dominant harmony preceding the return nor the expansiveness of the last reprise of the E-major theme, beginning in m. 67, is to be found in the first movement. In this manner, the Adagio engages the dual capacity of the piano, one section a literal transcription and the alternating section utilizing color devices nearer the soul of the instrument.

Through imitation, the energy of the neighboring tone permeates the Scherzo. If the short slur over the upbeat of three eighth notes is extended over the bar, the effect is merely facile; if, on the other hand, the upbeat is separated from the staccato quarter over the bar, as the articulation slur indicates, the tempo can be controlled more effectively and the impetus of the downbeat released. In spite of the quick tempo, the separation can be guaranteed by using the same finger over the bar (Ex. 15.4). Like the articulation, the accented quarter-note upbeat in m. 29 also has a braking effect (Ex. 15.5).

Ex. 15.4. Op. 2 No. 3, III, mm. 1–3.

Ex. 15.5. Op. 2 No. 3, III, mm. 28–30.

Among the early sonatas having a large-scale, brilliant opening movement—Op. 2 No. 2, Op. 7, Op. 10 No. 3, and Op. 22—only Op. 2 No. 3 concludes with a brilliant, sonorous finale; this is not surprising, in view of the conventional manner in which the piece has unfolded. The theme (comprising symmetrical phrases, tonic to dominant and dominant to tonic, like the first movement) receives its initial impulse of energy from the neighboring tone (Ex. 15.6), as does the semi-sequential sixteenth-note group (Ex. 15.7) and the descending sequence (Ex. 15.8). In each instance, the energy is derived from a half step. The phrase shown in Ex. 15.9 also begins with a stressed half step.

The parallel sixth chords in the theme become the pattern for much that follows. There are passages of unison writing of considerable length (Ex. 15.8 and its parallel passage). Ex. 15.9 is a kind of reinforced unison writing, in addition to which there

Ex. 15.6. Op. 2 No. 3, IV, m. 1.

Ex. 15.7. Op. 2 No. 3, IV, m. 9.

Ex. 15.8. Op. 2 No. 3, IV, mm. 45–46.

Ex. 15.9. Op. 2 No. 3, IV, mm. 119–21.

are numerous passages of parallel motion (Ex. 15.10). The particular appeal of the F-major theme (beginning in m. 103) lies in part in moving in longer note values. Its motion contrary to whatever the other hand is playing distances it further from the principal theme and contributes to its individuality. The reason the ritornello (Ex. 15.9) sounds disruptive is not solely the *sforzandos*; again, part of the reason is the reinstatement of parallel motion—a reminder that it is impossible to play a Beethoven sonata meaningfully without thinking.

Ex. 15.10. Op. 2 No. 3, IV, mm. 65–66, 269–70.

"Unison" being duplication, the equivalency of these types of writing to the spun-out, uncomplicated character of the finale is easy to understand. The finale is not the type of piece in which individual measures are crowded with musical events; quite the opposite, one such event soars over broad expanses of many measures and then repeats itself. The result is an uncomplicated piece in which the pleasure of playing is one we share with the gymnast.

Op. 14 No. 1

In his letter to Breitkopf & Härtel complaining about the "mania" for transcriptions, Beethoven maintains that only the composer or someone with "the same *skill and inventiveness*" would be equal to the challenge, because there would be not only alterations but also omissions and additions to the original material. "I have arranged only one of my sonatas for string quartet. . . ."[2] That sonata was Op. 14

No. 1, published as a string quartet earlier that same year of 1802. The sonata itself sounds like a string quartet—little wonder, for Nottebohm tells us:

> If one fixes one's gaze upon separate places in the sketched piece, it can appear questionable whether it was conceived for piano or for more instruments. Beethoven later set the sonata for four string instruments, and it is not impossible that such an application was being considered in the conception of the piece.[3]

The fact that the piano is a touching imposter makes it an interesting instrument; hence a comparison of the solo sonata and the quartet version ought to benefit the pianist. Throughout their history keyboard instruments have absorbed the sounds of other media and of the natural world. If the pianist ignores this rich heritage, the instrument remains just a piano. The difference in sound production between piano and strings is obvious—between striking and rubbing and between decay and controlled continuation of sound. C. P. E. Bach wrote that there are many things in music that cannot be fully heard but must be imagined.[4] Ideally, the possible range of timbres is limited only by the pianist's imagination. The imagined range of timbres must always be wider than what is actually possible on the instrument.

The first discovery in comparing the two versions of Op. 14 No. 1 is that the writing in the sonata, for the most part, consists of a set number of voice parts that matches the parts in the score of the quartet. The pianist, with ten fingers, is expected to reproduce not just the number of notes (in itself not a great feat in quartet writing) but the sum of the intensity of four individual players. The pianist's aural concentration must match the aural concentration of four individuals. Thus, the first benefit from comparing sonata and quartet is the exercise of the ability to hear, think, and play linearly as well as horizontally, an ability that represents a major plateau in becoming a musician at the piano.

Following Nottebohm's conclusion that the quartet was the original medium the composer had in mind, the sonata should be considered a transcription of the quartet, an approach far more helpful to the pianist. The following differences in dynamics occur in the quartet:

I:

m. 3, *crescendo*, ending as a *sforzando* on the downbeat of m. 4;

mm. 7 and 8, *fp* on the whole note in the bass;

m. 10, *crescendo* to a *piano* on the first beat of m. 11, duplicated in mm. 12–13;

mm. 16–20, *sforzando* on the third beat of each measure; no indication of *piano* within these measures;

m. 21, *ff* on the third beat;

m. 40, fourth beat, *crescendo* to a *piano* on the first beat of m. 42, duplicated in mm. 44–46;

m. 51, *sforzando* on the first beat;

m. 53, *p* on the eighth note following the *sforzando* on the first beat;

mm. 59–60, *crescendo* to *piano* on the downbeat of m. 61;

m. 65, *fp* on the first beat; likewise in mm. 67, 69, 75, and 77;
mm. 69–70, no *crescendo;*
m. 71, no *piano, crescendo* throughout the measure;
m. 75, *fp* instead of *piano;*
m. 77, *fp* instead of *pianissimo;*
m. 80, *sforzando* missing;
m. 81, *piano* on the first beat;
mm. 85–86, *crescendo* from *piano* to *pianissimo* on the first beat of m. 87;
mm. 89–90, *crescendo* instead of *decrescendo;*
m. 91 (recapitulation) *piano* on the first beat, *sforzando* on the third beat, duplicated in the next measure;
m. 150, *crescendo;*
m. 155, *pianissimo;*
m. 157, *crescendo;*
mm. 158–60, *sforzando* on the third beat of each measure;
m. 161, *piano* for two beats, then *pianissimo.*

II:
m. 2, *crescendo* to *sfp* at the beginning of m. 3;
mm. 9–10, *crescendo* to *sforzando* in m. 11, followed by *decrescendo* in mm. 11–12, ending with *piano* at the beginning of m. 13;
m. 29, *crescendo;*
m. 31, *decrescendo* to *piano* on the fermata in m. 32;
m. 47, *sforzando* on the second beat;
m. 49, *piano* beginning on the second beat;
mm. 52 and 54, *sforzando* on the first beat (first violin and cello) and on the second beat (second violin and viola);
m. 62, *crescendo* lacking;
mm. 77–78, *crescendo* to *piano* at the beginning of m. 79;
m. 97, *crescendo,* instead of *decrescendo,* to *piano* in m. 99.

III:
m. 4, *sforzando* on the downbeat, *piano* beginning on the second beat (¢), duplicated in m. 12;
mm. 18–19, *sforzando* on the second beat of each measure;
m. 29, instead of *decrescendo, crescendo* to *piano* on the first beat of m. 30;
mm. 42–45, *sforzando* on the second beat, in addition to those on the first beat and the second half of the first beat;
m. 75, *pianissimo* on the first beat;
mm. 76–79, *sforzando* on the second half of the first beat;
m. 82, *forte* (no *decrescendo*);
m. 106, *crescendo* to *pianissimo* on the fermata in m. 108;

m. 112, *forte*, instead of *fortissimo*;
m. 119, *decrescendo* beginning on the second beat;
mm. 128–29, *sforzando* on the second beat;
m. 130, *fortissimo*.

This summary illustrates that Beethoven's piano writing, when compared with his writing for strings, exhibited the unique qualities of the piano, compensated for its limitations, or avoided potentially unmusical results. For example, in the first movement, the *sforzando* in m. 4 in the quartet would merely protrude on the piano, disrupting the smoothness of the line, even if one added < and > respectively, as did Czerny.[5] A *sforzando* in the strings could be more easily made an accent of quality (Ex. 15.11). As an example of compensation, pedaling the appoggiatura broken chord in m. 8 and then releasing the pedal on the whole note b produces the effect of an *fp* (Ex. 15.12). As another example of compensation, quartet writing offers contrast of timbre in the exchange of parts, as in mm. 16–22. Since this is possible on the piano only through exaggerated voicing, Beethoven chose, in the sonata, to alternate *forte* and *piano* phrases. Furthermore, the *forte* phrases in the sonata are supported with more notes than is the parallel phrase in the quartet (Ex. 15.13).

Ex. 15.11. Op. 14 No. 1, I, mm. 3–4.

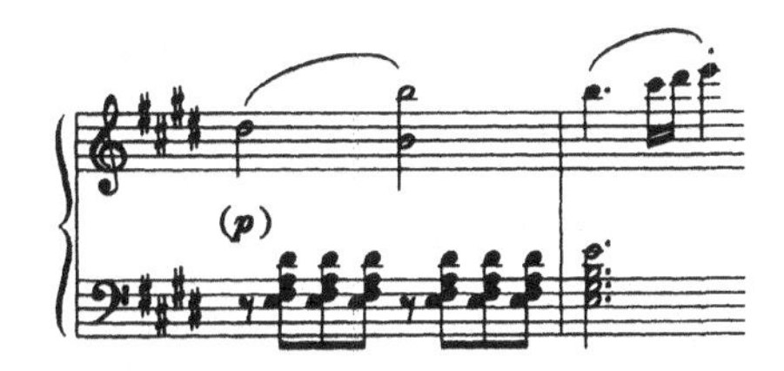

Ex. 15.12. Op. 14 No. 1, I, m. 8.

Ex. 15.13. Op. 14 No. 1, I, mm. 18–20.

In mm. 40–42, given the decay of piano sound, the peak of the melodic line would have been lost if a *subito piano* had been placed under the octave e^2–e^3, as in the quartet (Ex. 15.14). In mm. 50–55, the *crescendo* in the sonata is carefully measured, accounting for the absence of an *sf* on the first beat of m. 51; in mm. 54–55, the

Ex. 15.14. Op. 14 No. 1, I, mm. 40–42.

piano is again given dense chords to match the intensity of the strings (Ex. 15.15). In the quartet, the *piano* on the eighth note in m. 53 sets off the strength of the preceding *sforzando* (Ex. 15.16).

Ex. 15.15. Op. 14 No. 1, I, mm. 51, 53–55.

Ex. 15.16. Op. 14 No. 1, I, m. 53.

The *crescendo* in mm. 59–60 of the quartet may have been intended to parallel the *crescendo* in mm. 89–90, leading into the recapitulation. In the development, the repeated sixteenths replacing the broken chords in the sonata would, alone, have sounded tedious. The added broken-chord cello line achieves the forward movement of the repeated broken chords in the sonata (Ex. 15.17). A percussive accent in the sonata on the first beats of mm. 65, 67, 69, 75, and 77, like the *fp* in the quartet, would draw attention away from the ongoing line; the stress is saved for two high pitches in this line (Ex. 15.18). In Ex. 15.19, the lines and the dynamics are straightforward in the sonata. Again, the *sforzandos* would easily sound forced on the piano, changing the character of the movement, making it more impulsive and aggressive.

Ex. 15.17. Op. 14 No. 1, I, mm. 65–66.

Ex. 15.18. Op. 14 No. 1, I, mm. 73–75, 79–81.

Ex. 15.19. Op. 14 No. 1, I, mm. 89–92.

In the quartet, Beethoven's dynamic indications in the measures leading to and at the reprise are the reverse of those found in the sonata. At the point of reprise, the element of newness is startling in either version. Perhaps, the piano being a percussive instrument, Beethoven considered *forte* at the return of the principal theme more convincing and, likewise, a *crescendo* over the preceding single half notes less practical. The same half-note chords in the quartet would have been effective either *crescendo* or *decrescendo.* However, within a level of *piano,* the sixteenths in the three lower strings project more clearly, not to mention the stronger effect of the *sforzandos.* At the end of the movement, the *sforzandos* indicated over full chords in the strings are more effectively realized than such accents would be with the single notes in the sonata (Ex. 15.20).

Ex. 15.20. Op. 14 No. 1, I, mm. 158–60.

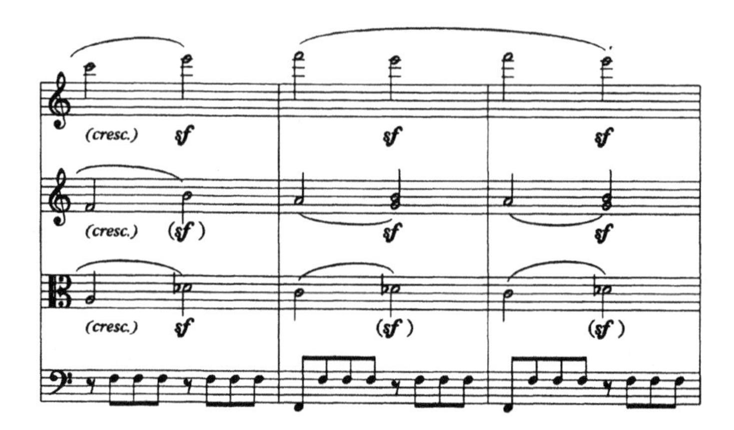

The difference in the articulation of the theme of the second movement in the strings may have been due to a desire to make the rhythmic pattern more vital (Ex. 15.21). As mentioned in a previous example, the presence of *sforzandos* in the quartet and not in the sonata may have indicated a desire for an accent in quality (Ex. 15.22). This is not to say that such an accent is not possible on the piano, but one must consider here the number of accents in the string version in mm. 45–58. On the piano (where Beethoven saves *the sforzandos* for mm. 57–58) such a cluster of *sforzandos* might distort the passage, covering its substance with an effect. In m. 62 Beethoven asks the pianist to imagine a crescendo throughout a held note (Ex. 15.23), an indication lacking in the quartet. However, in mm. 97–100 and 109–12 the dynamics follow the natural capacities of the piano and the strings respectively (Ex. 15.24)—an indication that Beethoven used the pianistically impossible marking sparingly.

Beethoven's realization of the theme of the finale on the piano is another lesson in the virtue of clarity. The descending thirds in the viola and second violin are reproduced by the broken chords in the sonata. In the strings, where a triplet figure would be less distinct, the contrast of staccato and held offbeats preserves clarity. The triplets in the piano naturally sound more distinct, if pedaled sparingly (Ex. 15.25). Clarity was also Beethoven's intent when realizing the imitative passage beginning in m. 14 on the piano. In the sonata, two voices appear, giving the listener only the essentials (Ex. 15.26).

Ex. 15.21. Op. 14 No. 1, II, mm. 1–3.

Ex. 15.22. Op. 14 No. 1, II, mm. 45–59.

Ex. 15.23. Op. 14 No. 1, II, m. 62.

Ex. 15.24. Op. 14 No. 1, II, mm. 97–100, 109–12.

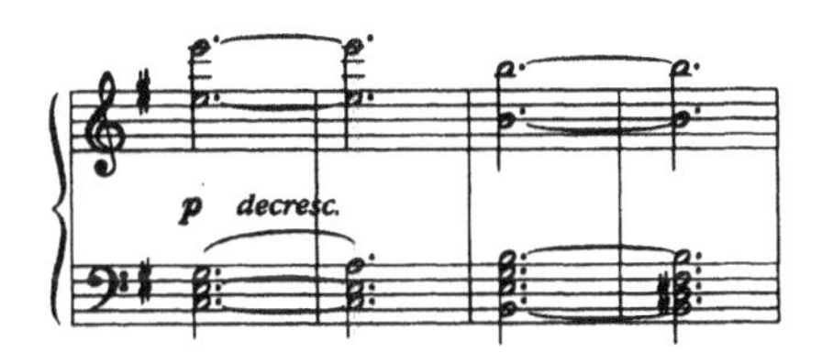

There are a number of examples of *sforzandos* in the third movement of the quartet that are not indicated in the sonata. These include the close of the first half of the principal theme (m. 4), the transition to the B-section (mm. 18–19), and passages toward the end of the G-major section (A♭ major in the quartet, mm. 76–79). These indicate, on one hand, that accent as emphasis in general was Beethoven's natural manner of musical speech, but on the other, that a string *sforzando* has a different effect and that the composer's sensitivity prevented unnecessary roughness. What would have become commonplace jabbing and pounding on the piano, without any musical purpose, was simply avoided.

The *fortissimo* in Ex. 15.27 from the sonata can be understood on two levels, the more immediate being a symbol of Beethoven's temperament, the other as the wisdom of craft: the most effective way to realize the fullness of sound in the *forte* triplet octaves of the quartet.

Ex. 15.25. Op. 14 No. 1, III, mm. 1–4.

Ex. 15.26. Op. 14 No. 1, III, mm. 15–18.

Ex. 15.27. Op. 14 No. 1, III, mm. 112–13.

Little has been said about the music itself, specifically, its germ motive, an interval of a rising fourth or a descending fifth, either filled in or an open leap (Ex. 15.28).

In the central part of the development, mm. 65–81, the stepwise motion and the presence of the germ interval may lead one's ears to believe that the episode is really a working-out of the second theme, mm. 22–30. The same use of fourths and fifths occurs in the finale (Ex. 15.29), and there is a likeness of shape and melodic direction between these phrases in the outer movements (Ex. 15.30).

Ex. 15.28. Op. 14 No. 1, I, mm. 1–4, 5, 16–18, 22–23, 38–39, 46–47, 65–67, 71–75, 80–81.

Ex. 15.29. Op. 14 No. 1, III, mm. 1–4, 121–24.

Ex. 15.30. Op. 14 No. 1, I, mm. 8–10; III, mm. 12–14.

Czerny's prose reveals his balanced manner of thinking:

> This movement [first] is of a serene, noble character and is to be executed in a lively but comfortable manner. The middle section (from the 23rd bar) must be played ex-

pressively and certainly not dragging, in which case it would sound somewhat empty. The melody line that follows (from the 49th bar) very delicately and harmoniously. [Czerny's term *harmonios* may be interpreted as a totality of sonority produced by the pedal.]

The character of this scherzo [second movement] is a sort of angry mood, and therefore it must be played in a serious but lively fashion, however in no way humorous or mischievous.

In contrast, the Trio (C major) is gently calming, and the performance in like manner.

Very lively and happy [the Rondo], but with a certain frivolous ease. The middle section (in G major) very brilliant and powerful, through which the top notes in the right hand are to be well marked.[6]

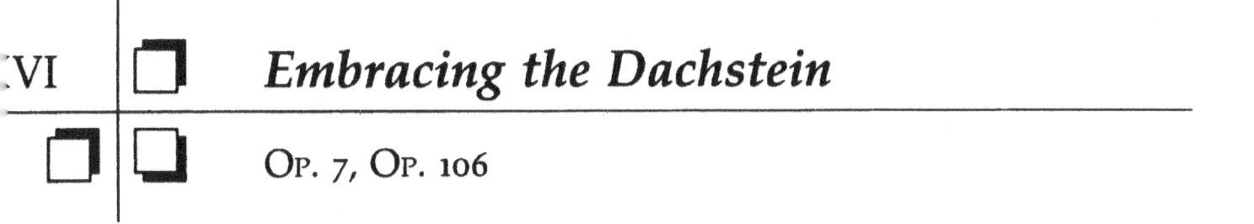

VI Embracing the Dachstein

Op. 7, Op. 106

Op. 7 and Op. 106 would not seem to have much in common, one sonata from the early years of Beethoven's creative life and the other from his last decade. What the two share is a breadth of conception and, aside from the Op. 106 Adagio, a spirit of assertiveness that overflows their many bars. The earlier work is perhaps the less self-assured of the two, lacking the cerebral armor of Beethoven's maturity. Nonetheless, each is colossal in its own way, peculiar to the time of life in which it was written.

Op. 7

With the exception of the *Hammerklavier,* the E♭ Sonata is Beethoven's longest piano sonata. However, length calculated in minutes has little meaning for the imagination, which tells time by a different clock, on whose face the hours are marked by sensations and impressions. Op. 2 No. 3 might seem to be longer because each movement is equally imposing, or Op. 111, because its philosophical answer sums up a lifetime of thought.

The first movement of Op. 7 is more unified than that of Op. 2 No. 3. It develops one character and was, as Czerny wrote, conceived in a passionate state of mind.[1] Clues in the first four measures define its character: 1. an Allegro molto in 6/8, seemingly swifter than duple subdivision; 2. repeated eighth notes; 3. a dynamic marking of *piano*, interrupted only by the *sforzando* on the E♭ chord in m. 3; and 4. unslurred tonic chords, making the passage harmonically stationary.

Because of the static harmony and the plainness of the melody line, the listener's attention is drawn to the unthinking bustle of repeated notes and the strange, single *sforzando*. Thinking about these measures away from the piano is like "listening" to a Bourdelle bust of Beethoven, with the mouth and eyes pressed shut, as if straining to create order out of chaos. Silent listening frees the imagination to survey the conflict within this music, namely, between mindless energy and containment. On the one hand, the rhythmic force, sounding more wild and driven than goal-directed, mounts in circling repetitive patterns (Ex. 16.1) that are repeated and arranged like fragments in a kaleidoscope (Ex. 16.2). Sequential passages (Ex. 16.3) and slurred figures (Ex. 16.4) assist the rhythmic drive. In addition, lightened resolutions clear the way for forward sweep, as in Ex. 16.5, where rests and a staccato weaken the downbeat, and the tied-over anticipation tempts the player to "anticipate the anticipation."

Ex. 16.1. Op. 7, I, mm. 4–6, 41–42.

Ex. 16.2. Op. 7, I, mm. 35–39, 215–19.

Ex. 16.3. Op. 7, I, m. 45–47.

Ex. 16.4. Op. 7, I, mm. 39, 49–50, 73–75, 93–94, 109–11.

Ex. 16.5. Op. 7, I, mm. 59–61, 127–29.

As the opening measures indicated, on one level the piece goes, while on another it either stands still or is restrained. Prolonged pitches and dynamic stress on dominant harmony suspend forward movement by delaying resolution, against which the force of energy and will is directed. In Exx. 16.1 and 16.2, a fixed note, held or implied, provides such a stationary point within the context of great activity. Stress and prolongation of dominant harmony, in a sense, throw the natural thrust of the music off balance (Ex. 16.6). In mm. 209–12. (Ex. 16.7), the descent in dominant harmony thrashes about with *sforzandos* and *Pralltriller.* Even the heavily marked tonic pedal in Ex. 16.8 acts briefly as the root of the dominant of the subdominant. Again, with respect to throwing the rhythmic drive off balance, it is significant that the dynamic marks in the final measures are placed on the second half of the measure (Ex. 16.9).

Beyond this, the generally fragmentary and rhythmically energetic melodic material is often confined to the range of a small interval. The restriction augments the force of an effect, such as the *fortissimo* over the chords outlining a major third in m. 25, following eight measures of E♭ scales that escaped the confines of an E♭ triad. Similarly, the outlines of the sixteenths in Ex. 16.8 separate into small fragments that turn back and forth within the interval of a third.

The internal conflict between opposing forces is the stuff of the dramatist who develops the point of the play in the person of one character. In Shakespeare, it might be the conflict between action and reflection or between ambition and con-

Ex. 16.6. Op. 7, I, mm. 9–11, 16–17, 25–28, 41, 63–67, 127–29, 137–41.

Ex. 16.7. Op. 7, I, mm. 209–12.

science. That the greatest of these characters belong to the highest political stratum and play for huge stakes magnifies the struggle within the individual. The first movement of Op. 7 is likewise approached by highly gifted and able pianists, yet the music is about a flesh-and-blood experience: turbulent energy that, confined, soon breaks through the bounds of propriety. At such a point, music as art has been redefined as the delineation of human wildness.

Ex. 16.8. Op. 7, I, mm. 111–15.

Ex. 16.9. Op. 7, I, mm. 351–62.

There is no "nice" way to play the passage in Ex. 16.10 without sounding dull. There is no "far enough." Only by submitting to the music in unrestrained involvement can one hear what it is saying. Reverence for Beethoven may convert him into a musical pet, while the spirit within the music is that of someone deranged and demanding that we admit that we know him, an answer we are afraid to give because we might recognize the same madman in ourselves.

Ex. 16.10. Op. 7, I, mm. 79–81.

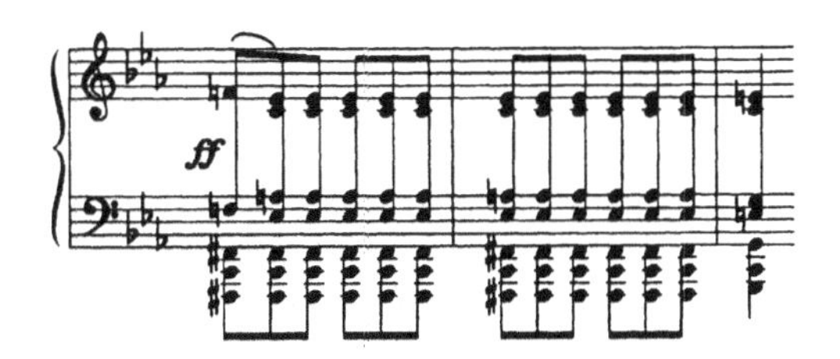

No doubt it was difficult to write sonatas after the phenomenon of Beethoven. Perhaps this is what Tomaschek was thinking after he had heard Beethoven play in Prague in 1798: "Beethoven's magnificent phrasing and particularly the daring flights in his improvisation stirred me strangely to the depths of my soul; indeed I found myself so profoundly bowed down that I did not touch my pianoforte for several days . . . ." Subsequent hearings did not renew the initial impression, for, while Tomaschek admired Beethoven's "powerful and brilliant playing," the coherence suffered through too abrupt changes in direction and dwelling on the "singular and original."[2] Nonetheless, the impression—it would seem a shattering one—had been made, and no doubt Tomaschek, like many another, was never the same musician thereafter. It is as though, after the first movement of Op. 7, the nineteenth century, whose descendants we are, grasped in every direction for associations to support a belief in its own music—virtuosity, literature, painting, nature, nationalism, miniaturism, intimacy, and even the specialization we observe as performers, scholars, composers, critics, and teachers.

The best definition of *con gran espressione,* the marking of the second movement, is the music itself. First of all, the movement is in C major, a third relationship to E♭, which sets it apart from the rest of the sonata, much like the C-major phrase in the first movement of Op. 27 No. 1 that interrupts the E♭ tonality as though with a chilling thought. Here, in Op. 7, the third relationship is analogous to spaciousness, unlike a simple change of mode, as in the slow movements of Op. 2 No. 1, Op. 10 No. 3, Op. 14 No. 1, Op. 27 No. 2, and Op. 28. Furthermore, additional third relationships abound. The B-section, which begins in m. 25, is in A♭, a third relationship to C major. A few bars later, D♭ major becomes a third relationship of sorts to F minor. Finally, although it does not follow immediately, the next significant idea, a statement of the principal theme in B♭ major, is a third relationship to D♭.

Like key quality, silence defines *con gran espressione*. Fully half of each of the opening three measures consists of silence. Czerny mentions the rests, saying that the sublime character must be expressed through all the powers of the most deeply felt performance, although the theme must be played in strict tempo, so that it does not become unintelligible to the listener through the many rests. In a footnote he adds:

> One can well take for granted two kinds of performance. The one for the player himself, when he is alone and plays for his own pleasure. The other for the listener, and first and foremost for that person who does not know the piece at all. The second kind is naturally the more important, and there is no question that between the two there can and must be a great difference.[3]

A rest, then, is a potent effect to be treated with great care, for the progress of the movement is measured in the duration of silence as much as in note values. Rests give dignity to the two-note slurs descending into the return of the theme (Ex. 16.11) and make possible the tension of mm. 20–21, in which the abruptness of the staccato chords, *fortissimo*, is followed by the moving legato of the three upbeats, *pianissimo* (Ex. 16.12). Silence permits us to hear the orchestration of the *sempre tenuto—sempre staccato* in the A♭ section (Ex. 16.13), and the precise calculation of silence permits us to enter into the mystery of the *subito* dynamics in Exx. 16.14 and 16.15. In each instance, rests are more than a part of the notation of the score; they represent a conscious search for inner silence and the voice of one's own individuality.

Ex. 16.11. Op. 7, II, mm. 14–15.

Ex. 16.12. Op. 7, II, mm. 21–22.

Ex. 16.13. Op. 7, II, m. 25.

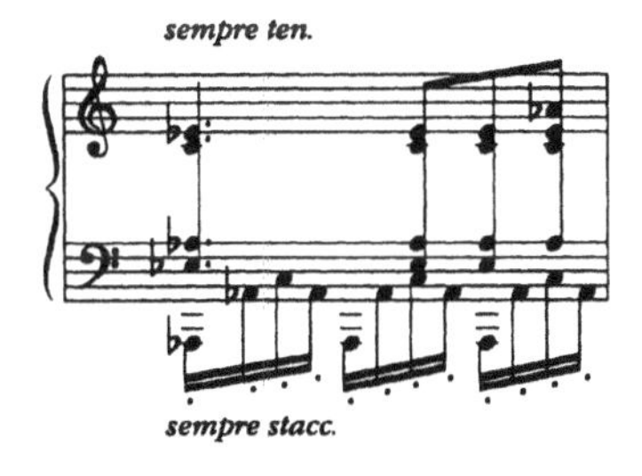

Con gran espressione is further defined by the dynamic plan. Because of the movement's serene beginning, its character becomes self-conscious through dynamic eccentricity. Not unexpectedly, most of these markings are associated with dissonance. The *sforzando* in Ex. 16.16 occurs over the longest note value thus far in the movement. In Ex. 16.17, the *sforzando*, placed over an a♭, darkens the color of major. The *sforzandos* in mm. 27, 30, and 35 mark dissonance in the form of ascending appoggiaturas (Ex. 16.18). The *sforzandos* in Ex. 16.19 are also associated with dissonance, but, as in the realization of all dynamic markings, the repeated *forte* and *fortissimo* are effective only in proportion to the involvement of the player.

The effect of the dynamics is a loss of equilibrium, as though the music were moving from one excess to another, which Exx. 16.12 and 16.19 illustrate. Another is the string of *sforzandos* in Ex. 16.15, preceded by a *pianissimo* and followed by rests and staccato sixteenths. Still another illustration of imbalance occurs in the final four measures of the movement, in which a *ffp* bursts with great intensity from an

Ex. 16.14. Op 7, II, mm. 37–38.

Ex. 16.15. Op. 7, II, mm. 46–47.

Ex. 16.16. Op. 7, II, m. 4.

Ex. 16.17. Op. 7, II, m. 7.

Ex. 16.18. Op. 7, II, m. 27.

Ex. 16.19. Op. 7, II, mm. 75–78.

otherwise *pianissimo* level, as do the *forte* and *forte-piano* in Ex. 16.11 and the *rinforzando* and *sforzandos* in mm. 17 and 18. The *crescendo* over a half note to a *sforzando* over the a in m. 39, which must be imagined on the piano, projects tension to the degree that the player believes it can be made to sound.

The presence of double-dotted rhythm, usually—but not always—at emotional peaks in the music, is a final definition of *con gran espressione*. The loftiness of the Largo originates in its manner of being silent and immovable for precisely measured units of time, just as it sounds dynamically exaggerated at precisely calculated points. The narrator in the music always speaks in a manner of restrained agitation.

Czerny devotes only brief comment to the Allegro ("tenderly playful and lively") and the Minore ("the trio *legato* and harmonious," followed by a direction to use the pedal with the *ffp* in m. 3 and retain it for two measures[4]). According to Nottebohm, sketches for the movement indicate that it was originally to be one of a group of four bagatelles (so-called by Beethoven on the margin of the sketch) and was only later incorporated into the sonata, for which the pages in question contain no sketches.[5] The broken-chord figure unifies the Allegro, providing stability against which the fragmentary motives play like shadows on a wall and giving prominence to the pitch b, which continues throughout the movement.

Ex. 16.20. Op. 7, III, mm. 22–26, 41–43, 68–70, 139–43.

It may be because of pitch structure that Beethoven altered the opening of the second section from  in the sketch to the present form;[6] perhaps for the same reason, Czerny places an *arpeggiando* beside the first chord of the movement.[7] In mm. 25–30, the broken diminished chords in the left hand, the leader in the canon, are slurred in pairs of measures, while an unbroken five-measure slur extends over the right-hand voice, the follower, apparently to avoid a bland sameness of diminished seventh color. The beginning phrase of the Minore recalls the first movement (Ex. 16.21), although the passion of the moment is a far stronger reminder of the two preceding movements.

Ex. 16.21. Op. 7, I, m. 93.

The absence of any break in the sound throughout the considerable length of the Rondo—except for the single mm. 40 and 133—is remarkable. Again, the musical character grows out of features introduced in the first eight measures: the repeated notes (relating to the continuous quality of sound), the harmonic attachment to the dominant, and the numerous appoggiaturas. Conditioned by the continuous variation with each reprise of the theme, the recurring pause on the dominant, the sequential patterns and tendency to dwell on the dominant in the B-section (the overall form being a rondo, ABACABA coda), and the spun-out figuration preceding each reprise, the main episodes of the movement linger and sometimes dream, moving in large circles rather than in straight lines.

The impact of the C-minor episode is its tonality, the repetitious block chords, *sforzando,* on weak beats, and the subdivision in furiously active thirty-seconds. This section, like the Minore of the preceding movement, establishes a kinship with the first movement. Possibly the most moving event in the Rondo is the transformation in the character of the C-minor section at its reappearance in E♭ major at the close of the movement. All the energy has disappeared. The half steps are replaced with the evenness of simple broken chords (Ex. 16.22) and the full chords, *fortissimo,* with broken octaves in a much more subdued dynamic level. The change is like an answer to an earlier outcry, bringing a peace to the close of the movement and the sonata that is even deeper than that of the opening of the Rondo. This view is supported by dynamic detail: The original section in C minor is introduced by held octaves, b♭–b, *p* < *sf,* the latter section with the same pitches, *f* > *pp* (mm. 154–55). The shock of the *ffp* indicated separately in each hand returns one forcibly to the original key (Ex. 16.23).

Ex. 16.22. Op. 7, IV, mm. 64, 166.

Ex. 16.23. Op. 7, IV, m. 161.

The indication *ffp* over a single note occurs in only five of the early sonatas: Op. 2 No. 2 (I, II), Op. 2 No. 3 (I), Op. 7 (II, III, IV), Op. 10 No. 1 (III), and Op. 10 No. 3

(I, II). The extreme nature of the marking is typical of the spirit of Op. 7. Like adolescence in its searching for balance amid excess, the effect of the work as a whole is unbalanced, in that the third and fourth movements depart, except—typically—for isolated outbursts, from the persuasive straightforwardness of the first two movements. Unless the imbalance is recognized for what it is, the unity of the piece will remain elusive, and the sonata will appear inconsistent, as two strong movements with two pretty ones tacked on. Op. 7 is a work that remains for all time "in progress," not finished or complete in the usual sense, but more like a day in the life of the adolescent spirit.

Op. 106

It would be difficult to imagine two more dissimilar spirits than Louis Moreau Gottschalk and Ludwig van Beethoven. Consequently, it is hardly surprising to read Gottschalk's claim that Beethoven fell below mediocrity as a composer for the piano because he neither understood the instrument nor how to adapt his ideas to it.[8] Rimsky-Korsakov said much the same in less-inflated language, referring to Beethoven's "leonine leaps of orchestral imagination" and maintaining that his technique "remains much inferior to his titanic conception."[9] Debussy, also, considered the sonatas "very badly written for the piano" and viewed the later ones as transcriptions of orchestral scores.[10]

Stravinsky, on the other hand, saw Beethoven as "the indisputable monarch of the instrument," the instrument that "inspires his thought and determines its substance." Some composers, he said, "compose music for the piano" while others "compose *piano music*." For Stravinsky, Beethoven belonged in the second group.[11] Regarding the treatment of the keyboard, Beethoven himself wrote:

> As for the title of the new sonata, all you need do is to transfer to it the title which the Wiener Musikzeitung gave to the symphony in A, i.e., "The symphony in A which is difficult to perform." No doubt my excellent L[ieutenan]t G[enera]l will be taken aback, for he will think that "difficult" is a relative term, e.g., what seems difficult to one person will seem easy to another, and that therefore the term has no precise meaning whatever. But the L[ ]t G[ ]l must know that this term *has a very precise meaning, for what is difficult is also beautiful, good, great* and so forth. Hence everyone will realize that this is *the most lavish* praise that can be bestowed, since what is *difficult makes one sweat.*[12]
>
> Does he believe I think of a wretched fiddle when the spirit speaks to me?[13]

The preceding may be read as a verbal exchange, a face-off between Beethoven and succeeding generations. What each says reveals the tastes and creative philosophy of the time. We recognize Gottschalk as a gifted entertainer and not as one interested in works rooted in life at its most problematic. His reaction to piano writing such as Op. 106 could be anticipated; one should commend him for his honesty. When writing for the piano, Debussy had far more in common with Beethoven than he may have been willing to admit; like Beethoven, he defined for himself what piano music *is*.

Pianists may readily subscribe to Stravinsky's characterization "monarch of the instrument" but, concerned as they are with sounding respectable, may distance themselves from Beethoven's ideas about difficulty, beauty, and sweat. Pianists themselves belong to one or the other of two categories. Does one's playing of a Beethoven sonata spring from an inner need, or is it a demonstration of competence? Is the purpose of playing the piano "how you do it" or "why you do it"? When we play, we are debating the value system of piano playing.

Op. 106 is not a problematic work in the same sense as Op. 110. When the fugue theme enters in Op. 110, based on the same pitches as the falling thirds in the opening phrase of the sonata, the ascending fourths rise from the dense writing—the darkness—of the arioso like a still, small voice of hope. When they become falling fourths in the inversion of the fugue subject, the character turns resigned. The rising third, a–c♯, that Beethoven added to the beginning of the Adagio of Op. 106 makes the motivic pattern at the beginning of each movement uniform. Was Beethoven's purpose an intellectual integration of the work or an expressive intensification of it? Does the motivic relationship have a greater expressive potential than the motivic opening of each of the four movements of Op. 2 No. 3? The purely technical problems in Op. 110 do not become more difficult because it is an interpretively problematic work. On the other hand, in Op. 106 Beethoven made the interpretive solution dependent on the technical challenge.

Op. 106 is a work of extremes in terms of its length, its technical difficulty, and the cerebral concentration it requires. Its allure is its dimensions, a keyboard Ninth Symphony and Grosse Fuge combined under one's ten fingers. The sonata begins with a daunting situation: the initial leap of approximately two octaves, the *fortissimo* chords, a top voice that must speak over the *fortissimo* chords while reaching a ninth, the long pedal, pausing so soon with a fermata over a rest, the melodic crowding and reaches of a ninth in the subsequent lyrical phrase, and the range of five octaves and a fourth between outer parts in m. 16. The lyrical phrase sounds as though it had been lifted from the theme for a set of variations given Archduke Rudolph by his teacher (Ex. 16.24). The text, "O Hope, you steel the heart and drive away sorrows," is appropriate for the spirit of the sonata.

Ex. 16.24.

The situation is made truly extreme by the composer's metronome marking, 𝅗𝅥 = 138. Although relieved by *ritardandos* and fermatas, the extraordinarily quick tempo puts the content of the movement constantly in conflict with the torrent of bars and beats. Considering that not every measure or phrase or passage can or should be played at 138 to the half note, is it realistic to try to reach that tempo at all? Was the marking intended to be understood as an absolute or as a gesture to invoke the spirit of the piece?

By indicating a virtually impossibly quick tempo, Beethoven was exhorting pianists to reach beyond their grasp technically and mentally. Play the movement comfortably in a judicious tempo, and the point of the music—pitting keyboard space and musical content against time—will be lost. Therefore, the opening leap, if divided between the hands to eliminate risk, eliminates the will to play the leap in the shortest length of time that is symbolic of a personal will to overcome whatever the challenge.

Reaching beyond one's grasp, and especially suggesting that Beethoven reached beyond his grasp, is heresy to the performer whose ideal is to sound impeccable, or even merely respectable. Yet, the breadth of thought that Beethoven is attempting to portray through the use of extremes is too vast to be framed by any instrument or any form, and therein lies its grandeur. The piece breathes immensity in the juxtaposition of dissimilar styles:

- the rhythmic *fortissimo* chordal theme versus the lyrical phrase;
- the widely spaced triplets and melodic line in the middle section of the Scherzo versus the more compact writing of the outer sections;
- the contrast between the flurry of three-beat phrases in the Scherzo proper with the relative harmonic immobility of the middle section;
- a passionate Adagio, the longest and darkest of any Beethoven slow movement for the piano, following a bagatelle-like Scherzo;
- an improvisatory Largo comprising differing keyboard styles, reminiscent of the beginning of the finale of the Ninth Symphony;
- in the fugue, the calm (*sempre dolce—cantabile—una corda*) of the D-major section, mm. 250–78, following the frenzy of leaps and trills in mm. 243–46;
- the introduction of the lyrical D-major section (the exposition and development of a fourth countersubject[14]) after the first measure rest in 248 measures of intense fugal development

and in the exploiting of the range of the keyboard:

- the expanding lines of the lyrical segment of the principal theme of the first movement (mm. 4–17), extending at its widest point to five octaves plus a fourth;
- similar expanding lines in each hand, mm. 31–34 of the first movement, two octaves apart in each hand, and five from top to bottom notes;

the melodic line of the second theme (in G major, mm. 46–63 of the first movement) ranging almost three octaves;
extended use of the high treble;
accompaniment figures extending beyond an octave (mm. 99–111);
reaches of a tenth in each hand in the fugato in the development of the first movement (mm. 159–61);
the six-octave ascending scale in the Scherzo;
numerous passages of a range of four octaves or more in the Adagio, mm. 31, 43–44, 45–52 (a span of four octaves and a sixth in the right hand from the treble to the bass phrases), 64–68, 81, 87–91, 102–103, 108–109, 114–21 (except for m. 180, the five-octave span between AA♯ and a^3 in m. 118 is the widest such expanse in the movement, marked *con grand' espressione*—four measures later than the same marking in the earlier parallel passage), 128–29, 130–36, 151–54, 156–60, 170, 176–77, 179, 180, 185–86.

Although tallying measures only reinforces intuition, the total number of such measures in the Adagio is approximately sixty, out of a total movement length of 187. The sound ideal, in any event, suggests the aloneness of great expanses, as in the Robert Frost poem,

> They cannot scare me with their empty spaces
> Between stars—on stars where no human race is.
> I have it in me so much nearer home
> To scare myself with my own desert places.[15]

There are three instances of a five-octave range in the Largo, after which spans of four octaves or more occur less frequently in the fugue (mm. 108–109, 112–17, 238, 241–42) until one approaches the climax preceding the D-major exposition. Instances of a five-octave span occur in approximately one-third of the remainder of the fugue, as one would expect in the climax of a fugal movement of such proportions. These include the joining of the subject with the subject in inversion in m. 345, the final statement of the subject in mm. 359–60, and the span between the "drum roll" in the left hand and the top of the arpeggio in the right in m. 371.

Formal dimensions alone create "titanic" proportions. Closing material in the first movement begins with the dominant seventh broken-chord theme in G major (Ex. 16.25), just over halfway through the exposition. Although the next closing segment sounds like a new theme, it is derived from the principal theme (Ex. 16.26). The *cantabile* theme follows, itself followed by the *fortissimo* chordal theme in m. 112. The fermatas and *ritardandos* from the beginning of the movement through m. 69 make that portion of the exposition longer than it actually is in number of measures, balancing the considerable length of the closing section.

Ex. 16.25. Op. 106, I, mm. 75–76.

Ex. 16.26. Op. 106, I, mm. 91–92.

As in the first movement, the extension of single harmonies in the trio of the Scherzo fosters the impression of hugeness; so do the thirty-five measures of F♯-minor tonality with which the Adagio opens, interrupted only by the G-major phrases that are an extension of the Neapolitan. These thirty-five measures would not seem so prolonged were it not for the half cadence in m. 26, followed by a new theme in the same key.

Related to long harmonic breaths, postponing harmonic change over the barline (Ex. 16.27) and harmonic side-stepping from the dominant or dominant seventh to the dominant ninth, or simply superposing the diminished seventh over a dominant pedal, are signs of music that does not want to "go further." The impact of m. 165 depends on a muscular experience of effort (Ex. 16.29). Just as it sounds harmonically weak, passages such as Ex. 16.27 feel like a weakened body that drags its feet instead of walking purposefully, had Beethoven written it as shown in Ex. 16.28.

There are approximately sixty-five such harmonic/melodic postponements prior to the "Bebung" effect in m. 165 (Ex. 16.29), the apex of all the postponing and side-stepping and unwillingness to go further. In fact, the same harmonic "redundancy" can be heard in the first measure of the Adagio. Again in such well thought-out music, the first measures of a movement usually foretell what the piece is going to be "like" musically.

The Adagio is in sonata form. The two-measure G-major phrase mentioned earlier occurs twice in the opening section of the exposition and again in the parallel position in the recapitulation. The phrase sounds straightforward and fresh, compared to the body of the writing in the section. The difference between the exposition and recapitulation should be noticed: the *espressivo* in m. 26 becomes a lengthy

Ex. 16.27. Op. 106, III, mm. 4–6, 9–13.

Ex. 16.28.

Ex. 16.29. Op. 106, III, m. 165.

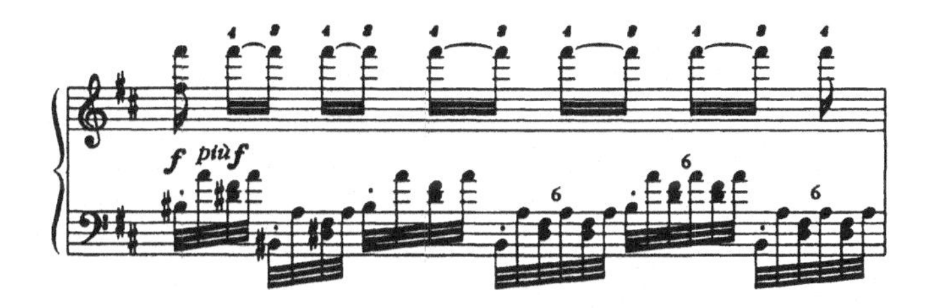

ritardando in mm. 107–12, during which the G-major phrase becomes, so to speak, more subjective with the addition of sixteenth-note anticipations of the main beats (Ex. 16.30).

Ex. 16.30. Op. 106, III, mm. 108–10.

Melodic and/or harmonic progressions based on an extended sequence of descending thirds are another dimension of spaciousness. In the development of the Adagio, mm. 78–87, *sforzandos* falling on weak beats draw attention to the long descending melodic line in thirds (Ex. 16.31).

Ex. 16.31. Op. 106, III, mm. 78–87.

Beethoven's sketch for the Largo is based harmonically on chordal roots that likewise descend in thirds (Ex. 16.32), and the subject of the fugue outlines descending thirds (Ex. 16.33). Although they are not harmonically identical, the chromatic descent in mm. 70–74 of the first movement and a harmonic/melodic descent in mm. 39–44 of the Adagio (Ex. 16.34) are similar enough to be remembered, much as one looks at a distant peak from the top of another. One can hear in the earlier passage the same anticipation of harmony over the bar that gives the Adagio its encumbered quality.

The improvisatory Largo itself presents and discards four different ideas, each concluding on a fermata, before leading into the fugue subject. The discarded ideas give the beginning of the fugue, in a sense a fifth new idea, a significance it would have lacked if not preceded by the Largo.

The fugue must be played to appreciate the qualities that make it larger than life. Like the original metronome setting for the first movement, that for the fugue once more places the quickness of the tempo at odds with the technical difficulty of the writing and the concentration of detail. The leap of a tenth in the fugue subject that was present in all the sketches ensures that it will be recognizable whenever it appears, not to mention the unusual length of the subject. Other factors include the placing of *sforzandos* on the motive from the countersubject in the high treble (Ex. 16.35a); doubling of voice lines in thirds, sixths, and octaves; the scattering of trills at widely separated points of the compass (Exx. 16.35b and c); the long notes of the counterpoint to the subject in retrograde (Ex. 16.35d); the *fortissimo* clusters of voices outlining the beginning of the subject in mirror (Ex. 16.35e); the thick sound of the low B♭ trill and pedal on FF (Ex. 16.35f); and the trills over the beginning of the subject in octaves (Ex. 16.35g), the same device Brahms used in the D-minor Concerto.

Ex. 16.32. Op. 106, sketch from Nottebohm.[16]

Ex. 16.33. Op. 106, IV, mm. 16–20.

In our era of the revival of the early piano, how do we rationalize the "embryo" instrument with a titanic conception? Stravinsky said that to write piano music is to find qualities in the instrument that heighten the uniqueness of one's musical ideas, and vice versa. "What is difficult makes one sweat," Beethoven wrote, and "what is difficult is also beautiful." Whether or not Beethoven found it an expressive opportunity, the insufficient sonority of his piano, as compared with the present day piano, itself reveals the "titanic conception" in a way that we, with our technologically more highly developed instruments, may fail to perceive. Our applause is reserved for those able to make Op. 106 sound possible, but the spirit of the music speaks through those who behold it as one would a grand natural phenomenon.

Ex. 16.34. Op. 106, I, mm. 70–74; III, mm. 39–44.

Ex. 16.35. Op. 106, IV: a. mm. 44–45; b. mm. 103–105; c. mm. 111–15; d. mm. 153–55; e. mm. 333–34; f. mm. 372–74; g. m. 389–90.

b
c

d
p
cantabile

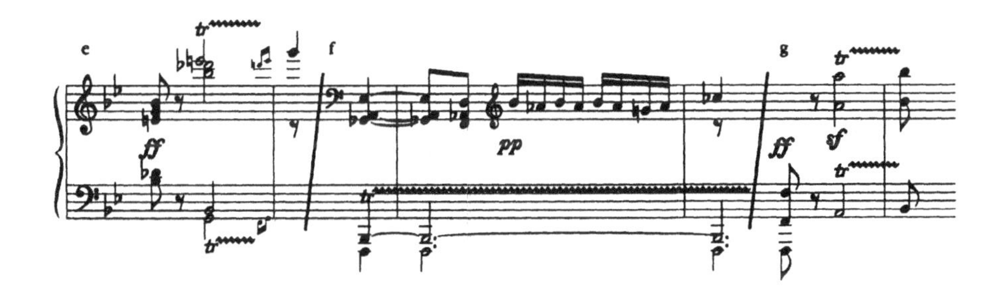
e
f
g
ff
pp

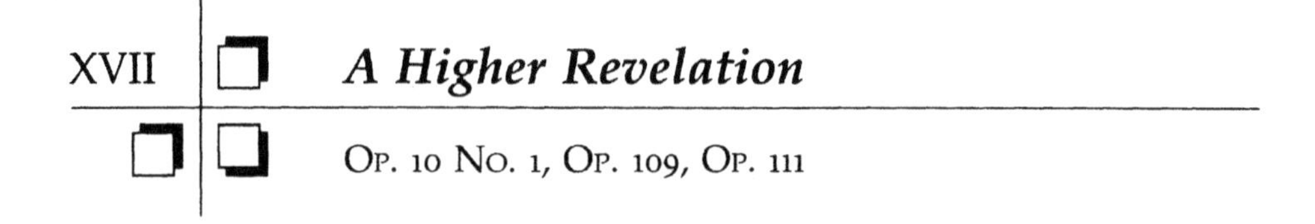

XVII A Higher Revelation

Op. 10 No. 1, Op. 109, Op. 111

I must despise the world which does not intuitively feel that music is a higher revelation than all wisdom and philosophy.

Beethoven

Assuming that the foregoing quotation received second hand from Bettina von Arnim is not apocryphal,[1] Beethoven was saying that the creative experience, originating deep within the self, discloses that which was not previously realized through one's intellectual powers. The creative experience is the experience of what something is "like." We can more easily define the phrase "I am" by describing what a particular facet of being is like. Describing what something is like is the role of imagery and the function of adjectives and adverbs.

Imagery gives the abstraction a perceivable body. To give an idea of the depth of her feelings of guilt which the audience can neither see nor measure, Shakespeare has Lady Macbeth sleepwalk through the corridors of the castle while the voice of her subconscious reflects that "all the perfumes of Arabia will not sweeten this little hand." Lincoln, writing a letter of sympathy to a Boston widow who reportedly had lost five sons in the war, referred to "the solemn pride that must be yours to have placed so costly a sacrifice on the altar of freedom," sublimating the carnage of the battle to an image of a spiritual ritual for the survival of the nation. Or one might recall, as a moving example of imagery in everyday speech, the Civil War soldier who, thinking of the possibility of his death, wrote his wife that, were she to feel a cool breeze on her face, it would be his spirit passing by.

If one is not to play like a note accountant, an awareness of imagery is as necessary for the pianist/interpreter as for the dramatist or the Civil War president expressing constitutional distinctions in legal poetry. Imagery for the interpreter is recognizing musical adjectives and adverbs and the implications of a calculated manner of musical speech. In Beethoven, the use of keyboard space immediately comes to mind, the most memorable example of which is the spacing of single lines, *piano*, five octaves apart, as in the second movement of Op. 111. As another example of the interaction between space and line, the expanding and contracting lines of Op. 101 may be conceived as what "yearning" is like. Or, one might point to the space of approximately two octaves between the hands in the Arietta theme of Op. 111, or the tumultuous effect of widely spaced single lines, *fortissimo*, at the close of the exposition of the first movement of the same sonata. In Op. 109 the space of more than five octaves between the fifth fingers of one's hands during the reprise of the principal theme, when compared with the opening measures of the movement, is the culmination of a sweeping visual perspective. That which at the beginning was tender and naive is transformed, following the shock of the Adagio espressivo and the ensuing climb up a scalar staircase in the development, into a vision of triumph. Not only in character, the breadth of the spacing represents a triumph as well over the limitation of the number of notes a pianist can play simultaneously. As another example of distance imagery in Op. 109, the space of almost two octaves between the hands at the beginning of Variation VI of the third movement produces the effect of transcendent calm within one's consciousness. Here, as in the Arietta theme and the opening of Op. 110, the four-part writing contributes to the image of composure, in Op. 109 and the Arietta theme, a composure found following turmoil.

In the fourth variation of the second movement of Op. 111, the measured triplet thirty-second tremolo (also forming a pedal point) becomes an image of stillness and suspendedness following the joyous syncopated uproar of the preceding variation. When the stationary quality drifts to the treble of the keyboard for the alternating half of the fourth variation, the imagery is that of contemplation, far removed and undisturbed by anything that has preceded. One senses a mystical quality that, in the A-minor segment (beginning in m. 89), lifts the listener to a still higher plane of understanding.

Then there is the imagery of the trills, not cadential formulas or pretty ornamentation, but the creation of atmosphere. Or does the extended treble trill at the close of the movement place the final statement of the Arietta theme above the atmosphere? One notices also that this statement sounds unfinished, comprising only the first half of the theme and ending on g, the dominant of the C-major scale. Perhaps omitting the A-minor phrase (the second half of the theme) at this point is also part of the imagery of reaching inner peace and happiness that can never again be disturbed. Finally, there is the imagery of effort and struggle that appears in Beethoven's treatment of the piano, sufficient mention of which has already been made.

Just as Beethoven's words quoted above, even if they are not entirely accurate, represent a *knowing* distilled from intuition and subjective impulses that stirred within, the hours of practice one dedicates to achieving a finely honed and brilliant technique will be for nought unless there are ideas beyond the notes to communicate.

Op. 10 No. 1

Comparing the early C-minor Sonata with mature sonatas such as Opp. 109 and 111 separates the impulsiveness of youth from the accumulated wisdom of age. The first two movements of Op. 10 No. 1, though clothed in a relatively spare keyboard style, maintain a level of seriousness comparable with the two later sonatas. The integration of character and form in Opp. 109 and 111, however, differs from the willful indulgence in imaginative play for its own sake in the earlier sonata, where the freakishness of its finale departs from the forthright earnestness of the first movement. As such, it differs from other sonatas in minor, such as Op. 2 No. 1, Op. 13, Op. 27 No. 2, Op. 31 No. 2, and Op. 57, which end in a far more emotionally charged state of mind. The three sonatas Op. 10 No. 1, Op. 109, and Op. 111 may be imagined as three ascending steps toward a higher revelation.

Because it is concise and unequivocal in manner, the C-minor Sonata is relatively accessible to the younger pianist. Its forceful character is projected with a minimum of technical difficulty, so that teacher and student together can begin studying the musical language sooner. Only by consulting scores, as Schumann advised, can study be diverted from obedience to an outside authority—whether the teacher, the "master" class, or the recording—to belief in the composer as teacher.

It should not be difficult to identify immediately with the youthful impulsiveness of this sonata. The opening theme typifies this aspect of the composer's personality. The suddenness of the C-minor chord, *forte;* the snatching of breath in the sixteenth rest; the dotted broken chord grasping upward and ending like a huge question mark, the answer of the two-note slur, *piano;* the second *forte*—together these define impulsiveness, a quality sustained throughout the entire sonata.

Ex. 17.1. Op. 10 No. 1. I: a. mm. 9–14; b. mm. 31–33; c. mm. 78–82; d. mm. 86–90; e. mm. 93–95; f. mm. 154–58; g. mm. 108–10; II: h. mm. 5–7; i. mm. 17–18; j. m. 28; k. mm. 39–40; l. mm. 44–45; III: m. mm. 14–16; n. mm. 20–22; o. mm. 44–45; p. mm. 113–14.

e
sf
fp
ff
f
ff
sf
sf
g
p
h
fp
i
f
p
j
12
6
k
rinf.
f
sf
sf
l
m
ff
f
sf
sf
sf
n
o
ff
(p)
ff
sf

Impulsiveness is the spirit of broken chords that sound torn off (Ex. 17.1a); the *fp* in m. 32, following a pause (Ex. 17.1b); the *sforzandos* on the third beat of mm. 78, 80, and 81 (Ex. 17.1c); as well as the insistent *sforzandos* on the three e♭'s in mm. 87–89 (Ex. 17.1d). By breaking the slur at the barline (Ex. 17.1d), was it Beethoven's intent to jab the e♭'s with a *sforzando*? The *sforzandos* in mm. 93–94 throw the listener off balance metrically (Ex. 17.1e), while those in mm. 155–56 (Ex. 17.1f) have an emotional pull like the experience of intense longing. Even the *piano* on the first beat of m. 110, where a *forte* might have been expected, sounds impulsive (Ex. 17.1g).

In the Adagio, after four measures of calm, the line suddenly reaches upward (Ex. 17.1h). The *forte* and descending arpeggio in mm. 17, 19, and 21 are impulsive (Ex. 17.1i), as is the sudden flourish in sixty-fourth notes (Ex. 17.1j) and the placement of the *sforzandos* in m. 39 (Ex. 17.1k). The arpeggiated dominant seventh chord, *fortissimo,* in m. 45 (Ex. 17.1l) *is* the transition back the A♭ major and the reprise. The finale is equally impetuous: the *sforzandos* on offbeats in mm. 14–15 (Ex. 17.1m); the *subito fortissimo* in m. 22 (Ex. 17.1n); the repetition of the marking *ff* in mm. 34, 37, and 41 (when the indication is already in effect); the brusque offbeat *sforzando* in m. 45 (Ex. 17.1o); and the abrupt return to *fortissimo* and Tempo I in m. 114 (Ex. 17.1p).

Impatience is projected by the pressure of dynamic force on the haste with which the musical plot unfolds; in the outer movements, especially, there is little time for reflection. While bar forms are not peculiar to this sonata alone, the pattern of breaking away from repetition in the aab structure is here given physical meaning through dynamics. In mm. 9–16 of the first movement, "b" is marked *rinf.* (Ex. 17.1a). In mm. 17–22 and 22–30, the last segment is marked *ff.* Did a bar form dictate Beethoven's choice of a *forte* in m. 22 (Ex. 17.2), following the *fortissimo* in the preceding measure?

Ex. 17.2. Op. 10 No. 1, I, mm. 21–22.

The bar form in mm. 32–48 includes a more expansive "b," which is marked *crescendo—diminuendo,* while, in mm. 142–58, a combination of expressive devices—use of extreme registers (on the piano of the period), a forceful dynamic level, and harmonic "fulfillment"—make this "b" the dramatic peak of the movement. Possibly because the formal organization sounds so closed and repetitious, like a mosaic of small, intense patterns, the movement ends just as unceremoniously as it began, without extension or further development.

The bar form in the opening eight measures of the *Adagio molto* likewise rises suddenly through dotted rhythms and a *crescendo* to an arpeggiated subdominant chord (Ex. 17.1h). As in the first movement, the bar form is the prevailing unit in the Prestissimo, the first sixteen bars dividing into measure groups of 4 + 4 + 8, each four-measure section dividing again into 1 + 1 + 2, and the eight-measure segment into 2 + 2 + 4. Even the final part of the eight-measure segment, beginning in m. 12, is clearly another such formal subdivision, as are those beginning in mm. 16, 22, 28, 37, and 115. The bar form in mm. 46–57, which comprises the complete development section, must be pointed out in particular as an illustration of a formal unit that communicates breathless haste.

Like the impulsiveness of the dramatic pauses in the outer movements, the pauses in the slow movement (in mm. 17–21 and 44–45) are typical of the restless spirit of the piece. The double-dotted rhythms, fragmented thought, and dynamic outbursts make this a less august piece than, for example, the slow movement of Op. 13. Not until the coda, knit together by the syncopation in the accompaniment, does one find a sustained calm. Otherwise, the silences injected into the stream of musical thought are like declamatory punctuation in stage speech, a personal involvement with a theatrical projection of meaning.

The character of this sonata becomes more complex if one does not confuse its impulsiveness with strength. Continuing by fits and starts, waiting here and then bolting in another direction, suggests a personality that is anything but strong and poised. Impulsiveness of this sort is much like aggressiveness that compensates for inner insecurity. Such an interpretation of the sonata makes the whimsical nature of the finale (which Czerny described as written "in jenem fantastischen Humor" so peculiar to Beethoven[2]) seem in character; so does the way the piece rumbles to its close, its energies seemingly spent.

Following the workings of Beethoven's mind beyond the outward character into the actual choosing of the notes—by analogy, the actual words the actor will be given to speak—the opening theme of the first movement is:

a rising figure, *forte,* made more singular by being
a C-minor broken chord, made more singular by breaking
the intervals of the chord into pairs, made more singular by introducing
a dotted rhythm, creating a jagged effect, made more singular by adding
a legato slur, connecting and containing the line, made more singular by culminating in

two staccato quarters at the top of the ascent.

The answering phrase is:

a falling figure, *piano,* made more singular by
the narrowness of its range, a second (compared with the octave and a sixth in the ascending broken chord), made more singular by
its rhythm, longer note values (compared with the preceding dotted rhythm).

If the foregoing seems tedious, so also must have been the actual process of revision after revision in the composer's mind, until the idea had been stripped of everything superfluous that might detract from its singularity; an important lesson for one of any age is that ideas that took Beethoven's mind months to shape cannot be fully understood in thirty minutes of learning the notes. Thus, in the first movement, the dotted figure always ascends (again an impulsive gesture), and, for that matter, a rising line in this movement is often associated with leaps. For example, the transition beginning in m. 32 rises the interval of a sixth and descends in an ornamented stepwise fashion (Ex. 17.3a); the second theme closely resembles the opening theme in rising through a broken E♭ chord and descending a minor second (Ex. 17.3b).

Ex. 17.3. Op. 10 No. 1, I: a. mm. 33–36; b. mm. 56–59; c. mm. 118–33; d. mm. 140–43.

In the development, what appears to be a new theme (Ex. 17.3c) is an assemblage of motives found in mm. 32–45 and in the second theme, mm. 56–63. While the stepwise twisting melodic movement seems to go neither up nor down, the distinctive melodic leaps ascend. The direction within the twisting segment recurs unchanged in mm. 136–37; 138–39, and 140–41, until, in m. 142, its direction changes (Ex. 17.3d), at which point Beethoven introduces a *crescendo.* During the ensuing twenty-six measures, the emotional climax of the movement, the large ascending line moves in leaps, slurred seconds descend, and the large descending line moves stepwise. It is possible that the last fact alone should decide the uncertainty surrounding the reading in m. 161 in the original edition (Ex. 17.4).

Ex. 17.4. Op. 10 No. 1, I, mm. 161–62.

Within the shadow of the huge climax in mm. 154–56, the originally strong profile of the theme is softened through the absence of a *forte* on the first beats of mm. 110 and 114 (Ex. 17.1g), permitting the long melodic line beginning in m. 118 (Ex. 17.3c) to sound more important, even new. The other detail, the placing of the *crescendo—diminuendo* at a different point in the transposed repetition beginning in m. 125, has been mentioned earlier.

Throughout the movement, the interpreter must decide how explicit the separations in the articulation should be. An intentionally clear separation between mm. 4 and 5 (Ex. 17.5) and all similar instances requires physical doing and conflicts with what feels musically natural—but interpretively careless. The young pianist may need encouragement to learn a fingering for the legato in the left hand in mm. 13–16 (Ex. 17.6), above which pedal changes can be made to preserve the articulation. A clear separation would be logical between mm. 55 and 56 in Ex. 17.7, in view of the eighth rests in the preceding measures and the entrance of the second theme in m. 56 on the downbeat. It would be effective also to separate between mm. 83 and 84, as indicated by the slur that begins simultaneously with the entrance of the *fortissimo*.

Ex. 17.5. Op. 10 No. 1, I, mm. 3–5.

Ex. 17.6. Op. 10 No. 1, I, mm. 13–16.

Ex. 17.7. Op. 10 No. 1, I, mm. 55–56.

Ex. 17.8. Op. 10, No. 1, I, mm. 83–84.

In spite of its minor key, this sonata is written in a different vein from that of Op. 2 No. 1, Op. 13, Op. 27 No. 2, Op. 31 No. 2, Op. 57, and Op. 111, possibly in the same spirit as the improvisation Beethoven produced when he was in an unpredictable mood such as Czerny described:

> frequently not an eye remained dry, while many would break out into loud sobs. . . . After ending an improvisation of this kind he would burst into loud laughter and banter his hearers on the emotion he had caused in them. "You are fools!" he would say. Sometimes he would feel himself insulted by these indications of sympathy. "Who can live among such spoiled children?" he would cry. . . .[3]

Other, very serious sonatas have their moments of irony also: the Allegro molto of Op. 110, or the rippling Allegro following the funeral march of Op. 26. In the present sonata, the bitterness of the descent from the climax in the development of the first movement can be easily recalled, as can the self-conscious seriousness of the slow movement. The finale, on the other hand, sounds neither tragic nor heroic. Instead, the stringing together of short ideas, the retention of major for the second theme in the reprise, the startling effect of *subito* dynamics, and the rhetorical pauses picture a wild frolic of the imagination that will not permit a more serious sequel to the preceding movements.

Also unlike the preceding movements, the finale exhibits an ambiguity in metrical stress. If one places the natural stress within the three-note, lower neighboring-tone figure in the theme and makes a clear separation before the repeated f's ♪♫♩♩ | ♩, the neighboring tone will receive the greater weight. In fact, when Beethoven adds a *sforzando* to the downbeat in the development, the figure feels awkward. The pulling against the natural stress of the downbeat occurs again in the two-note slurred figure in the left hand in mm. 12–14 and in the *sforzandos* on the offbeats in mm. 14–15 (Ex. 17.1m). Stress on the downbeat is weakened by the melodic overshooting of the tonic in the second theme (Ex. 17.1n). As noted earlier, the *sforzando* on the tonic in the final cadence of the exposition puts the listener off balance by occurring on the second quarter of the measure. Czerny wrote of this movement:

> This finale is written wholly in that fantastic frame of mind that was so typical of Beethoven. This mood manifests itself particularly in the middle section (from measure 17 on) through a whimsical *ritardando* of single notes, although one must generally remain true here to the very quick tempo.
>
> However, the character of the piece is by no means happy [a better translation of *heiter* is possibly "pure fun"], and therefore the wantonness of the player cannot be permitted to become trivial and distorted.
>
> The whimsical performance can only be attained through the most masterful control of all mechanical difficulties. Anything to the contrary will change the performance into an unintelligible, laughable caricature.[4]

Op. 109

Op. 109 is a frequent choice of pianists of college age perhaps because, compared with Op. 110, it is a more concise and active work. Eight bars into the piece one encounters a musical crisis, as tempo and character change from one well-defined section to another. The Prestissimo immediately makes its statement, also within eight bars, the thrust of which recurs throughout the movement. The third-movement variations, each dissimilar to the previous one, are easier to project than are the broadly alternating arioso and fugue of Op. 110. Beginning with a deeply private mellowness and ending with the resigned repetition of the variation theme evokes the maturing sensitivity of the young adult. Beethoven's letter of dedication to Maximiliana Brentano seems to be written in the same nostalgic vein:

> Vienna, December 6, 1821
>
> A dedication!!! Well, this is not one of those dedications which are used and abused by thousands of people—It is the spirit which unites the noble and finer people of this earth and which time can *never* destroy. It is this spirit which now speaks to you and which calls you to mind and makes me see you still as a child, and likewise your beloved parents. . . .[5]

The same richness of remembrance issues from the happy-sad character of Op. 109. The first sign that all is not right occurs at the moment when the smooth lines and unbroken rhythm of the opening Vivace collapse in the fragmentation of the Adagio. The diminished seventh chord introduced chromatically in m. 9 falls short of the cadential goal. When this progression from g♯ through a♯ to b is not consummated, the result is musical unfulfillment, a symbolic structural crisis followed by melodic/dynamic bits and pieces. There is now a plot to develop, and each note of the arpeggiando diminished seventh chord must be played with genuine effort to match the weightiness of the event. In music that is greater than it can be played, any facilitation, such as crossing the left hand over the right to thump the a^2, obscures the point of the piece.

The apparent simplicity of the opening measures conceals much sophisticated thought. The first melodic interval is g♯–b, the two pitches that will constitute the framework for the musical plot of the sonata. The melody line of the first phrase begins and ends on g♯, perhaps bringing to mind the sensuousness of other themes in E major that also begin on the third of the chord: Op. 2 No. 3, II; Op. 53 I; and Op. 37, II. In the left hand, the lowest notes descend, with one exception, through an E-major scale, from which is derived the tetrachord building block found in the Adagio. The dynamic indications that Beethoven used to mark off these tetrachords (Ex. 17.9) distinguish the four-note groups from each other; like two characters in tense suppressed excitement, they interrupt each other with incomplete comments. The return of the diminished seventh harmony in m. 12 begins three measures of variation, each starting with the corresponding pitch in mm. 9–11 (a–f×–f♯). If "rhapsodic" is construed to mean loosed from all rational restraint, the purposeful, if rather fitful, strangeness of the *subito pianos* and the ascending motive f♯–g♯–a♯–b (followed by a *sforzando* on another b in the bass in m. 15) rules out any such understanding of the music. In the final measure of the Adagio, a premature and concealed resolution to b and B major is achieved.

Ex. 17.9. Op. 109, I, mm. 9–11.

This, then, is the situation as of page one: a beginning of innocent sensitivity that, interrupted by the troubled Adagio, cannot resume in exactly the same manner at the beginning of the development; the naïveté of the opening sounds tempered here, as if sobered by the character of the *Adagio espressivo.* Within the g♯–b relationship, the first pitches we hear in the sonata, the drifting upward to g♯ in m. 21 sounds hushed and solitary, as though one were gaining a new insight that will alter the understanding of everything to follow. The impression of gazing into new regions involves a number of factors: the higher compass, the unchanging dynamic level of *piano,* the half cadence in C♯ minor, and, perhaps most of all, the sound of g♯ as part of G♯-major harmony, a third relationship to E major. Thereafter, the longest unbroken line in the movement begins in m. 25, where a sudden *piano* alerts the ear to a new beginning, and extends through a sequential unfolding of tetrachords (Ex. 17.10) to the point of preparation (m. 42) for the reprise. At the point of reaching b (m. 33), the dynamic level drops to *piano*, a *sforzando-piano* marks the offbeats, and the slurred sixteenths in the left hand alternate direction—all to permit the line to ascend another octave without continuing the *crescendo*. The breadth of the theme at its return is not in its dynamic marking alone, but as much in the range between top and bottom, from four octaves plus a fifth to five octaves plus a third.

Ex. 17.10. Op. 109, I, mm. 25–27.

The musical achievement of reaching b, which has just been accomplished so convincingly, is momentarily set aside with the reentry of the Adagio, in which d–b♯ (spelled c♮ in the variation, m. 62) descends again to b. The difference between the sound of this resolution and that consummated in mm. 41–48 represents a development of character, the earlier resolution reached by force of will, the later one almost passively. Throughout the remainder of the movement, first b, then g♯, then b again becomes the pitch of finality. The broken-third sextuplets in mm. 63–64 are not a decorative frill, but constitute the substance of the passage, like the principal theme of the movement and the theme of the third movement. The E-major broken chord in m. 65 reaches g♯³ as its highest pitch, again passively, as though the music drifted up toward that pitch. At the Tempo I the slurs connect tetrachords (Ex. 17.11). The naturally stronger sound of b is tempered by alternating phrases that end on g♯ and by incompletion (m. 74). B is approached from c♯ and c in mm. 89–92; the dynamics are carefully coordinated with the slurs, making the two-note grouping clear, as though one were fondling the pitch. The repetition of c♯–b in m. 97, the *sforzando,* and the position of the final chord confirm b as the pitch on which the movement ends. Is the movement a sonata form with a coda, or should it be described ABX (development) ABX (further development)? Interpretively, it may be more persuasive to regard it as a two-part movement, the first resolving with great conviction on b, the second confirming that resolution in a much less direct and self-confident manner.

Ex. 17.11. Op. 109, I, mm. 67–73.

Within this context, the impact of the Prestissimo can hardly be overstated. The pedal that joins the close of the first movement to the opening of the second is as much a means of connecting as preparation for interruption. The shock results from the *fortissimo* dynamic level, beginning the movement on the third of the parallel minor, the new "as possible" tempo, and the conflict between two diverging lines—the rock-solid statement of the tetrachord *ben marcato* in the left hand against the rhythmic subdivision in the right hand articulating the *prestissimo* tempo. All the inwardness of the opening of the first movement, in which g♯ ascends to b while the tetrachord begins to move downward in the bass, is swept away as though by a pent-up power being released into this conflict of pitch primacy. The musical imagery portrays an inner contest between two forces whose reality is more perceivable than that of the finale of Schumann's *Carnaval*, even with—and perhaps because of—its extramusical titles. It is the same Beethoven as the composer of Op. 2 No. 1, in which bodily force is the agent through which the intellectual craft delivers its message—here the entrance on g♮ challenging the preceding resolution on b.

Following these threads of thought through the movement is necessary, since each potential insight must be questioned, in order to avoid an academic clutter in which details conceal rather than reveal the piece. For example, the appearance of a tetrachord pattern inverted and in retrograde in m. 7 (Ex. 17.12) could never be convincingly heard. However, the tetrachords in the left hand do establish an aural parallel with the opening of the sonata. At the same time, the melodic interval g♮–b in the first two measures reinforces the parallel. To hear filled-in thirds in mm. 9–10 is possible, although other features are more important and clearer: the strangeness of the fourth scale step (the seventh of the dominant seventh) rising to the fifth, the sudden *piano* level, the dominant pedal, and the division of the phrase by the dynamic swell and the slurred and unslurred measures (in mm. 19–20 and 23–24 with "legato" added above the slur). Here the principal point is once again the polarity between the third and fifth of the chord: two measures pointing to b, followed by an ascent to g (the pitch at which the *crescendo* ends). Furthermore, the melodic ascent in the right hand pulls against the bass, as in the first eight measures of the movement (Ex. 17.13).

Ex. 17.12. Op. 109, II, m. 7.

Ex. 17.13. Op. 109, II, mm. 9–12.

The motive in m. 25, beginning on g and ending on b and announcing a transition (Ex. 17.14), is derived from the figure in the left hand at the beginning of the movement; the *poco espressivo* divides the steadiness of the preceding eighths from the next thrust of energy. The second theme, beginning in m. 33, closely resembles the opening theme in its rhythm and melodic shape, while the dominant pedal point in the left hand parallels the dominant pedal in mm. 9–24. As another example of an insight that is more apparent than real, the octaves in mm. 39–41 (Ex. 17.15) unfold as tetrachords, as in the development section of the first movement; here, one hears them as a repetition of the minor second. On the other hand, the three statements of the descending tetrachord pattern in mm. 43–48, like that in the left hand at the beginning of the Prestissimo, are hardly mistakable as such. Unlike the slurring of the parallel passage in mm. 145–50 (possibly because the reach upward is a tenth instead of a sixth), Beethoven's slurring in the exposition attaches the syncopated last eighth of the bar to the preceding tetrachord (Ex. 17.16).

Ex. 17.14. Op. 109, II, mm. 25–28.

Ex. 17.15. Op. 109, II, mm. 39–41.

Ex. 17.16. Op. 109, II, mm. 43–49.

In order that the recapitulation produce the same shock as the beginning of the movement, the development lies entirely within a range of *piano* and *pianissimo*, and, at the last moment, the theme reenters following a harmonic slash (Ex. 17.17). Two additional details involving tension between g♮ and b♮ include the strange cadential afterthought, mm. 168–69, in which the dominant seventh with f♯ in the top voice resolves on the tonic with the fifth of the chord on top (Ex. 17.18), and the tetrachord that occurs in an inner voice in the last three measures, which resolves on g (Ex. 17.19).

Ex. 17.17. Op. 109, II, mm. 102–105.

Ex. 17.18. Op. 109, II, mm. 168–69.

Ex. 17.19. Op. 109, II, mm. 175–77.

The length of the variation movement, compared with those of the first two movements, and the fact that it begins after a complete stop, invites comparison with a two-movement sonata, specifically Op. 111. The variation theme of each work has a sensuous melodic line of great composure, although the widely spaced writing of the Op. 111 Arietta gives it a detached profundity, next to which the theme of the variations in Op. 109 retains its personal, human warmth. The lengthy Arietta falls into two (or, at most, three) large sections; in comparison, the third movement of Op. 109 resembles a mosaic of character pieces. Thus, the variations continue the pattern of sudden changes of character that mark the preceding movements, but here they are based on tempo and dynamic levels, not tonality. There is no passionate rending of the musical cloak with a broken diminished seventh chord, no sudden shift to the parallel minor, and no abrupt interruption of the tonal train of thought, as in the recapitulation of the Prestissimo.

Establishing a balance between the pitches g♯ and b, the theme can hardly *not* be heard as a philosophical answer to the preceding movements. The line rises to b in the first half of the theme and then settles back to close on g♯. Gone is the striving toward b that occupied the first movement. The dynamic swell accompanying the ascent to the dominant in mm. 4–5 is balanced by a *subito piano* in mm. 7–8, where the modulation to the dominant is effected; the dynamic swell over the resolution on g♯ in mm. 11–12 is likewise balanced by an uninflected *mezza voce* in mm. 15–16. (In the final statement at the close of the sonata, the swell in mm. 4–5 and the final *mezza voce* are omitted.) The theme and the first variation (including, of course, the final statement of the theme) are the only sections of the movement to sound like a "slow" movement, so that the variations form a large departure and return, an excursion taking us to the El Greco–like upward sweeps of the final variation.

Although the harmonic plan of Variation I generally follows that of the theme, the melodic line traces only the movement from b to g♯ in the second half of the theme. The melodic line begins on b² and returns to that pitch at the beginning of the two succeeding phrases, each time marked with an accent. The only accents indicated in this variation are placed over these b's and, in mm. 25–27, over the descent through a to g♯ (Ex. 17.20). Dwelling melodically on the second half of the theme by means of accents is an intellectual device directing the listener's concentration to the idea of conclusion, since the plot of the sonata is now concerned with a return to g♯.

Ex. 17.20. Op. 109, III, mm. 25–27.

Variation II is a double variation, in which the keyboard pattern in the first statement of each half resembles the Vivace of the first movement. Perhaps these passages, marked *leggiermente,* were meant to sound like an etherialized *Vivace, ma non troppo.*

In the furious manner in which its lines charge in opposite directions, Variation III recalls the Prestissimo. The marking *piacevole* at the beginning of Variation IV describes the effect of the tempo indication *Etwas langsamer als das Thema.* Beyond that, the marking reminds us to listen to elements of its peaceful character, such as the position of this variation following the Allegro vivace; the stretching of the quarter-note beats with a sixteenth-note subdivision in 9/8 time; the slow, repetitive harmonic movement from tonic to dominant and back; and the loosely imitative writing. Less strictly attached to the theme, this variation becomes more color-oriented. One may feel that color is the purpose of the imitative pattern and certainly of the sensuous pedaled ninth chords in mm. 105–106.

The first pitches of Variation V, which the ear hears as separate voice parts, echo the Credo of the *Missa solemnis* (Ex. 17.21). Following the contrapuntal treatment in mm. 133–34, the writing never sounds as dense or the polyphony as severe, no doubt in preparation (as is the extra repetition, *piano,* in mm. 145–52) for Variation VI, the first sixteen bars of which concern balance, introducing g♯ and b (as a pedal) simultaneously. Whether the individual eighth in m. 157 is equal to the eighth of the preceding bar seems academic. The rhythmic quickening: 𝄽 ♩, ♫, 𝄾 ♫♪, ♬♬♬, 𝄽 ♬♬♬♬ leads naturally to *tr*~~~ . Are we to hear a reminder of the Adagio of the first movement in the diminished seventh with d in the soprano in m. 169, followed by a gradual descent to a in m. 173?

Ex. 17.21. *Missa solemnis,* Credo.

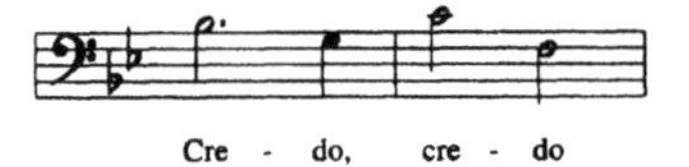

The movement may be heard as a summing-up of the first two movements: the pitch relationship g♯–b–g♯ in the theme of the variations; the rising bass line in the first half of the theme, encompassing an octave, like the range of the descending bass line in the openings of the first and second movements; the keyboard writing of the second variation; and the interruption of the character with the *Allegro vivace* of the third variation. The movement as a whole, with its quick variation in the middle and the restatement of the theme at the close, would seem to reestablish inner balance after the uncertainty and turmoil preceding it. The final statement of the theme is now more withdrawn, with the first dynamic swell and the arpeggiando of the E-major chord of the sixth missing. In the Henle edition we are told that the rolled chord in m. 200 is a simple chord in the autograph.

Like the first phrase of the first movement, which begins on g♯ and ends on g♯, the conclusion of the sonata returns in deepest peace to the g♯ in the final chord—strange as this resolution is, with the tonic chord placed on the third beat of the 3/4 measure with a new pedal indication, as though its end were a continuation. One of the meanings that can be read into the final measure is that the weakening of the cadence has to do with balance, b being the pitch that is left in returning to g♯, the importance of g♯ is thus diminished. Or are we to think of the sonata as a never-ending circular movement, its end its beginning and its beginning its end? Or is the dominant seventh in the last measure a dim memory of the ascent in dominant-seventh harmony in mm. 173–74, at the height of the striving?

The last word can never be written about music such as this, nor can the last interpretation ever be played.

Op. 111

The mature years of life are the coda of the piece. Last words, last acts, last wishes hold the imagination as spellbound as did the plans of youth. Will it be a time of keener insight, or disillusionment, or joy, or peace?

Even if Op. 111 is Beethoven's last piano sonata, it still precedes his final musical statements for the piano by at least two years. Because of its movement order—a linear Allegro of great forcefulness and passion, followed by an Adagio almost fifteen minutes in length—and the concentration of mind within each movement, the piece relates to struggle and resignation. Each movement is "about" one idea, and therefore the sonata represents a pairing of opposites:

an Allegro	an Adagio
a movement in minor	a movement in the parallel major
a sonata-allegro	theme and variations
common time with duple subdivision	compound time with triple subdivision
frequent interruptions and fluctuations in tempo	one tempo, with no interruption in sound from the first note to the last
a generally linear style, with many fugal passages	great variety of keyboard writing

Despite the opposing character, there are formal similarities between the two movements. Although a variation movement is not built on a large-scale plan of departure and return, as is a sonata-allegro, the beginning of the fifth variation (following the modulatory digression) sounds like a reprise. Conversely, the sonata-allegro, which is largely monothematic, relies more heavily on variation procedure and contrapuntal development than departure and return, for which reason one is justified in viewing each movement as a monumentality of thought rather than action. Finally, while there is no indication of tempo change in the second movement, the progressively smaller note values produce a gradual acceleration to a level of wild excitement, followed by an extended and profound peace.

An interpreter—one who actually plays the sonatas—needs the analytical skills of the theorist, the breadth of understanding of the music historian, and, beyond this, the physical skill to play the instrument. However, the playing of this music demands still more, namely, a philosophical bent. Whether or not the music has a philosophical meaning depends upon the attitude of the pianist who plays it. Ries remembered:

> If I missed something in a passage or incorrectly played notes and leaps that he wanted to have consistently accurate, he seldom showed anything; only if I showed a lack in expression, in *crescendi*, etc., or in the character of the piece did he become aroused, because, he said, the former is an accident, the latter a lack of knowledge, feeling, or attention. The former happened quite often to him, even when he played in public.[6]

As to why Beethoven considered expressive elements, character, knowledge, feeling, and attention (presumably to content) more important than consistent accuracy, Op. 111 provides the answer. Czerny wrote that the first movement of Op. 111 should be played with all the passion that the difficulty of its passages demands.[7] To Czerny's teacher Beethoven, passion was not a make-believe act. Whatever Beethoven's motivation or impulse or personal need, his frustration found a physical release in wrestling with the "difficulty of the passages" and intellectual release in equating the release of passion with the intense process of development. As Alan Pryce-Jones wrote in his introduction to Thayer's biography,

> Music is an abstract art, and there is thus a significant point to be taken in all that touches Beethoven's character. So long as he could move in the sphere of abstraction, he could fulfil himself amply. Large themes, like liberty or friendship or disappointed passion, awakened an immediate response in him. The embodiment of these themes in action was a very different matter. [One should not] interpret the Ninth Symphony, or *Fidelio*, or the quartets, as though they were fragments of experience translated into a musical idiom. The abstract concept which inspired each of them was all the more real to Beethoven—we must suppose—because it compensated for a deepening sense of disappointment with the realities of life.[8]

Conflicts and problems, "the realities of life," and abstract thought are just as much a part of the human condition now as in the year 1821. Czerny did not say the music was to be played "with all the brilliance" or "with all the virtuosity"; and he could have said, instead of passion, with all the "involvement" its difficulty demands. Passion knows no limits and leads to excess, and excess leads to unpredictability, and, under pressure, unpredictability can turn a performance into a disaster. Czerny might have said that one should play this music like an inspired fool.

Risking failure and humiliation out of passion for a musical image is a redemptive experience, breaking down the wall of pretense between player and listener. Lili Kraus called it being "touched by grace." Paradoxically, the pianists who set out to demonstrate that their technique has mastered the difficulties merely reduce Op. 111 to their own size, and the result is invariably uninteresting.

When the spirit of Op. 111 takes control of Beethoven's keyboard writing, the pianist can expect to feel inadequate. If not, the piece being played is not Op. 111. The linear style of the writing, including unison passages and fugal sections, frequently lacks sufficient body to produce the level of sonority that the spirit of the piece calls for. Instead, this linear style, under the pressure of the fast tempo and the dynamic intensity, requires genuine physical effort, as shown by sixteenths in which *sforzandos* fall like hammer blows on each beat (Ex. 17.22), by the duration of fugal passages at a *forte* level, by sixteenths involving quick changes of hand position and stretches (Ex. 17.23), and by note repetitions as one voice follows in the tracks of another (Ex. 17.24). Had the composer provided more notes, and more conveniently placed, the playing of the movement would have required less effort, but, as it is, a lack of intensity will be perceived as detached and bland. It is the sort of piece whose spirit dwells just beyond the limits of the technical ability of the player and the capacity of the instrument. The pianist who does not risk shame will never move anyone.

Ex. 17.22. Op. 111, I, mm. 26–28, 67.

Ex. 17.23. Op. 111, I, mm. 55–56, 61–64, 82–83, 89–90.

Ex. 17.24. Op. 111, I, m. 111.

The octave leaps at the beginning of the Maestoso, when played with one hand, as notated, also provide moments of risk. Why take the chance of missing the f♯

octave, when the figure might be divided between the hands? *Maestoso* implies having overcome an opposing force, and therefore the octaves ought to sound disdainful of risk. To "play it safe" is to begin out of character—as though Beethoven had given the Heiligenstadt Testament to a copyist practiced in cursive writing, in order that the document written in the darkest night of his soul would look neat to posterity.

Playing this music "with all the passion that the difficulty of its passages demands" is also an intellectual passion to understand the score. The opening phrase encloses several important details: the double-dotted rhythm, the leap in octaves, the diminished-seventh harmony, the trill on c resolving to b♮, and the rising melodic line through a third, separated by rests and ending with a drum-roll–like arpeggio. The significance of the double-dotted rhythm is that it sounds self-conscious, as the rests do in a slow tempo, and the arpeggio that delays the beat. Perhaps this is reason enough to begin the arpeggio on the beat, for the opening line of the play is a consciously defiant cry. The player may be reminded also of the sequence of three diminished seventh chords in the slow movement of Op. 10 No. 3 (mm. 23–24 and 62–63), in each instance, "nowhere" harmony. In the Maestoso, there are two attempts leading nowhere before finding a harmonic progression with which to continue. In the first phrase, the *sforzandos* over e♭ and c, together with the trill on c, mark two of the important pitches in the theme of the Allegro, the b♮ in m. 2 being the third of these pitches and the same note of resolution as in mm. 11, 13, and 15. Is the melody line g–a♮–b♮–c, appearing twice in the Maestoso, a prefiguration of the sixteenth-note triplet in the principal theme of the Allegro?

When the time comes for the theme of the Allegro, it emerges in fragments—first arising out of the written trill, then the upbeat to c, then the segment concluding with the fermata, followed by the complete theme—as though assembled from preceding embryonic material. The leap downward a diminished fourth to the leading tone derives stature from its link with the leaps in the Maestoso and the melodic resolutions on b♮. The fermata becomes a rhetorical pause, while the *poco ritenente* and, subsequently, the *meno allegro, ritardando* and *adagio* have a flagging effect on the forward thrust of the music. In fact, the tendency of the Allegro periodically either to stop or to cadence (mm. 30–31, 34–35, 51–52, 53–55, 64–66, 94–95, 99–100, 117–18, 119–21, 125–26, 141–43, 151–52, 153–54, 156–58) may originate in the rhythmic waiting in the Maestoso and the pause and *poco ritenente* within the theme. Compared with the sophistication of the contrapuntal writing, the unison writing that recurs throughout the movement sounds barren, a primitive, back-to-nature style.

The A♭ major six-four in m. 9 is the first indication of a shift toward major, an effect of momentary relief, friendly in tone, from the prevailing minor. The same chord in the same position in m. 50, in the exposition, produces a similar sense of relief following the fugal passages; it introduces a brief second theme, whose appoggiaturas lead to the rhythmic "lostness" of the *meno allegro*. Here, as in the Maestoso (where it is treated as a passing chord), the six-four remains unresolved and the musical thought stands still, as though contemplating what is to come next, before resolving chromatically in a deceptive cadence.

When speaking of the passion demanded by difficulty, Czerny may have been thinking primarily of the fugal passages, where counterpoint provides a framework for rising sequences. That these passages develop the principal theme makes the style also an intellectual passion. The range of the melodic line in mm. 48–49 (just short of five octaves, although five and one-half octaves in the recapitulation) is another intellectually conceived passion; neither the human voice nor any single-line instrument can realize such an expanse. The approximately three- to five-octave space between the lines moving in opposite directions, *fortissimo*, in mm. 64–65 challenged Beethoven's piano to create an illusion of size and force far beyond that which it actually possessed—the sort of passage Gottschalk would have cited as evidence of knowing "only imperfectly" how to write for the instrument.

Though the turmoil is difficult to play, it is not very difficult to interpret. Music with such bold lines can be understood even by an uninitiated listener who listens not to piano playing but to "something" that is vital, like life itself, and therefore unlikely to be perfect. A letter Bartók wrote in the spring of 1923 to his mother and aunt following a concert, is relevant. The conditions, which would have upset the most seasoned performer, included improvised steps (a chair and a kitchen stool) to the stage; a rickety, creaking stage that caused everything on it to sway and that was so small there was hardly room for the page-turner's chair; and lighting so dim the page-turner could scarcely read the score. At one point, the violinist forgot to remove the mute and, with a *fortissimo* approaching, Bartók finally had to shout, " 'Take off the mute!' The crown of all misfortunes occurred, however, when the page turner threw my music from the music stand and had to gather it up from the floor. . . . The hall was nevertheless full; we had nice applause. . . . "[9] An audience in an urban "cultural center" where rituals of concert giving were more formal might not, at that time, have given the performers "nice applause." Bartók's audience may have reacted as did Voigt, in Schumann's aphorism, after hearing the Ninth Symphony: "I am the blind man who is standing before the Strasbourg Cathedral, who hears the bells but cannot see the entrance."[10]

A further intellectual element involves the role of the diminished seventh. The Maestoso opens with the three possible diminished seventh chords, a diminished seventh broken chord introduces the closing theme in the exposition and recapitulation, and the three diminished seventh chords reappear in the rising sequence leading to the reprise and again in the coda, mm. 146–48. Diminished-seventh harmony occurs at heights of agitation preceding a musical solution of one kind or another, like a scream before the return to rational thought.

The time spent establishing C major at the close of the movement (mm. 150–58) within a *pianissimo* dynamic level suggests that a harmonic/extramusical decision has been made. The peaceful ending is like a tunnel leading into the self, where the spirit of the Arietta waits to speak. The character of the Adagio has been aptly described as resignation following struggle. With its closed structure, the Arietta theme itself projects the definiteness of an answer that has been reached through great trial and that, in its metrical breadth, has become a bedrock of strength. Resignation, as we follow the quickening subdivision of the first three variations, is not sadness but joy. The even subdivision of the remainder of the movement departs from the rhythmic definition of resignation, becoming the canvas on which the composer spread keyboard colors that seem to transcend rhythmic patterns. One might say that there is something beyond joy, that joy has become self-forgetting, distilled. In its representation of the infinite nuances of character and spiritual progress, the Adagio is a long journey of thought-elaboration.

Yet, for a number of reasons, the movement sounds shorter than its actual length in minutes would suggest. One is the drifting quality of the triple subdivision. The descending fourth with which the theme begins is metrically ambiguous. The stress on the c^2 and the g^1 over the bar being virtually equal, what does it matter, in this timeless circumstance, what beat is the most important, that we should "lead" to it?

The tripartite division of the movement also makes the piece sound shorter than its actual length: the theme and first three variations, the double variation that dissolves into an improvisatory section and a chain of trills, and the recapitulation, consisting of one complete and the final incomplete variation accompanied by an extended trill. At the same time, the meter divides the movement in two parts, the first three variations forming a tier in which $\frac{9}{16}$ ♫ becomes $\frac{6}{16}$ ♬♬ (the L'istesso tempo easily felt by subdividing the 9/16 meter in 32nds) and then $\frac{12}{32}$ ♬♬ ♬♬. Thereafter, an absolutely steady subdivision is retained—with the important exception of the improvisatory section—to the end: Like the visual pattern of a heartbeat on an oscilloscope that turns into a straight line at death, the subdivision beginning in the fourth variation projects a peace that is not altered fundamentally throughout the remainder of the movement.

The tonal plan also beguiles the listener from an awareness of length: The movement is entirely in the keys of C major and A minor, except for the digression to E♭ major with voice lines lingering five and one-half octaves apart and the chromatic modulations that follow returning to C major. If the lack of movement in tonality makes the music seem to stand still, the rhythmic pattern of offbeats beginning in the fourth variation and the melodic directionlessness of the alternate halves of that variation also project timelessness. It is the second of these passages that drifts into a development of sorts (beginning in m. 96), in which the highly placed triplets cease to be functional variation and become color, in and for itself. Broken chords in mm. 100–105 summarize the two tonalities of the movement.

There are few passages in the Beethoven sonatas or the piano repertoire generally that attain the regions of the chain of trills, the triple trill, the going apart and drifting back together of lines at the very extremes of the piano's compass, and the modulatory path back to the theme. The working-out of the *espressivo* phrase (beginning in m. 120) with the tenderness of its falling interval, has a touchingly consolatory quality, the rests and offbeat placement of the melody much like the *ermattet* second arioso of Op. 110. The scale steps 7–1–2 of m. 122 first appeared, also separated by rests, in m. 2 of the Maestoso; again in the closing phrase of the Arietta theme; and now following the most elevated passage in the movement, as the music finds its way back to the key of C major and the eventual conclusion among the trills and atmospheric drifting in thirds. In m. 174 the descending sixths, marked *crescendo,* fill in a three-fold repetition of the falling motive at the beginning of the movement (Ex. 17.25). Is it significant that the motive is reversed thereafter in the left hand, rising instead of falling?

Ex. 17.25. Op. 111, II, m. 174.

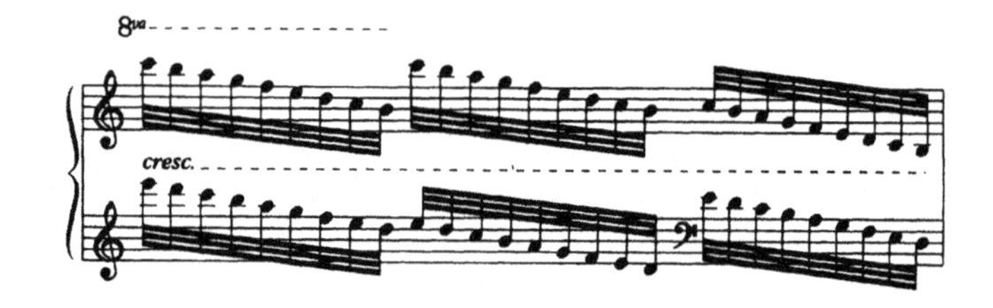

In its projection of passion through difficulty Op. 111 bears a kinship with many other Beethoven sonatas. One need only think, for example, of Op. 106. However, this last sonata of Beethoven is more deeply involved with the ultimate answers of life—with a discerning of ultimate purpose—than its fellows. In that sense, its difficulty is sincere beyond all question; it is as far removed from virtuosic display as the east from the west. The sonata becomes the measure against which the interpretation of any other sonata of Beethoven—or, for that matter, the depth of any other sonata—is judged.

In actual fact, Op. 111 becomes the standard beyond measure to which one's own idealism as a musician and depth as a human being will be compared.

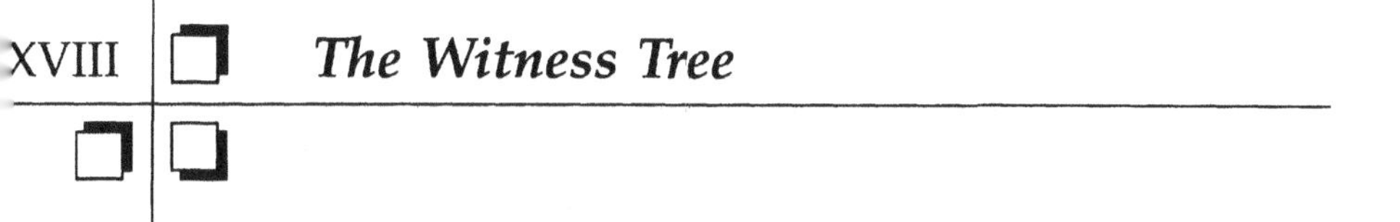

XVIII The Witness Tree

> *Wem meine Musik sich verständlich macht, der muss frei werden von all dem Elend, womit sich die andern schleppen.*
>
> BEETHOVEN

In a field requiring sustained dedication with no guarantee of reward, the serious interpreter becomes obsessed with finding reassurance of valid accomplishment and self-worth. Within the vastness of musical creativity that has preceded us, the phenomenon of Beethoven, like the witness tree (a marker from which nineteenth-century surveyors made their measurements), becomes a living point of orientation for establishing aesthetic boundaries and clarifying one's professional values. One would like to believe in the accuracy of the quotation above ("The one to whom my music makes itself understandable will, as a matter of course, become free of all the misery that others drag around with them"), which was included in a letter from Bettina Brentano to Goethe.

What scholarly research cannot prove or disprove, personal experience can. The comment attributed to Beethoven is remarkable, first of all, in personifying the music as an active agent: it "makes itself understandable." The German modal *muss* is problematic, not to be understood "that the listener must (first) become free of all the misery," but that it will happen unavoidably as a result of the experience. Above all, the statement is remarkable for linking the music inseparably to the human condition, although following this concept to its logical conclusion presents unsettling implications for our profession.

One may analyze a work until every note has been explained or practice it until every detail can be heard and yet not discover the spirit of the music. A Beethoven theme or motive remains inert until, like the composer, one exerts the will to comprehend the uniqueness of its form and content. As music that cannot ignore its own power, it demands that one make room for its stature within oneself by asking the reason for each compositional turn of events. The Poco Andante at the close of Op. 81a can be puzzling, all the more so as its harmonic life becomes motionless. Why did Beethoven not end the movement with the upward sweeping E♭ scale, *fortissimo*? A Taiwanese graduate student, asked what she thought was Beethoven's reason for this seemingly unnecessary interpolation, said that it was "more than happy." In the sustaining of E♭ tonic harmony, the return is depicted as consummated in the deepest and most treasured sense of two becoming one—spiritually or, in the observance of marriage, of two becoming one flesh. The music, if one is willing to follow its spirit unreservedly wherever it may lead within the self, has the capacity to establish within each of us who play it a standard for genuineness, honesty, and truth.

It is a spirit that raises piano playing to the significance and reality of life, leading one away from a simple veneration of piano playing to preoccupation with the needs of human beings. Playing a sonata such as Op. 2 No. 1 can be for some a psychological safety-valve—a complex musical symbol, at once earthy and learned—for the working-out of the insoluble in daily life. In transforming overwhelming problems of body and mind into abstract polarities, Beethoven's musical speech taxes the capacity of the instrument and challenges the player's will to rise to the level of its content. Haydn and Mozart, Beethoven's two elders in the art, though no less possessed of human passion, never feel frustrating to the player's muscles, as does, for example, the *Appassionata*. In their many moments of light, they share with him a buoyant optimism; however, when faced with the darker side of reality, they become fatalistic. Beethoven, nourished by a different soil, contests his circumstances, imbuing his works with a philosophical content.

> Wer immer strebend sich bemüht,
> Den können wir erlösen,
>
> [Whoever continually takes pains to strive,
> Him we can redeem,]

Whether or not Goethe fully appreciated Beethoven or would have had an understanding for our role as *re*-creators, for the musician/interpreter these lines from *Faust* are the door to the world of the Beethoven sonatas, a body of repertoire that Artur Schnabel described as "music that is always greater than it can be played." Thus, in a passage such as that shown in Ex. 18.1, the imagination always perceives more than the fingers can project. In the physical effort of realizing so much with so little—the few notes widely spaced between the hands, the *sforzandos* over single notes, the separation indicated by the slur and the staccato, and the shift from minor to major—the interpreter encounters the *likeness* of emotional stress. When is the *sforzando* strong enough? The pianist cannot swell sustained pitches dynamically, as can a string or wind player; once the note has been played, any imagined change in dynamic intensity can only be projected agogically. How much must one extend the dotted half note to communicate great effort? Exactly how short should the staccato quarters be played in order that the millisecond of silence before the whole note will increase its weight? How much should this downbeat be delayed? Should the second *sforzando* be louder (more effortful) than the first? When the effect of the music depends on the sincerity of its association with human impulses that cannot be measured, the support of an accepted tradition or one's previous success vanishes. Reaching the point somewhere beyond the notes where playing mirrors and intensifies the totality of consciousness is, like Faust's striving for experience, the true measure of the interpreter's success.

Ex. 18.1 Op. 81a, I, mm. 35–38.

On the instrument, the two immediate determinants in projecting this sense of striving in Beethoven—or meaning or musical sense, generally—are dynamics and pacing. Muscular perceptions inform the mind, leading to bodily movements that produce the sounds and the subtle modifications of tempo that communicate meaning. It is the perception of reaching that internalizes Op. 49 No. 1, or the articulation of the theme of the Allegro of the first movement of Op. 81a that feels held back. Were one's sinews strained to accomplish a superhuman feat in a moment of great crisis, the experience of anxiety in overcoming what seems to be insuperable odds would be the same anxiety one feels at beginning the first measures of Op. 106 or approaching its fugue. The kinesthetic experience gives a Beethoven score the added dimension of a tablature—one might say, a tablature of trials—indicating not only positions of the hands but also the sensation of muscular contortions and effort. Beethoven may never have used the word *kinetisch*, expressing the idea more simply by saying that "what is difficult is also beautiful." The objection may be raised that, following this line of reasoning, the less developed one's technique, the better one will play Beethoven. On the contrary, the spirit of the music requires a technique that is more than facility, challenging one to reach higher to a point of inadequacy, thereby to respond to the sorrow of sorrows or the ecstasy of happiness, or an unquestioning strength of will. Were this music not interwoven with the experiences of living, it would not seem greater than it can be played. Once this is understood, one regards inadequacy, even failure, with a more realistic and forgiving attitude.

An awareness of the intensity of expressive detail is nowhere so critical as in the beginning measures of a movement, where the character of the musical plot is introduced to the listener. Whether line, propulsive rhythmic energy, segmented form, or the pitting of time against space, it is the interpreter's responsibility to sculpt the musical elements with the utmost clarity. Here, and in the unfolding of the musical drama, dynamics may become signposts pointing to important statements, structural pitches, or decisive junctions in the music. One may recall the *fortissimo* and *sforzandos* marking the descending hexachord in the first movement of Op. 2 No. 1, the *sforzando* on g♯ in the theme of the finale of Op. 27 No. 2, or the *sforzando* on e♮ at the reprise of the principal theme of the first movement of Op. 13. Each instance illustrates an approach that will always remain revolutionary: the visceral projecting the cerebral. Dynamics, after all, are produced by physical force.

From a purely musical point of view, the result is often unnaturalness, the symptoms of which, besides finding expressiveness in difficulty, include pursuing a tempo that borders on the impossible, forcing dynamic levels with too few notes, devising uncommon keyboard figures to communicate uncommon thought images, and notating articulation phrasing that wrings expressiveness from the briefest phrase. It is music that, if not always beautiful, is always meaningful. In contriving intellectual figures to convey an inner passion, Brahms, among the Romantics, approaches most closely the spirit of Beethoven. Here also, as the subjective surge passes the border checkpoints of the mind, the cerebral manipulation of sound results in an unnatural, often awkward, feel to the fingers.

For all this unnaturalness, however, one does not experience the same "reaching beyond one's grasp" in Brahms as in Beethoven. The musical ideas of Romantic piano repertoire are clothed in the increasing sensuousness and sonority of the instrument. Tonal half-tints, the aura created by undamped strings, and a homogenized tonal quality throughout the compass provided a means of escape into a beguiling dream world of fantasy, removed from the realities of everyday living. Beethoven takes us into a world of fantasy also, although, in exerting the force of his personality against the lesser strength of his instrument, he defines for us more realistically the quality of the crises of life. Chopin is as logical a craftsman as Beethoven, yet, because of the nature of the writing, it is impossible to make Chopin sound like Beethoven. By exploiting the total richness of piano sound, Chopin's keyboard writing sounds deceptively less structured, encouraging a self-indulgence that in itself is not necessarily unhealthy. However, as a style understood by all, musician and nonmusician alike, the Romantic piano sound is only too readily accepted as the norm for keyboard music of all periods. Such an approach results in a casualness in which the preciseness and the unnaturalness of Beethoven's dynamic indications and marks of articulation, the structure of the piece in the separation of ideas, and the silence to be perceived between voice parts are lost.

When one has been led by the learning of a Beethoven sonata to that point in one's growth that the philosophical content of the music is woven into the fabric of one's thinking, professional values become inseparable from ethical ideals, instilling within one's conscience the severest judge of one's motives and purposes. Op. 111 represents an arduous, lifelong spiritual journey, culminating in being granted an inner peace after striving against all that life is not; it was for Beethoven, as it should be for us, one of the most profound statements about human existence. Without having personally traveled the journey, or feeling compassion for one in the process of doing so, one may play the notes, but the thought within, beyond and above the notes, will remain untouched. As representative of difficult repertoire from the Classic period, the work is undoubtedly useful in a competition as a vehicle for demonstrating that one is a better pianist than the next person. However, playing Op. 111 to win a prize or mount a career is at cross-purposes with playing Op. 111 to celebrate the deepest sentiments of one's life. It is reasonable to ask why one cannot have both the demonstration of pianistic skill and the thought beyond the notes. The answer involves purpose. Op. 111 was written to define an answer to a dilemma of epic proportions. It is not to be performed, it was written to be lived. To use it for any other purpose is as flawed as it would be to have contestants from the clergy declaim the Beatitudes before a jury who would weigh diction, memory, the pacing of the delivery, and stage presence to decide which one won.

Pianists who cannot accept the existence of the philosophical content of a Beethoven sonata will find their satisfaction in playing the notes cleanly and intelligently and comparing editions and recordings. On the other hand, if it is accepted, the philosophical content implies an appreciation for the totality of the human experience, from the common denominator of each of us (which is the desire to be understood—in this case, through the playing of a piece of music) to our diversity. Despite the objectives of the institutions within which we work, the expectation of uniformity among human beings is no more indicative of high standards than the recognition of varying strengths in our students and ourselves proves the absence of standards. There is indeed a very real competition and upholding of standards, but these have to do with perceived growth measured against perceived personal potential. If we believe that potential will always exceed growth, everyone who perseveres in this lifelong competition may aspire to the prize—and to the exclusion of no other competitor—that prize which is a wholeness of the self in the integration of artistry and personal need. Here, fortunately for each of us, there is no "final" decision.

Whether or not the words Bettina Brentano remembered constitute Beethoven's very utterance, as Alexander Ringer has remarked, is less important than the ideas to which she responded—the evidence of which is inherent in the music. Beethoven might have found a kindred being in the words of the ancient psalmist: I will solve my riddle to the music of the lyre.

Notes

I. The First Raptus, and All Subsequent Ones

1. Carl Czerny, *Vollständige theoretisch-practischen Pianoforte-Schule, Op. 500* (Vienna, 1842), Vol. IV, p. 38.
2. Ibid., p. 51.
3. Ibid., pp. 55–56.
4. Ibid., p. 62.
5. *The Letters of Beethoven*, translated and edited by Emily Anderson (New York: St. Martin's Press, 1961), Vol. II, p. 527.
6. Ibid., p. 578.
7. C. S. Lewis, *The Great Divorce*, from *The Best of C. S. Lewis* (Washington, DC: Christianity Today, Inc., 1969), p. 162.

II. Technique as Touch

1. Sandra P. Rosenblum, *Performance Practices in Classic Piano Music* (Bloomington and Indianapolis: Indiana University Press, 1988).
2. Anton Schindler, *Beethoven as I Knew Him*, edited by Donald W. MacArdle (Chapel Hill: The University of North Carolina Press, 1966), p. 498.
3. Carl Czerny, *Pianoforte-Schule* (Vienna, 1839), Vol. III, pp. 26–27.
4. Paul Mies, *Textkritische Untersuchungen bei Beethoven* (Bonn: Beethoven House, 1957), pp. 85–86.
5. Carl Czerny, *Pianoforte-Schule* (Vienna, 1842), Vol. IV, p. 53.
6. Ibid, p. 63.
7. Ibid., pp. 106–107.
8. Ibid., p. 111.
9. *Beethoven Sonatas*, edited by Harold Craxton, with commentaries by Donald Francis Tovey (London: Associated Board of the Royal Schools of Music, 1958), Vol. II, p. 124.
10. Hugo Riemann, "Secrets of Artistic Phrasing," *The Etude*, June 1913, pp. 397–98.
11. Carl Philipp Emmanuel Bach, *Essay on the True Art of Playing Keyboard Instruments*, translated and edited by William J. Mitchell (New York: Norton, 1949), p. 155.
12. Czerny, Vol. IV, p. 52.
13. Ibid., Vol. III, p. 21.

III. Tempo and the Pacing of Musical Ideas

1. Adolph Bernhard Marx, *Anleitung zum Vortrag Beethovenscher Klavierwerke* (Berlin, 1875), p. 69.
2. Carl Czerny, *Pianoforte-Schule* (Vienna, 1842), Vol. IV, p. 59.

IV. Dynamic Nuance and Musical Line

1. J. S. Bach, *Well-Tempered Clavichord* [sic], edited by Carl Czerny (New York: Schirmer, 1893), Preface.
2. Walter Georgii, *Klaviermusik* (Zürich and Freiburg: Atlantis Verlag, 1950), p. 37.
3. Thomas Mann, *Sämtliche Erzählungen* (Frankfurt: S. Fischer Verlag, 1963), p. 414.

V. The Role of Silence

1. Alfred Einstein, *Music in the Romantic Era* (New York: Norton, 1947), p. 15.
2. Edmund Carpenter, "Silent Music and Invisible Art," *Natural History* 87/5 (May 1978): 92.

VI. Sound as Color

1. Carl Czerny, *Pianoforte-Schule* (Vienna, 1842), Vol. IV, pp. 109–10.
2. *Beethoven Sonatas*, edited by Harold Craxton, with commentaries by Donald Francis Tovey (London: Associated Board of the Royal Schools of Music, 1958), Vol. II, p. 125.

VII. Descriptive Music

1. *Thayer's Life of Beethoven*, edited by Elliot Forbes (Princeton: Princeton University Press, 1967), Vol. II, p. 620.
2. Ibid., Vol. I, p. 261.
3. Ibid., p. 436.
4. Gustav Nottebohm, *Zweite Beethoveniana* (Leipzig: Peters, 1887), pp. 374–75.
5. Ibid., p. 376.
6. *The Letters of Beethoven*, translated and edited by Emily Anderson (New York: St. Martin's Press, 1961), Vol. I, pp. 337–38.
7. Adolph Bernhard Marx, *Anleitung zum Vortrag Beethovenscher Klavierwerke* (Berlin, 1875), p. 142.
8. Ibid., p. 140.
9. Alfred Einstein, *Music in the Romantic Era* (New York: W. W. Norton, 1947), p. 6.
10. Alfred Christian Kalischer, *Beethoven und seine Zeitgenossen* (Berlin and Leipzig: Schuster und Loeffler, 1909–1910), Vol. IV, p. 44.

VIII. Motivic Development

1. Gustav Nottebohm, *Zweite Beethovenia* (Leipzig: Peters, 1887), pp. 564–66.
2. Ibid., p. 566.
3. Alfred Christian Kalischer, *Beethoven und seine Zeitgenossen* (Berlin and Leipzig, 1909–1910), Vol. IV, p. 44.
4. Anton Schindler, *Beethoven as I Knew Him*, edited by Donald W. MacArdle (Chapel Hill: University of North Carolina Press, 1966), pp. 76–77.
5. Carl Czerny, *Pianoforte-Schule* (Vienna, 1842), Vol. IV, p. 62.
6. Nottebohm, pp. 437–42.
7. Czerny, p. 62.
8. Nottebohm, p. 438.
9. Martin Cooper, *Beethoven, the Last Decade* (Oxford and New York: Oxford University Press, 1985), pp. 190–91.

10. John V. Cockshoot, *The Fugue in Beethoven's Piano Music* (London: Routledge & Kegan Paul, 1959), pp. 95–120.

IX. Quasi una Fantasia

1. Frederic Corder, "Beethoven's Sonatas and How to Play Them," *The Etude*, December 1926, pp. 897ff.
2. Carl Czerny, *Pianoforte-Schule* (Vienna, 1842), Vol. IV, p. 51.
3. Ibid.
4. Nottebohm, *Zweite Beethoveniana* (Leipzig: Peters 1887), pp. 236–43.
5. Ibid., p. 238.
6. Robert Schumann, *On Music and Musicians*, edited by Konrad Wolff, translated by Paul Rosenfeld (New York, Pantheon, 1952), p. 142.
7. Czerny, p. 50.

X. Line and Space

1. Paul Nettl, *Beethoven Encyclopedia* (New York: Philosophical Library, 1956), p. 300.
2. Anton Schindler, *Beethoven as I Knew Him* (Chapel Hill: University of North Carolina Press, 1966), p. 209.
3. *The Letters of Beethoven*, translated and edited by Emily Anderson (New York: St. Martin's Press, 1961), Vol. II, p. 671.
4. Carl Czerny, *Pianoforte-Schule* (Vienna, 1842), Vol. IV, p. 65.
5. Schindler, p. 209.
6. Adolph Bernhard Marx, *Anleitung zum Vortrag Beethovenscher Klavierwerke* (Berlin, 1875), p. 146.
7. Alfred Christian Kalischer, *Beethoven und seine Zeitgenossen* (Berlin and Leipzig: Schuster und Lopfflen, 1909–1910), Vol. III, pp. 121–23.
8. Schindler, p. 437.
9. Marx, p. 147.
10. Ibid., p. 147.

XI. Movement as Energized Color

1. Gustav Nottebohm, *Ein Skizzenbuch von Beethoven* (Breitkopf & Härtel: Leipzig, 1880), pp. 58–66.
2. Carl Czerny, *Pianoforte-Schule* (Vienna, 1842), Vol. IV, pp. 58–59.
3. Ibid., p. 59.
4. Ibid., p. 59.
5. Nottebohm, pp. 63–64.
6. Ibid., p. 64.
7. Czerny, p. 59.

XII. The Moment of Creation

1. Carl Czerny, *Pianoforte-Schule* (Vienna, 1842), Vol. IV, p. 53.
2. Ibid., p. 55
3. *Beethoven Sonatas*, edited by Harold Craxton, with commentaries by Donald Francis Tovey (London: Associated Board of the Royal Schools of Music, 1958), Vol. II, p. 124.

4. Carl Czerny, *Über den richtigen Vortrag der sämtlichen Beethoven'schen Klavierwerke* (Vienna: Universal, 1963), p. 11.

5. Johann Wolfgang von Goethe, *Faust* (Boston: Heath, *Boston*, 1892), pp. 56–57 (lines 1224–37).

6. Czerny, *Pianoforte-Schule*, Vol. IV, p. 55.

7. Tovey, p. 125.

8. Czerny, p. 56.

9. Ibid.

10. *Beethoven Sonatas*, edited by Eugen d'Albert (Leipzig: Otto Forberg, 1902), p. 113.

11. Czerny, p. 56.

12. Ibid., p. 57.

13. Tovey-Craxton, Vol. II, p. 150.

XIII. Facing Two Directions

1. Carl Czerny, *Pianoforte-Schule* (Vienna, 1842), Vol. IV, p. 60.

2. Ibid., pp. 62–63.

3. Gustav Nottebohm, *Zweite Beethoveniana* (Leipzig: Peters, 1887), p. 298.

4. Ibid., pp. 366–68.

XIV. The Enjoyment of Fluency

1. Carl Czerny, *Pianoforte-Schule* (Vienna, 1842), Vol. IV, p. 43.

2. Ibid., p. 44.

3. Anton Schindler, *Beethoven as I Knew Him* (Chapel Hill: University of North Carolina Press, 1966), p. 406.

4. *Thayer's Life of Beethoven* (Princeton: Princeton University Press, 1967), Vol. I, p. 208.

5. Czerny, p. 47.

6. William Barrett, *Death of the Soul* (Garden City: Doubleday, 1986), pp. 23–24.

7. Kinsky-Halm, *Das Werk Beethovens—Thematisch-Bibliographisches Verzeichnis seiner sämtlichen vollendeten Kompositionen* (Munich-Duisburg: Henle, 1955), p. 57.

8. Eric Blom, quoted in *The Beethoven Companion*, edited by Thomas K. Scherman and Louis Biancolli (Garden City: Doubleday, 1972), p. 287.

9. Czerny, p. 54.

10. Kinsky-Halm, p. 77.

11. Donald Francis Tovey, *A Companion to Beethoven's Pianoforte Sonatas* (London: The Associated Board of the Royal Schools of Music, 1948), p. 191.

XV. The Cosmopolitan Impostor

1. *The Letters of Beethoven*, translated and edited by Emily Anderson (New York, St. Martin's Press, 1961), Vol. I, pp. 74–75.

2. Ibid., pp. 74–75.

3. Gustav Nottebohm, *Zweite Beethoveniana* (Leipzig: Peters, 1887), p. 47.

4. Carl Philipp Emanuel Bach, *Essay on the True Art of Playing Keyboard Instruments*, translated and edited by William J. Mitchell (New York: Norton, 1949), p. 106.

5. Carl Czerny, *Pianoforte-Schule* (Vienna, 1842), Vol. IV, p. 46.

6. Ibid., p. 46.

XVI. Embracing the Dachstein

1. Carl Czerny, *Pianoforte-Schule* (Vienna, 1842), Vol. IV, p. 40.
2. *Thayer's Life of Beethoven* revised and edited by Elliot Forbes (Princeton: Princeton University Press, 1967), Vol. I, p. 207.
3. Czerny, p. 40.
4. Ibid.
5. Nottebohm, *Zweite Beethoveniana* (Leipzig: Peters, 1887), p. 509.
6. Ibid., p. 511.
7. Czerny, p. 40.
8. *The Beethoven Companion* edited by Thomas K. Scherman and Louis Biancolli (Garden City: Doubleday, 1973), p. 1157.
9. Ibid., p. 1161.
10. Ibid., p. 1165.
11. Ibid., p. 1167.
12. *The Letters of Beethoven*, translated and edited by Emily Anderson (New York: St. Martin's Press, 1961), Vol. II, p. 661.
13. *Beethoven, the Man and the Artist, as Revealed in His Own Words*, compiled by Friedrich Kerst, translated by Henry Edward Krehbiel (New York: Dover [abridged edition], 1964), p. 25.
14. John Cockshoot, *The Fugue in Beethoven's Piano Music* (London: Routledge & Kegan Paul, 1959), pp. 86–89.
15. *The Poetry of Robert Frost*, edited by Edward Connery Latham (New York: Holt, Rinehart and Winston, 1967), p. 296.
16. Nottebohm, p. 135.

XVII. A Higher Revelation

1. *Thayer's Life of Beethoven*, revised and edited by Elliot Forbes (Princeton: Princeton University Press, 1967), Vol. I, p. 494.
2. Carl Czerny, *Pianoforte-Schule* (Vienna, 1842), Vol. IV, p. 42.
3. *Thayer's Life of Beethoven* Vol. I, p. 185.
4. Czerny, p. 42.
5. *The Letters of Beethoven*, translated and edited by Emily Anderson (New York: St. Martin's Press, 1961), Vol. II, pp. 931–32.
6. Franz Gerhard Wegeler and Ferdinand Ries, *Biographische Notizen über Ludwig van Beethoven* (Coblenz, 1838), pp. 94–95.
7. Czerny, p. 69.
8. Alexander Wheelock Thayer, *The Life of Ludwig van Beethoven* (Carbondale: Southern Illinois University Press, 1960), pp. iv–v.
9. *Béla Bartók Letters*, edited by János Demény (New York: St. Martin's Press, 1971), pp. 161–62.
10. Robert Schumann, *On Music and Musicians*, translated by Paul Rosenfeld (New York: Pantheon, 1946), p. 98.

Index

BEETHOVEN

Sonatas

Op. 2 No. 1: 4, 18, 23, 31–32, 43–44, 46, 48, 50, 84–96, 112, 128, 130, 264, 282, 288, 292, 306, 308
Op. 2 No. 2: 4, 16, 23, 34, 43, 48, 50, 84–85, 122, 128–135, 215, 219, 243, 269
Op. 2 No. 3: 1, 46, 48–49, 50–51, 57–59, 84–85, 128, 239–244, 259, 269, 271, 290
Op. 7: 4, 11, 17, 27, 37–38, 49, 122, 219, 243, 259–270
Op. 10 No. 1: 44, 46, 49, 204, 224, 269, 282–289
Op. 10 No. 2: 37, 43, 46, 49, 211–215
Op. 10 No. 3: 17, 20, 45–46, 49, 122, 211, 215–220, 243, 264, 269, 301
Op. 13: 10–12, 15, 17–19, 29, 49, 67, 77–85, 91, 114, 127, 204, 211, 282, 285, 288, 308
Op. 14 No. 1: 12, 16, 31, 49, 239, 244–258, 264
Op. 14 No. 2: 37, 211, 220–224
Op. 22: 15, 211, 220, 224–231, 243
Op. 26: 13, 16–17, 23, 39, 45, 59–61, 114, 121–127, 288
Op. 27 No. 1: 27, 29–32, 45–46, 60, 62, 84, 113–121, 122, 264
Op. 27 No. 2: 1, 25, 30, 60–61, 82, 84–85, 113–122, 127, 169, 264, 282, 288, 308
Op. 28: 30, 38, 49, 57, 84, 159–169, 264
Op. 31 No. 1: 14, 49, 211, 231–235
Op. 31 No. 2: 1–2, 4, 13, 25, 31, 38, 45–46, 62, 114, 159, 169–182, 240, 282, 288
Op. 31 No. 3: 12, 15, 19, 38, 47, 49, 159, 182–190, 224
Op. 49 No. 1: 47, 49, 191–195, 307
Op. 49 No. 2: 24–25, 49, 84, 191–195
Op. 53: 35, 45, 47, 49, 60, 62, 82, 114, 121, 144–158, 231, 234, 290
Op. 54: 49, 191, 195–199
Op. 57: 2, 49, 60–61, 82, 84–85, 96–104, 114, 127, 169–170, 282, 288, 306
Op. 78: 14, 24–26, 57, 60, 84, 114, 191, 199–204, 224
Op. 79: 49, 211, 224, 235–238
Op. 81a: 11, 21, 25, 34–35, 60, 67–77, 114, 306–307
Op. 90: 4, 43–44, 49, 191, 204–210
Op. 101: 22, 60, 62, 128, 135–143
Op. 106: 60, 84, 114, 135, 200, 236, 259, 270–279, 304, 307
Op. 109: 4, 26, 53, 60, 84, 237–238, 281–282, 289–297
Op. 110: 4, 12–13, 21–23, 26, 53, 59–60, 84, 104–112, 114, 240, 271, 289
Op. 111: 3, 39, 53, 60, 114, 204, 210, 236, 259, 281–282, 288, 295, 297–304, 309

Bagatelles

Op. 33 No. 2: 20
Op. 33 No. 6: 51–52
Op. 126 No. 1: 26, 28–29
Op. 126 No. 5: 237

Concertos

No. I, Op. 15: 24
No. III, Op. 37: 60, 290
No. IV, Op. 58: 24, 45, 84, 144
No. V, Op. 73: 45

Other Beethoven W orks

Andante favori, WoO 57: 147, 153
Bonn Sonata, WoO 47: 78–79
Für Elise: 179
Piano Quartet, WoO 36: 93–94
Rondo, Op. 51 No. 1: 14, 16, 30

JOSEPH HAYDN

Sonatas

No. 15: 55
No. 31: 50–51
No. 33: 11, 54–56
No. 54: 54–56
No. 60: 58
No. 62: 36–37

WOLFGANG AMADEUS MOZART

Adagio in B minor, K. 540: 2–3
Fantasie, K. 475: 20

Sonatas

K. 279: 45
K. 283: 18
K. 284: 39, 43
K. 309: 43
K. 311: 35–36
K. 330: 59
K. 331: 59, 122
K. 333: 90
K. 457: 51, 170–171
K. 533: 56–57
K. 570: 31

Kenneth Drake is Professor Emeritus of Piano at the University of Illinois and author of *The Sonatas of Beethoven as He Played and Taught Them.* He is active as a performer on period pianos.